Uncle Cy's War

The New Brunswick Military Heritage Series, Volume 14

◼ Uncle Cy's War

THE FIRST WORLD WAR LETTERS OF MAJOR CYRUS F. INCHES

Edited by Valerie Teed

GOOSE LANE EDITIONS and
THE NEW BRUNSWICK MILITARY HERITAGE PROJECT

Edited by Brent Wilson and Barry Norris.
Front and back cover illustrations from the Cyrus Inches Collection.
Cover and interior page design by Julie Scriver.
Printed in Canada on paper containing100% post-consumer fiber.
10 9 8 7 6 5 4 3 2 1

Library and Archives Canada Cataloguing in Publication

Inches, Cyrus F.
    Uncle Cy's war: the First World War letters of Major Cyrus F. Inches /
Valerie Teed, editor.
(The New Brunswick military heritage series; v. 14)
Co-published by: New Brunswick Military Heritage Project.
Includes bibliographical references and index.
ISBN 978-0-86492-542-8

1. Inches, Cyrus F. — Correspondence.
2. Canada. Canadian Army — Officers — Correspondence.
3. Canada. Canadian Army. Heavy Battery, 1st — Biography.
4. World War, 1914-1918 — Personal narratives, Canadian.
I. Teed, Valerie, 1945- II. New Brunswick Military Heritage Project.
III. Title. IV. Series: New Brunswick military heritage series v. 14.

D640 I622 2009   940.4'8171   C2009-903339-9

Goose Lane Editions acknowledges the financial support of the Canada Council for the Arts, the Government of Canada through the Book Publishing Industry Development Program (BPIDP), and the New Brunswick Department of Wellness, Culture and Sport for its publishing activities.

Goose Lane Editions
Suite 330, 500 Beaverbrook Court
Fredericton, New Brunswick
CANADA E3B 5X4
www.gooselane.com

New Brunswick Military Heritage Project
The Brigadier Milton F. Gregg, VC,
Centre for the Study of War and Society
University of New Brunswick
PO Box 4400
Fredericton, New Brunswick
CANADA E3B 5A3
www.unb.ca/nbmhp

This book is dedicated to the memory of Uncle Cy Inches,
a generous, gregarious man, whose military and
cultural contribution through these letters and through
his farewell message to the N.C.O.s and men
of the 1st Canadian Heavy Battery in France,
deserves a place in New Brunswick's history.

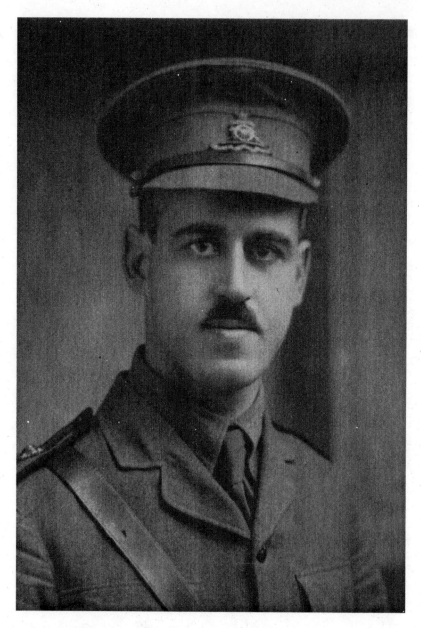

Cyrus Fiske Inches — B.C.L., L.L.B., D.S.O., M.C.

Contents

Who's Who in the Inches Letters

Buff — Hugh Mackay (and Katie* [Hazen] Mackay)

Bumps — Malcolm McAvity (and Frances* [Hazen] McAvity)

Chacker — the name Cyrus and his sister Connie used to refer to
        each other

Frank — Frank C. Magee, O.C. of the 1st Heavies, Cy's battery

Fraser — Fraser Campbell

Hall — Frank Hall, Cy's batman

Harry — Lieutenant-Colonel Wm. Henry Harrison, barrister, Cy's
        brother-in-law

Hughie — Hugh McLean, barrister and son of Major-General
        The Hon. H.H. McLean

Jack — J.H.A.L. Fairweather, Saint John barrister

Jim Harrison — Harry's brother

Kelly — Lieutenant Lawrence Kelly

King — Douglas King Hazen, Cy's law partner*

Len — Leonard Tilley, grandson of Sir Leonard Tilley

May Harrison — Harry's sister

Sandy — Alex MacMillan

Semi — Colin Mackay

Walter Harrison — cousin to Harry

*children of Sir J.D. Hazen

Introduction

I said to my husband that if the First World War were still on, his Great Uncle Cyrus would still be there. I had been transcribing a collection of nearly two hundred letters written by Uncle Cy to his mother and siblings, from Quebec, England, France, and Belgium during the full term of that atrocious war. At least I was under the impression that it had been an atrocious war, although you'd never know it from reading the letters to "Dear Ma."

The First World War was presented to my generation, the leading edge of the baby boomers, as a war of mud and slaughter. We were shown film clips of young soldiers climbing out of sodden, muddy trenches, rifles thrust forward, leaning toward the invisible enemy as they advanced through barbed wire and shell-torn fields. We watched them fall and die where they ran or stood, knee-deep in muck. We were told about the bombs and poisonous gases that maimed and killed them and their precious horses by the thousands. We eventually understood that their courage had often been based on a naive understanding of what they were up against and was fuelled by a resolve to be part of the glory that went with serving one's king and country. We saw the images of the horrendous carnage that was the "Great War," the "war to end all wars." Uncle Cy's letters, however, show a different side to the war, especially the camaraderie among the soldiers and their devotion to duty.

Backyard of 179 Germain Street, Saint John, N.B., circa 1905. Standing (from left to right): "Ma" (Mary), Dr. P.R. Inches, Elizabeth, Ken, Connie, unknown, Cyrus. Sitting (from left to right): unknown with cat and Charlie.

Cyrus Fiske Inches was among the first to sign up. He knew where his duty lay. He was the third son of Dr. Patrick "Peter" Robertson Inches and a grandson of Dr. Cyrus Fiske, Cyrus's namesake — both practising physicians in Saint John, New Brunswick. Born in Saint John on January 21, 1883, Cyrus descended from the Inches-Small-Spalding family of Dunkeld, Scotland, and the Fiske family of Boston, Massachusetts. (see Appendix) He grew up in the family home at 179 Germain Street in Saint John and spent summers at their country home in Westfield. He was educated at Saint John High School, Kings College Law School (B.C.L.), and Harvard Law School (L.L.B.).

In the summer of 1914, Cy was thirty-one years old, unmarried, and had a thriving law practice in partnership with D. King Hazen, son of Sir J.D. Hazen and a close friend of his family. He loved life, his family, and the ever-expanding broad circle of friends and associates with whom he surrounded himself. He was also a member of the militia, serving in the 3rd New Brunswick Regiment of the Canadian Garrison Artillery in Saint John.

Cy intended to make the best of the war and to survive it, and he was completely committed to the cause. He faithfully kept a diary chronicling the movements and battles of his battery. As he waited at Borden Camp in England for his clearance and sailing orders home to Canada in May 1919, he wrote and later published a booklet called *The 1st Canadian Heavy Battery in France — Farewell Message to the N.C.O.s and Men*. He made it his business to know where he was and what was happening. Because of his background and his status as an officer, he knew some of the people who were "running the war" and was occasionally privy to its strategies and politics. He was a contributor for the Saint John *Globe* and *Daily Telegraph* and regularly sent these papers descriptive letters about his war experiences. He lived and fought near the frontline trenches, eventually by choice. He had an enthusiasm for the fight, like many of his ilk, and lamented in a letter from Quebec's Château Frontenac in September 1914, "I am now told we are not to go to Salisbury Plain until April . . . I am beginning to despair of getting to the front." He twice refused leave to Canada, preferring to remain on active service until the conflict was over. When his mother, Mary Dorothea, died of pernicious anemia on July 24, 1917, he wrote to his brother Ken: "Harry is urging me to apply for three months leave to Canada but I can't quite see my way clear to do so at the present time. The temptation is great, though,

A very pleasant affair took place at the Union Club on Thursday evening, when the ~~L. M. Club~~ tendered a farewell dinner to Mr. Cyrus Inches, Mr. Lawrence Kelly, Mr. Ralph Hayes and Capt. Magee, officers of the artillery who left last evening for Valcartier on their way to the front.

Saint John Globe, August 29, 1914.

as I would dearly love to see you all again." His brother Charlie wrote that he could have been promoted to lieutenant-colonel at the Canadian School of Gunnery at Witley, in relatively safe England, but avoided it, choosing instead to remain with his battery.

Yet Cy seemed to ignore the intrusion of the war. His unshakable self-confidence blended masterfully with a brilliant mind, a deep empathy for his fellow man, and an impeccable sense of humour. Besides, he knew everybody. These traits and circumstances enabled him, in this atrocious war, to be the person he had always been. Socially, he simply superimposed the patterns of his civilian life on his military camp existence. The result was a more civilized level of social interaction, sprinkled with humour and kindness. It made life more like home for him and certainly more bearable for the officers and men in his battery. In a January 1918 note to Cy's brother Ken, a mutual officer and friend at the School of Gunnery wrote, "Several cadets taking this course worked in Cy's battery or know him. They all swear by him and would do anything for him . . ."

The letters in this volume represent slightly over half of those Cy wrote during the war.[1] His formal language, peppered with the terminology of his legal profession, often creates a dichotomy as he describes ordinary things and situations. On April 10, 1917, for example, he talks about "the frequency of my dinner engagements," referring to his habit of inviting officer friends to "dine" regularly at his mess, whatever that might have been. "Cloth Hall" was the name the officers in his battery gave to their mess in the summer of 1916. It was a dugout whose dirt walls were lined with burlap bags to retard wall cave-ins when it rained. The image of a mud-walled mess with table and chairs and guest officers "dining" is at the very least comical, and the most convincing evidence that Cyrus was making the best of a bad situation.

The letters reveal as much about Cy's nature as they do about the First World War. He was an academic with a voracious appetite for learning and mental diversion even in the wartime dearth of information. He was

---

1   I have compiled more of Cy's war letters to his sister, Connie (Inches) Harrison, in a book called *The Chacker Letters*.

a serious soldier whose contribution to the conflict was acknowledged by two wartime promotions to captain and major and command of the 1st Canadian Heavy Battery. He was twice mentioned in dispatches, awarded the Military Cross [M.C.] in January 1917 and a Distinguished Service Order [D.S.O.] in November 1919. Amid the thousands of soldiers who suffered from emotional breakdowns, he was a person who was able to cope with the privations and horrors of wartime life. He was a loyal New Brunswicker who knew his roots and his purpose and whose indomitable spirit prevailed for the four and a half long years of his active service with hardly a discernable lapse in his resolve.

Cyrus Inches is the real author of this book. Through his letters, the reader can read *his* mode of expression in the idiom of *his* day. I am only the transcriber and editor. In this role, I brought to light the letters, which had been kept, undisturbed, in dusty boxes for almost ninety years when I found them. Many of the 1916 letters had been written in indelible pencil and were stuck together, covered in purple blotching. I persisted in deciphering obscure and faint passages and came away feeling that my effort was worthwhile. The letters have merit, not only in content but also in style. I found Cy's superb sense of humour in his writing to be as fresh and clever today as it must have been ninety years ago.

Many more letters exist than I have chosen for this book. Space restrictions required that I edit out repetitious and superfluous material. However, I have included almost all of the text of Cy's retrospective booklet, which provides the historical context of this book — the battles, the movements, the technical details, the operational successes and failures. In contrast are the voluminous details of daily life seen in his letters, which often had nothing to do with the fighting and everything to do with survival.

The letters I chose for the book were those I felt would include the most broadly interesting subjects to a variety of readers. Historians will find value in the comprehensive nature of the information they contain, which covers the entire course of Canadian involvement in the war from Valcartier in August 1914 to Mons on November 11, 1918, and the many months of demobilization afterward. The letters make especially clear the

August 28. 1914.

ARTILLERY LEAVE
THIS EVENING

Will Start For Valcartier at 7 O'clock — Enthusiastic Send-off Arranged.

The last detachment of local troops from St. John, who will be in the first contingent leaving Canada for the defence of the Mother Country, will entrain this evening at 7 o'clock for Valcartier. The definite orders for the entrainment of the men this evening were received by Lieut. Col. B. R. Armstrong on Thursday evening. The artillery contingent will consist of 284 men and the men are all in the best of health and will compare favorably with the troops from any part of Canada. A few days ago it was thought that it would be rather difficult to recruit the detachment up to the required number of men, but when the news that they were going this week was received the recruits poured in as fast as they could be handled. Among those who will be in the contingent this evening are twenty-three who wear medals from the South African war and one who has a medal for service in Egypt. The men will leave the Island about 6 o'clock and will land at Reed's Point about 6.30 o'clock. On their arrival at Reed's Point the men will be met with a detachment of men from the 28th Dragoons, under command of Lieut. Morrisey, who will act as a guard of honor, a large number of the committee of the Soldiers' and Families' Relief Fund, by the mayor and commissioners and by other prominent citizens. The parade will be headed by the Temple Band, and the other four bands will be stationed at various points in the parade. The officers who are going are Major Frank Magee, in charge: Lieuts. C. F. Inches, R. Hayes and L. J. Kelly.

The men will be given an enthusiastic send-off by the citizens, who thoroughly recognize the sacrifice these men are making in going to fight for the empire.

Lieut. Inches left last evening for the general mobilization grounds at Valcartier. The scenes which have marked the departure of the other contingents will be in evidence again to-night.

contribution Canadian gunners made to the artillery's war. Readers may also be interested in finding their New Brunswick ancestors — surnames of men known to Cyrus Inches — alive and well in the pages of his letters.

Most of the letters were written to "Dear Ma," who, luckily for me, knew as little about the army and the conflict then as I do now. As a result, Cyrus "footnoted" explanations for her. In this book, I have done the same in an effort to provide background information for readers with limited knowledge of the war and the world as it was between 1914 and 1919.

Saint John Globe, August 28, 1914.

The 1st Canadian Heavy Battery in France —
Farewell Message to the N.C.O.s and Men

Before the battery is broken up for demobilization purposes,
I take this method to say to you a few words which may help
to keep green in your memory the record and traditions of the
Unit to which you belong. I will make no attempt to write a
complete history. My intention is to give you a short summary
of our career on the Western Front, in the hope that the main
features to which I will refer will recall to mind a thousand
and one other incidents which otherwise might be forgotten.

"Westfield," the Inches Family Summer Home, Westfield, N.B.

Chapter One

Valcartier to Salisbury Plain

*The battery was mobilized in Montreal in 1914 as a four gun
battery, went to the concentration camp at Valcartier, thence
to Salisbury Plain with the 1st Canadian Contingent, and
accompanied the 1st Division to France, landing there on
February 15, 1915. The pre-war establishment of a Division
provided for one Heavy Battery. It is a matter of no small
pride to us that at one time we were 1st Division men
personnel, men of "the old red patch."*

August 28, 1914
The Windsor Hotel
Montreal

Dearest Ma,

I arrived here all right and immediately ran into, in different places,
several Saint John people, including Aubrey Schofield and Tom Stewart.
I transacted considerable business this morning and in a short time will
go to lunch with Tom. I expect to go from here to Quebec this evening or
tomorrow morning and will meet the Saint John battery on their arrival
there on Sunday — and from thence to Valcartier.

Everything is uncertain as to just what disposition they will make of my proffered services, but as to that I will write you in due course. It is not likely the artillery will go across for some weeks and then it will, for them, be England — probably Oakhampton, according to what Colonel McLean told me yesterday morning.

I saw Connie and Charlie on the veranda as I went by Westfield. Please do not send me any money as I do not require it. Messrs. Barnhill, Ewing, and Sanford[2] will collect your mortgage interest while I am away. They have full particulars of everything. Mr. Ewing had a letter from Mr. Morrison a few days ago stating that the money would be forwarded to Saint John this week. As soon as the succession duties are adjusted, Messrs. Barnhill, Ewing, and Sanford will pay the legacies. They are the best family solicitors in Saint John, and you can trust them implicitly.

With much love,
Cyrus

September 9, 1914
Valcartier, P.Q.

Dear Ma,

This week has been rather uneventful because of the rain. The review of the troops before the governor general Sunday took place in a heavy rain and the men got pretty thoroughly soaked.

I got a letter from Connie yesterday, which is the first letter I have received from either you or Connie, and I take it your letters have gone astray like many others that the boys have been looking for. The snapshots of Pat and Janice are excellent and are a credit to Charlie's skill as a photographer. I suppose that when Charles goes back to college, you will be turning your thoughts to Saint John, even though you ought to

---

2   A law firm in Saint John.

stay out [in Westfield] as long as possible for the sake of Connie and the children. As Campbell is just leaving for the post office, I will close with love.

Cyrus

September 17, 1914
Valcartier, P.Q.

Dear Ma,

Very little of any movement has occurred since I wrote you last. There is nothing official yet as to who will be chosen or the date of sailing, but it will probably be near the first of next month.

Our daily routine of taking care of the horses still continues. Morning stables at 6 a.m., noon stables at 11:15 a.m. and evening stables at 4 p.m. Then the horses have to be branded and numbered, and likewise the wagons and other stores. I have a horse which is all right when allowed to go in the direction it wants to and when there are no automobiles around, so I am trying to get another which can adapt itself more thoroughly to the surroundings.

Kelly has been appointed paymaster to another corps, so I now have the tent to myself. My batman went to Quebec on leave yesterday, so the surroundings are in a state which closely resembles my room at home after I have been there by myself for a few days.

The worst baby of the lot over inoculation proved to be the doctor himself of our division. The way he complains of his sore arm is quite the joke of the mess. For two days now I have wagered whoever I happen to sit beside that he dare not ask the doctor how his arm is and have lost both times, but it has raised the subject for the doctor to dilate upon to the amusement of the others.

With much love,
Cyrus

September 21, 1914
Valcartier, P.Q.

Dear Ma,

Frank Magee, who was in command of the fourth section of our column, has been transferred . . . and his command, for a few days until a permanent appointment is made, has fallen on my shoulders. In the reorganization, it is expected that a captain from outside will command No. 4. Today Len Tilley spent an hour with me. He has been to Ottawa with reference to the formation of a rifle club of a hundred men and other similar clubs in Saint John. He introduced me to his brother-in-law from Winnipeg, who is a captain in an infantry battalion.

Yesterday was full of interest. In the morning we proceeded to the review ground, where a short service was held. The attendance was voluntary so there were not as many there as there were in the big review before the duke in the afternoon. In this review we were mounted. When one comes to think, it was quite funny from our standpoint. We turned out with fifty farm wagons . . . these being the vehicles for the ammunition. In my section there were nine wagons — two horses in each wagon with a driver and one gunner on the seat — two other lieutenants besides myself. Hoodless and Dunlop of Hamilton (known to me as Hoodlum and Dewdrop — both of them more experienced men than I am) were both immensely amused over the exigency which put me in charge for the day. The drill was new to me and I had to have one on each side to coach me in what commands to give. We had to go through some pretty rough ground before reaching the saluting point, which caused tremendous confusion, but by covering the wagons in the section ahead we managed to collect ourselves after a fashion and were in fairly straight formation by the time we reached the Royal party.

My horse was as entirely new to me as the situation was to him, and as I could have but one hand on the rein, while the other was saluting — the result was that my horse side stepped all the way past. I got off better than some officers in another battalion, who went by with both arms around their horses' necks to keep from falling off. I will always look back at the day I was in charge of farm wagons in a grand review of troops as one of the big days of my career.

Today two of the men in our section were brought up before me for being drunk while on leave in Quebec. The men had with them instructions from the provost marshal in Quebec that they be dealt with according to Camp Order No. 400 and something, which on looking up I found contained a pre-emptory order to discharge them and send them home, but curiously enough the instructions have been mislaid somewhere, and the men, both of them good soldiers, are now back again in the ranks.

Yours with much love,
Cyrus

September 25, 1914
Canadian Pacific Railway Hotel System
Château Frontenac, Quebec

Dearest Ma,

I received your fine long letter and also the express parcel and do not know how to express my gratitude. Consider that I have kissed you for it.

It is hard to keep the run of the days here but three days ago we got orders to embark — that is, to leave camp — as soon after noon as possible. These orders were shortly changed to a command to take all our horses in and put them on the *Montezuma*[3] together with a hundred men, so the whole column rode in that night starting at 10 and arriving in Quebec at 6:20 the next morning — nearly nine hours in [the] saddle. We got the horses on and went back by official train that afternoon, not stopping to load our stores because the men had gotten some liquor somewhere and were being arrested right and left. That night in camp there was a small riot between our section and No. 2 Section owing to the antipathy shown by some of No. 2 Section towards a few Saint

---

3   Sister ship to the *Mount Temple* sunk by German Submarine UC-41 on July 25, 1917.

John men transferred recently from 4 to 2. After this was quelled, it was discovered that two civilians had entered the tents while we were in town and they were put under arrest, the goods having been found on them. The next morning, court was duly held and drunks and thieves disposed of in dispatch, which would make Judge Ritchie green with envy.

In the afternoon, I was sent into the boat on some business, then to the Château [Frontenac] for general head scouring. When I came to pay the barber, I missed fifty dollars (which, by the way, has just been returned to me; by mistake I included it in some money I paid a lieutenant on board the boat). Had to borrow to buy a dinner ticket in the Château . . . and while waiting in line for the ticket, I felt my arm patted and, looking around, discovered Kelly, and we had a merry reunion. I wanted to stay all night and take in the theatre but could not get our headquarters on the phone and so did not care to take a chance, and returned to camp by the 9:00 p.m. train.

This morning the adjutant, Major Long, sent me in to the steamer again. When I got in two and a half hours late, I found the boat had been moved out into the stream four miles up the river opposite Wolfe's Cove, and by much good luck I happened to spy Colonel Good of Woodstock [who was] just leaving for the same steamer in a Fruemaker[4] boat belonging to the Quebec Harbour Commission, so I joined forces with him after counting the horses on board — an hour's job — pleasant aroma and all that. I climbed down the rope ladder — sure cure for a delicate stomach — and am now at 4 p.m. spending the few minutes before train time writing to you. I expect to get back in time for dinner, which will be appreciated, because I have abstained from food since 7 a.m., but don't worry about it, because we are already accustomed to missing a meal once in a while.

I should not be surprised on arriving in camp to find them packing up, preparing for the march in. I am now told we are to go to Salisbury Plain until April. I believe the position of our corps is four miles back of the firing line so *I am beginning to despair of getting to the front*. I don't

---

4   Boat built by the American Fruehauf Corporation.

know what boat we will be assigned to — there was just room left for one hundred men on the *Montezuma* after the horses had been put on.

Thanking you again and with much love,
Cyrus

September 27, 1914
Quebec, Onboard S.S. *Megantic*

Dear Ken,

I do not know just when you will get this letter as there are rumours of strict censorship of mail from Quebec at present and I am also a little dubious about several letters I mailed last evening in a box some distance up the wharf.

Our horses with one hundred men are in the *Montezuma*. We are on the *Megantic* with the 48th Highlanders and a field ambulance corps. I do not know whether they will be of much use when *mal de mer* sets in or not. We are not allowed to pick our staterooms. The consequence is that I am with two others in a very fine room — a centre one — air close and artificial light. The men who expected to sleep in hammocks are in the L and third-class staterooms, much better accommodations than most of them ever enjoyed before. Some of them even have first-class rooms, one of which I would very much like to acquire.

My roommates at present are McTaggart, an R.M.C. [Royal Military College] man, [and] Dawley, a bank man — the latter knows Charlie Gregory and is in some business deals with him. The saloon service is excellent, and we pity the rest of our officers on board the *Montezuma*. Colonel Sam Hughes and the Japanese consul have just paid us an official visit in his yacht. By the way, we are lying in the stream a little above the city, where we [sailed to] during the night sometime, a movement of which I was entirely unconscious, as I was enjoying sheets and pillows for the first time in a month. *I believe [Colonel Hughes] announced that the Allies have broken through the German line.* We do not know just when we will move off. Until we do, shore leave is restricted to officers only. I daresay it will take two weeks to cross owing to the slow speed of some of the transports.

If you will drop a line to me care [of the] Divisional Ammunition Column [D.A.C.], Canadian Overseas Expeditionary Contingent, England, I think I will get it all right. I will now close, as I want to write Mary and Connie before supper.

Sincerely,
Cyrus

October 1, 1914
Off Father Point
Onboard S.S. *Megantic*

Dear Ma,

We left last evening at 10 o'clock. The night was very fine and Quebec presented a pretty sight, the lights from the Château [Frontenac] and other steamers lending tone to the scene. Just at present the water is calm and prospects are that it will continue so.

Last evening Captain Foulkes of Victoria joined the party — he missed his own steamer. He was the tennis champion of Canada for some years and knows Bumps well. We do not know what port we are going to — I think the colonel has sealed orders as to that, which will not be made public until we get away from land. This is all very exciting, like the Henty stories we used to read.

Tell Ken the *Saturday Telegraph* with the social news came to hand all right. The account of the camp was very interesting. To me the camp seems a thing in the long distant past. The month here passed very quickly. I suppose we will not get any war news until we reach the other side. As a matter of fact, I don't read it much anyway. The baseball and football championships which are soon to be played are far more interesting. I have a date with Fraser Campbell for the Yale game at New Haven in November which I do not think I can keep.

> With much love,
> Cyrus

October 3, 1914
Gaspé Basin
Onboard S.S. *Megantic*

Dear Ma,

The sail down the river was very beautiful. We lay to in the mouth of the basin during the night. Friday — another very fine day — we moved farther up the basin and found ourselves in the midst of a fleet of about thirty-two steamers and four cruisers. The surrounding hills of coloured foliage formed a fine background and altogether it was an unusual sight and must have astonished considerably the villagers all along the coast on each side of the basin. We rather expected to sail this morning early but are still at anchor. There is snow in places on some of the hilltops, which suggests that over in New Brunswick you are in the dead of winter.

Yesterday I had to work for my living, being the officer detailed to look after the guard for the day. It consists of forty-five men divided into three shifts of fifteen each who mount sentry in fifteen different places throughout the ship for two hours or until relieved by the next shift. The guard also takes charge of the prisoners. We went on duty at 10 o'clock yesterday morning and left this morning at 10:30. As I had to personally visit each sentry once every hour during the night, I did not go to bed and am consequently a little sleepy at present, though towards morning I discerned a lounge near one of the sentries which I thought could just as well be monopolized by me instead of him, and snoozed off for a while during the intervals — getting him to wake me at the proper periods. About 5 o'clock I found one sentry sound asleep on a bench and reprimanded him severely — he was so thoroughly frightened that

I forgot to report him. The Divisional Ammunition Column supply the guard every third day — the Highlanders the other two, so my chances of getting selected for the position again, I'm glad to say, are not very great.

We took a stowaway into custody and kept him in limbo all night and then attached him to one of our sections. He had been in since we came on board a week ago, had been allotted a bunk and place at the table and altogether was having a fine time. He was a private in another battalion and had missed his ship. The second in command of the Highlanders is Major Marshall. I thought I had seen him before, so asked him if he had ever been in Saint John and found he had been there five years as assistant D.O.C. [district officer commanding].

I understand that it will take us nearly a fortnight to cross as we cannot go faster than the slowest boat, which is ten knots. I don't know how much of all this information is state's secret. Someone told me that we are at liberty to tell of anything that *has* happened but nothing that is *going to* happen. The only order out is that communication with the shore is absolutely prohibited, so there does not seem any chance of mailing this now. I think they ought to be taking advantage of the calm seas to get moving.

With much love,
Cyrus

October 4, 1914
Onboard S.S. *Megantic*
[see next page for the beginning of the letter]

There is supposed to be a distance of four hundred yards I am told between vessels in column, but this distance is increased at times, though our column seems to be maintaining the proper formation. Between columns there looks to be something like two miles.

Today is very fine with fresh breeze from the northwest. After breakfast I felt the first real symptoms of sickness and was soon obliged to retire to my cabin, where I relieved myself of the accumulations of many meals and since then, strange to say, have been quite comfortable. Did justice to an appetizing lunch and have been sitting out on deck all afternoon basking in the sun. I heard one man say it is the finest day he ever saw at sea.

The daily routine consists of two parades for the men — morning at 10:15, afternoon at 3 for an hour's drill each time. At 5 p.m. we generally have a lecture on some subject — military law, first aid, and whatnot — and then are off duty for the rest of the evening except those who are on some special duty such as captain of the day, officer of the day, commander of the guard, or subaltern in waiting. I had my turn two

Portion of a letter to brother Ken.

days ago when the ship was not capering and will not likely be chosen for some days.

We expect to be about fifteen days in crossing. Yesterday afternoon a boxing match of six rounds took place at 4:30 p.m. between two heavies for the championship of the 48th Highlanders. The ring was just outside my window, thus saving me the bother of fighting for a good position to view it. The match was refereed by a big fellow named Sinclair, subaltern in the 48th and a member of the Argonauts football team — perhaps the finest-looking specimen of a man on board. The fight caused a lot of excitement and ended in a draw.

This morning the first real news we have had since leaving Quebec was taken in by wireless and a summary of the war news posted on the bulletin board together with the baseball results yesterday, which was quite amusing to our table because last evening I had ventured to class baseball among the standard athletic sports and met with such ridicule and opposition from most of those present. Today we find the only news worthy of notice consists of war news and baseball. Don't forget to send me a paper containing the account of each game in the World Series and until the football season is over I would like to have the sporting section of the Sunday *Boston Herald* or *Globe*.

Sincerely yours,
Cyrus

October 9, 1914
Onboard S.S. *Megantic*

Dear Ma,

This is near the end of the week, and we find ourselves about halfway across. The weather all the way has been exceptionally fine and quite favourable for a quick voyage, but we did not exceed two hundred and fourteen miles a day until yesterday, when we went two hundred and fifty. Whenever I express an opinion that the sea is quite mountainous, I am scoffed at by the good sailors. . . .

The daily routine is as follows: breakfast at 8 a.m. signalling class at 9; parade of our section 10:30; lunch at 1 p.m.; parade at 3; sports at 4; dinner at 7. Quite a monotonous program. Every time you take up a book to spend a quiet hour you feel you ought to be doing some study in a military way, etc., and *the zest is thereby taken out of the holiday.* This continual undermining motion, you will note, is making me grouchy.

We are getting the war summary daily by wireless from Paldu, England. *The last report is that the Germans have discovered that they are not good on the attack, whatever that means.* At the present time we are in the Gulf Stream and the weather is quite balmy some distance off the Grand Banks of Newfoundland. Two whales disported themselves near the ship. I was in time to see the water spout and that was all.

We have been joined by more warships. Whenever a steamer heaves in sight, one of the war vessels steams out and shoos it away either to right or left. Some steamers must get thoroughly frightened the way they turn tail and run.

With much love,
Cyrus

October 14, 1914
Onboard S.S. *Megantic*

Dear Ma,

We passed the Scilly Islands[5] at 4 o'clock this morning and expect to be off Eddystone Light about 1 p.m. and from thence we proceed to Penlee Point outside Plymouth for orders. Night before last [the] wind commenced to blow and during the night the rain fell heavily. The wind continued strong all day yesterday and last night, and we got our first real rolling, but there was no sickness as far as I know among our officers.

---

5   Isles of Scilly, off Cornwall.

As we are fairly close to shore we are not affected now by the wind, although the spray is dashing high over several torpedo boats which now form our escort. The cruisers stayed with the main body of the fleet, from which, together with several of the faster boats, we broke away early this morning. I can't tell you yet just what my first impressions of England are because the coast is pretty well clouded over by haze.

To prevent indiscriminate tipping, the adjutant arranged for subscriptions to a fund which will be distributed among the stewards by the purser. Each lieutenant was assessed five dollars, which to my mind lets us out rather easily. From this [point] on every man is watching his property closely because several cases of stealing have come to light. (Captain Stern misses twenty dollars.) And it is expected a wholesale plunder will be attempted in the last few hours of the trip. Lunch bugle blows.

With love,
Cyrus

October 14, 1914
Plymouth, onboard S.S. *Megantic*

Dear Ma,

We arrived off the harbour about 2 p.m. and were towed to our anchorage, where we made fast to a buoy in the stream. Plymouth is evidently a naval base if one can judge from the training ships, old and modern, and the warships and docks round about. The city itself is a mass of slate roofs which we may be allowed to inspect from closer quarters. At present the order is that no one is allowed onshore tonight. Whether we embark here or not is not known. As soon as I get in touch with a cable office I will wire you that I am well.

All the way up the harbour, or it may be a river (I'll look up the geography), the shores on either side were lined in places with citizens and sailors who cheered and waved enthusiastically. Just inside the breakwater were two German steamers, one a very large one, both prizes. The forts all around looked very massive and indeed much like Quebec only on a more extended scale. Our boat was the second to come to anchor and since then several others have come up behind us. . . .

Love,
Cyrus

October 15, 1914
Onboard S.S. *Megantic*

Dear Ma,
Our arrival in Plymouth was evidently a surprise to the natives — several of the English morning papers are on board. Only one I believe [knew about] the arrival of the Canadians and states it was unexpected. The paper further says that we are to go to Bulford Camp, which is part of Salisbury Plain. Some of the transports have gone into the piers, and we will likely get orders to disembark soon. Am looking forward with keen interest to the trip through England

Orders came to dye our haversacks brown. In an oversight we were issued with white. The order came while we were at sea and at first coffee was to be used as there was no dye on board, but when it was reckoned how much coffee it would take to dye eighteen hundred haversacks, the plan was abandoned.

The weather last evening was cloudy with a chilly wind, and today it looks like rain. The landscape is green and the land is laid off in hedges in the manner of which you who have travelled several times through the country well know.

I sent a cable this morning early to Ken stating that I had arrived and was in good health. Although we are at anchor, the usual drill — physical exercise and signalling — is going on. When we get finally settled in camp, there will be a great shakedown and readjustment. It is probable that many of the provisional appointments made in Canada

Envelope
addressed to
Cy's mother.

will not be confirmed by the English authorities. And as the officers are considerably overstrength, there is some speculation as to what will be done with the surplus. For instance, in one section there are four officers at present attached, viz. Stern, Hoodless, Dunlop, and myself. Hoodless and Dunlop are well versed in battery drill and I am not, so it is likely that they will be sent up to the batteries and I will have to stick along with the ammunition column.

We got newspapers for the first time since leaving Quebec this morning and the situation looks rather hopeful. From a short piece I read in a London paper, I take it that all city lights are not turned on at night, which keeps the city in darkness to discourage attacks from airmen, and that the early closing moment — about 7 p.m. — is observed pretty generally throughout the land. I have written you several letters lately which I trust will pass the censor all right.

With love,
Cyrus

October 16, 1914
12:30 p.m.
Onboard S.S. *Megantic*

Dear Ken,

We drew into the dock this morning and the 48th Highlanders are preparing to leave the ship. The ammunition column has no definite orders yet. As we entered the basin (a dock known as Prince of Wales Basin) this morning we passed on one side a super-Dreadnought[6] getting ready to leave and another, the *Elizabeth*, in process of construction while on the other side was the *Tiger* — the largest in the fleet, one man told me — taking on coal. The piers are very substantial looking, being built of granite blocks and capable of accommodating many vessels.

The boxing matches referred to in the paper were very entertaining. Last Saturday evening a return match between the two heavies who had fought on deck the week previous took place in the third-class saloon and was most exciting — the ring roped off in the centre and the crowded room made a scene that will always be remembered. Yesterday afternoon several bouts took place on deck. The last one was between a lightweight from our column and the champion amateur lightweight of Canada, who came from the *Laurentic* and was quite enjoyable, the decision going to the *Laurentic*. The latest dope as to destination is Lavington Station, thence to South Down, Salisbury Plain, for training.

Sincerely,
Cyrus

6   By 1914, the Royal Navy had nineteen Dreadnoughts, or modern battleships, with thirteen more under construction. At the time, they were the biggest, fastest, and most heavily armed warships ever built, and the first major ones driven solely by steam turbines.

Gunners' tents on Salisbury Plain.

Chapter Two

Salisbury Plain

*Our warrant officer joined the battery on Salisbury Plain at
a time when things were more or less chaotic, and we needed
instruction in regimental duties. He had an uphill fight but
finally succeeded in getting things to run with smoothness. You
thought him stern and severe, but when you found that he was . . .
'just' in his dealings with you and a lover of fair play, he won
your respect and became your friend. He was a tower of strength
to the unit. No one had the interests of the battery more at heart.
He was continually asking me to do one thing or another for
your comfort. If the slightest thing seemed to work an injustice
to you, he let me know of it at once. He couldn't see anything
else but the 1st Heavies. No one put anything over on the 1st
Heavies when he was around.*

October 22, 1914
Salisbury Plain

Dear Ken,

   Things are going along quietly here. We are practically without any
equipment yet. Rather unadvisedly we left the Plymouth Docks without
leaving anyone behind to look after our wagons, saddles, harness etc.,

etc., and as everyone is playing the grab game, I don't think we will see much of it.

Some of my mail has evidently gone astray again because apart from a letter from Ma dated September 26 and another dated October 6, [I have] had no mail since Valcartier. An order has been made that all parties can have leave for not exceeding three days, and this will give us ample opportunity from time to time to see the surrounding country. I am going in a week or so to London to spend two or three days with Hughie McLean. He is staying with his father at the Savoy for a month and has my clothes there with him. I thought civilian clothes a nuisance so sent you all I had from Valcartier, but now I want them because a uniform attracts too much attention.

Will write you again soon,
Cy

October 26, 1914
Salisbury Plain

Dear Ma,

Please excuse the improvised writing implement but I find it [pencil] more suitable to tent surroundings than pen and ink. Today is fine and cool with wind blowing, which is just what we want after a spell of five cloudy and rainy days for the purpose of drying processes. There must still be a stack of letters lying for me somewhere. It was reported that the *Franconia*, one of the transports, was carrying an immense quantity of mail matter from Valcartier but it probably has not been sorted yet.

On Wednesday last we all gathered to receive a short talk from General Alderson, who has been appointed to command the Canadians. He is not a large man but still not as diminutive as Earl Roberts, who reviewed us on Saturday morning in the rain. Dr. Maclaren, Dr. Corbet, and Dr. Bridges are in the same mess tent with our column and it seems quite like New Brunswick to see them there. Tomorrow morning I am transferring myself and baggage to another ammunition column, that attached to the heavy battery, commanded by Frank Magee, and in future my address will be Ammunition Column Heavy Battery, West Down, North Camp, Salisbury Plain. I am rather glad to get somewhere near Frank again, although I have made a number of good friends where I am now. I think I can work in better with Frank than any other — he appreciates my capacities and incapacities better.

In a few days I expect to go into Salisbury for the afternoon. It is about as far from here as Westfield is from Saint John and is reported to be very quaint and old fashioned. Besides having a celebrated cathedral, the houses are most interesting. One man told me the second storeys overhang and can be reached easily from the sidewalk, but I think he must be kidding me.

So far my duties have consisted solely in the care of horse lines, and in trying to get the right number of horses to which our section is entitled, viz. 105 draught and 8 riding. These duties are not very onerous but occupy most of the time. I am a little disappointed in the English papers, although I am afraid American journalism is overdone and a few of our own papers are inclined to exaggerate, in particular the *Saint John Telegraph*. I think I prefer a paper with the real news on the front page.

Captain Stern is in London for a few days, and his command has descended on me in his absence. I have just held daily court at which two prisoners appeared. The first case was against a man for absenting himself since arrival at Plymouth — this I remanded to be dealt with by Captain Stern. In the second case the prisoner was charged with refusing to obey the order of a non-commissioned officer. He had already been in custody for two days so I discharged him from arrest and for so doing incurred the criticism of the officer who had overheard the refusal and who had put him under arrest — he wanted to give him three months!

With love,
Cyrus

November 2, 1914
Salisbury Plain

Dear Ken,

I received your letters and also the papers re baseball, which we drank in most rapidly. In fact it made me quite proud to give out the information. The Braves must be a wonderful team.

This is the tenth day of rainy weather, and this last day is much worse than the first, and the indications are not for better weather. The explanation given by the natives is that since April, until this damp spell, the weather was unusually fine with no rain and therefore it is time some rain fell.

I joined Frank Magee's ammunition column on Tuesday evening last and have not been very busy since. Their Majesties have decided to inspect the Canadians on Wednesday. This morning the troops held a rehearsal in the heavy rain before General Alderson. I stayed in my tent looking after the camp while the others were away and thereby escaped a good drenching. Yesterday afternoon — Sunday — Frank, Kel, and myself rode over to Tilshead village to five o'clock tea. One of our officers, Ryan by name, of the Montreal Cemetery Company, was followed over by his wife, who has taken rooms in the village, and were asked over to tea. Mrs. Ryan was a typist in the Royal Trust Company in Montreal and known to Kelly — it was quite a novel situation for him meeting her in an English village in this manner.

Will you kindly, without unnecessary delay, etc., ask Mary where she got the socks she gave me and buy a dozen pairs and forward them to me by mail *registered* together with the bill. Frank Magee wants some and another party has taken a great fancy to them.

I am doing considerable riding now and expect to be able to sit in my saddle fairly well soon. The opportunities for riding are most excellent and it is a fine pastime. I have a new man now to look after me. I took quite a fancy to him at Valcartier and when I left the D.A.C. I decided to [ask] for the other man's transfer. His name is Frank Hall and I had a hard time persuading Captain Stern to give him up. He was in the

Coast Defence Service in Nova Scotia for three years and was also in the Philippines. He knows a horse thoroughly and is invaluable to me in that respect. He is, besides, a native of Saint John. He is a quiet-going chap and the other officers did not appreciate his abilities, and so when I asked for him, Stern promised him to me. He soon regretted his promise and tried in every way to prevent him going. Even today when I sent Hall up to see if there was any mail at D.A.C., Stern got him and told him if he would come back he would make him a bombardier, which means one stripe (a corporal has two stripes, a sergeant three) but Hall refused the offer.

The bugle is blowing the first post — 9 p.m. — which means come into camp. Last post is 9:30 p.m. and 9:45 p.m. lights out. I want to get in between the blankets but I am doing orderly duty tonight, meaning the round of the sentries and horse picquet and to see that no lights are burning — sometime between 10 and 11. So I have to stay up for awhile longer. To my mind an oversight at Valcartier which has not been improved, as here, is the lack of some well-heated place in the evening in which the officers can congregate, as the only thing really to do after dinner is to go to bed. Frank and I are getting an oil heater — fourteen or fifteen bob [shillings] — which will be here any day now and then we can live like lords.

On the *Megantic* the D.A.C. officers were inclined to ridicule some of the 48th Highlanders who brought their stoves with them but that proves to have been a mistaken folly. It is surprising how really warm the stove makes the tent. Don't surmise that I am in a complaining mood — far from it. I am feeling grand and getting as strong as a prize fighter and eat like a cormorant. In fact there is nothing like life in the open for health. Our tent is a bell tent — that is, a round tent fourteen feet in diameter — wooden platform for a floor, the pole in the centre serves as a coat hanger. Frank has his sleeping bag with three blankets. I have a rubber sheet on the floor then a pelisse[7] stuffed with hay and straw and on top of that seven blankets, which makes a snug cot all together. Two boxes the

---

7   An outdoor garment with armholes or sleeves reaching to the ankles, worn over other clothes.

size of banana crates make a good set of shelves and Frank has a table for his office work, and that completes our outfit. The canvas has kept the rain out well.

When I take over my duties I expect to rise at 6 a.m. and attend morning stables at 6:15 — this consists of leading the horses out to water and then feeding and grooming them, which proceeding lasts until 7, when the men have breakfast. Morning parade is at 8:30 and my job will be to take the horses and drivers out for exercise and manoeuvre. Noon stables is at 11:45 a.m. The afternoon is a repetition of the morning. Evening stables is at 4:15 p.m. The men have their dinner at 5 and then those not on guard or picquet or in the clink for petty offences go off for recreation to the canteens, Y.M.C.A. tents, or to call on friends in other camps.

Sincerely,
Cyrus

November 17, 1914

Dear Ma,

I have all the underclothing I need so it will not be necessary for you to send any more. I have two issue suits of underwear — that is, clothing

Number 1 horse lines on Salisbury Plain.

issued for which we pay nothing — which are about three times as thick as anything I ever saw before, so it is unlikely I'll ever be tempted to put them on. [rest of letter missing]

December 5, 1914
Thackeray Hotel
Great Russell Street
London, England

Dear Ma,

I left camp at 11 a.m. with Dick Leach and my batman and rode to Lavington Station, arriving there in time to catch the 12:30 p.m. train. Just as the trains hove in sight I remembered that my grip containing *our* outfit was still tied to the back of Hall's saddle, so we rushed back to where we had dismounted only to find Hall and the horses had gone. We decided to take the 1:48 and retraced our steps to the village inn, and just as we got there Hall came galloping back with the three horses and bag with many apologies for having forgotten. The real joke came when the 1:48 came thundering past without stopping and we were obliged to wait for the 2:30, which, however, turned out to be a through train with but one stop on the way to London, namely at Reading.

We arrived in town at 4:30, took a taxi to Daly's Theatre to get seats for *The Country Girl*, found the house full up, and went to the Prince of Wales Theatre and got the last pair of seats for *Miss Hook of Holland*, a delightful comic opera with Miss Phyllis Dare in the title role. After securing our seats for the theatre, I insisted on having my hair cut and shampooed, a process which cost one shilling, just half the charge in Saint John. I then purchased a new tie and gloves, had the mud brushed off my boots by a boot black on the curb, and then felt quite respectable. After strolling along Regent Street for a while we went to Frascati's for dinner — a huge success. My order of meat was chicken, in contrast to the alternate diet of mutton and beef served up by Horrids — I mean Harrods.

It gets dark here shortly after four o'clock, and as the city is kept in practical darkness on account of the danger from Zeppelin attack, I have not been able to see much of it yet. But some motor busses with a top deck look to me as a splendid vantage ground for a sightseer and will probably receive their fair share of patronage from me in the morrow. We got off at Paddington Station, as this hotel is directly opposite the British Museum.

Just as I was leaving camp the post office orderly brought your parcel along with gloves, etc., for which please accept thanks. Luckily I had my riding breaches cleaned and mended on Thursday afternoon. I noticed a small tear in the knee and to prevent it getting any larger sent Hall to Tilshead with them to get the old lady who does my washing to mend them. This she did and helped Hall gasoline them, all for thruppence. Now for a hot tub.

Good night.

With love,
Cyrus

December 11, 1914
Salisbury Plain

Dear Ken,

You will have heard before this that I have had my initial visit to London, which I wish we could have made together. My visit to the Inns of Court with Hughie McLean was a delightful experience. He called at the hotel for me about half past twelve and we went to the law courts where I heard Mr. Justice Astbury in a Chancery case and the lord chief justice (Rufus Isaacs) in an appellate case. Counsel and judges wear wigs and look exactly like pictures that you have frequently seen of the English bar and judiciary — their polished style of speaking is quite noticeable.

Hughie has his desk in an office in one of the yards. The very atmosphere of the place is an incentive to study — a great contrast to some of the districts further along, viz. Piccadilly and Oxford Circuses and whatnot. After leaving the court rooms we went through the Temple Church, which is a very old place full of monuments of the Templars, then paid a visit to Goldsmith's tomb. I enjoyed very much my lunch in the Inner Temple where lawyers and students go for their noonday meal. It was not one of the dinners that Hugh has to eat as a prerequisite to his admission to the bar. I thought at first it was and offered to eat a good one for him. The regular dinners are more formal and are eaten at four named periods during the year. We then betook ourselves to the Cheshire Cheese, a small pub with restaurant, which is famous by reason of the fact that Dr. Johnston was an habitué of the place.

The weather of late has been improving — the last two days being fine and mild. The rain we get on the plain is by no means universal. The plain has a bad reputation and often when it is blowing or raining hard here it is pleasant in London.

Sincerely,
Cyrus

December 20, 1914
Heavy Battery

Dear Ma,
I am glad to report that at last I have a tent all to myself but as my furniture has not yet been selected, I am sitting on the floor with lantern on suitcase beside me doing my best to forget the first principles of handwriting. By the way, I think I mentioned once before in an early letter a farmhouse in a grove near our camp. I did not think then that we were to spend the winter there but so have events transpired. We had to move somewhere to get out of the mud and preferably to a wood where the horses can get some shelter from the elements, which at this time of year in this country stand fairly exclusively for rain, and as the promised land consisting of huts is apparently as far distant as ever, we

looked around for a likely spot and decided upon this grove. We found we could utilize the old farm buildings for stores, offices, and mess room with kitchen attached. As some solatium for our wounded feelings in not going into huts, a few additional tents were given us and now each officer has his own.

We have two large rooms for [the] men and, as we expect to fit one up with tubs for washing personnel and material, some of them will be compelled to undergo their first bath and will experience the novelty of getting used to clean clothing. But the mess room is what you should see. Instead of a marquee apologetically heated with oil lamp stoves, we have a room eleven by eleven feet square with a huge open fireplace. Alongside the fireplace is an alcove in which shelves are to be placed for our provisions, and opening off the room is the kitchen eleven feet long by five feet wide. I can't paint a picture of the cottage but it is just such a one in which [Robbie] Burns might have been born — thatched roof, thick walls, low ceilings.

The other building, which runs at right angles, has been taken possession of by the quartermaster sergeant and the sergeant major. Hearing sounds of revelry caused by the gramophone, I dropped into the store room last evening and found them with two privileged assistants comfortably ensconced before a large open fireplace with the logs

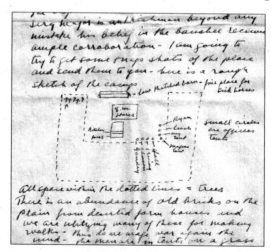

Sketch of camp
on Salisbury Plain.

burning merrily. They were certainly enjoying themselves. They have appropriated upstairs for their sleeping apartment and were looking forward to a sound sleep with some braggadocio. I am inclined to opine that their slumber was somewhat infringed upon by two owls that apparently have their domicile under the capacious eaves. I am going to try and get some snapshots of the place . . . here is a rough sketch of the camp.

There is an abundance of old bricks on the plain from deserted farmhouses, and we are utilizing many of these for making walks — thus do we wage war against the mud. The men are in tents on a grass slope back of the grove. They are taking pains to keep horses and vehicles out of their lines to keep the sod intact and have stretched wire on stakes for that purpose. Much to their delight a horseman from another battery, neglectful of warnings not to ride through and going at some speed with the easy assurance of an accomplished rider, did not see the wire. Result? His horse stopped at the wire and [the rider] stopped a considerable distance within the enclosure. Sympathy? Nil. Nor would you blame them for their lack of charitable feeling if you could see the result of indiscriminate trampling. The men average seven to a tent, and we have approximately two hundred men. The tent floors would prove a poor advertisement for Old Dutch Cleanser.

I was not present at the moving — the *locus in quo* of my alibi was Salisbury, to which good town I had been sent to purchase all kinds of utensils for fitting up our mess and an initial supply of provisions. I think I told you before that Harrods' ("Horrids") contract for messing ends tomorrow, and it is ordered that officers conduct their own messing in future. We are allowed 4s a day and rations or, if preferred, 5s 6d a day without drawing rations. My instructions were to buy utensils and supplement rations with a reasonable supply of staple diet. Rations consist of bacon, bread, coffee, tea, sugar, salt, and pepper with an inadequate allowance of vegetables. Note the absence of butter, eggs, and milk, to say nothing of plum pudding and turkey.

So to Salisbury I repaired, not without showing, as a matter of policy, an assumed reluctance to leave camp. *I find it is not wise to appear too eager to undertake anything in the army.* Left here at 9:30 a.m. on a motor lorry accompanied by the invaluable Hall — arrived 10:15 doing the fourteen miles in good time considering the means of locomotion. Went at once to Smee's Bookstore for some maps, then to the Old Grange, and then to Lloyd's Hardware Shop, where I remained till 1:15 p.m. undergoing much vexation of spirit because the return journey was scheduled to commence at 2 o'clock and I was counting on ample time for sightseeing. Thus you see how I have failed to appreciate the time you spend in the marts on King Street.[8]

After that I went to lunch at the Old Grange Hotel, and as I am sending you a pamphlet on the place I will not dwell on its antiquities farther. The motor lorry being delayed until 3:30 p.m. owing to the fact that the R.C.H.A. [Royal Canadian Horse Artillery] had a half interest in its use and were also purchasing stores, I was enabled to visit a wholesale grocer. Eggs are almost unobtainable, and if the milk we are getting at Harrods is not taken from the chalky subsoil which here abounds, then I'll eat my hat. However, after refusing some very good Danish eggs which were recommended for frying but which I was assured would pop on boiling, I located a dairy where I purchased all they had left — one and a half dozen at 3s a dozen. The proprietress stated she had refused one of her best customers a few moments before but let me have them because she has a son in the New Army. Such is the power of a uniform. I then found a place where they had four dozen left which I got at 2/6 a dozen.

The stove is a range which just fits the kitchen and goes against the wall with the pipe out. I hired it for 3/10 for as long as we want it with the condition that we can become the owners on paying another quid (slang for pound). The biggest problem is the cook but we expect to land one tomorrow.

I found I could get a seat in a Ford car which was leaving at 4:45 p.m., so I was afforded an opportunity of walking through the cathedral — thus squeezing into five minutes that which should take that many hours.

---

8   King Street, Saint John, N.B.

On getting back to camp I found that it had been decided to draw money instead of rations, so I am off on another jaunt to Shrewton tomorrow to make arrangements for meat and bread. I entirely accord with your description of the English puddings, and while I am sergeant of the mess I will scrutinize that department of the menu very closely.

Jack Ryan and I are remaining in camp for Christmas — as we both can't go to Tilshead, we are going to make merry in the mess and his wife is to join us, so that the dinner in Tilshead is off. I am thinking of supplementing turkey with pheasant *et al.*

> With much love,
> Cyrus

December 24, 1914

Dear Ma,

I have before me among a mass of letters yours of December 3, 7, and 11, and instead of trimming Christmas trees I am spending the evening answering letters and acknowledging cards.

I experienced in full measure the difference in travelling here between a through train and one which makes intermediate stops. The old accommodation train to Westfield is an express compared with a slow train here. My mission in Devizes (a very old, historic town) was first to buy suits of civilian clothes for the useless men in the battery who are being sent back to Canada and then to bring more hardware for putting up the mess. I thought I had sufficient materials but our cook, an ex-steward on a steamer and our waiter at Harrods, suggested additions which we don't need — however, they say a good cook must be humoured.

After shopping I had a grilled steak at the Haunch of Venison — six hundred years old — I mean the Venison, not the steak, though unfortunately, it seemed like it. I then hired a small motor car, collected my purchases at the different stores, and hied away back to camp, arriving there about 10 p.m.

If the cook keeps sober I think we will have a good dinner on the morrow. This afternoon I rode over to Shrewton and brought back the turkey and the ham which I had cooked at a local provisioners. Mrs. Ryan is to provide the plum pudding, mince pie, and various other delicacies. I arranged for the cooking of the meat before the cook came or, rather, before he had been tested out. He is to warm them up. The cook did not arrive until the middle of the first morning, so Dick Leach and I got the breakfast ready. I cooked the porridge, which everyone declared much superior to Harrods, while he poached the eggs.

Two days ago a parcel came containing chocolate bars and small boxes of sweets and a jar of apricot jam with a card of best wishes from Christine and Bertha Maclaren, who I take it are the Dr.'s sisters — am I right? I got a card from Dr. and Mrs. P.R. Inches which is a model of good taste.

I had my photo taken while in London and expected to make presentations to the family in that form but the photographer has disappointed me, and if they do not turn up soon I will sue him because he demanded my money in advance. It is now half past twelve and I have to go the round of the horse picquet and guard before turning in.

Mr. and Mrs. Ryan were in for a while tonight and I told Mrs. Ryan that I was going to hang up my sock tonight over the oil stove to test the Santa Claus theory thoroughly, as this is the first time I have ever been given an opportunity to solve the mystery. Though if there is nothing there I'll venture to say that you will claim he does not approve of oil stoves.

> With much love and good wishes,
> Cyrus

Crissus Eve

Dear Chacker,

It is getting towards two o'clock in the morning and I am still writing letters. I rode over to the Copse Farm today to invite Lawrence Kelly to dinner with me tomorrow but found he had gone to Salisbury. Just like the heavy battery, his brigade has settled around a deserted farm building. It is really in good repair and quite capacious, and they are living in much luxury with many rooms for messing, sociality, and offices — together with two pianos.

I hear a sonorous noise in the next tent, which is either Santa Claus operating or old man Reed snoring away in his sleep. As it may be Santa Claus, to bed for me or he won't leave me anything. Love to Patsy and Jan. Merriness to you and Harry.

> With love,
> Chacker

December 31, 1914
Salisbury Plain

Dear Ken,

This is probably the last letter I'll write from West Down for some time to come. I spent the day with Magee, Leach, and the sergeant major at Devizes, Marston, and Worton with reference to billeting the battery in private houses for the winter. We made a house-to-house canvas in Marston and Worton and found ample quarters for man and beast. At present I think that Leach, myself, and one other will go to Captain Peto's house — a fine large one with splendid stalls and garage. He is a Member of Parliament and has been at the front, to which he goes back shortly. He says that weather conditions make it undesirable to send more troops across for some months.

We had dinner at the Bear Inn at Devizes. We had with us the chief constable, who was very effective in impressing upon the people the necessity for billeting. He said that Worton took pride in having as a visitor at present the tallest man in the world, eight foot two inches, and after supper, hearing the man's voice in the bar, he went out and brought him in. He lately came back from Germany, where he was interned. It seems he was being exhibited in German towns at the opening of the war when he and his manager were made prisoners. He got quite emaciated for want of sufficient food and was allowed to go back on an American passport which he had. It is impossible to give you an idea of his size. It is quite alarming. He had to stoop to get in the door of the room and was broad enough to about fill the doorway. He sat down and even then was nearly as tall as Frank Magee, who was standing. With these fun remarks, etc.

Yours,
Cyrus

January 10, 1915
No. 1 H.B. Worton P.O.
Wilts

Dear Ma,

Your two letters, the last written on Christmas day, arrived on Friday, so you [see] the delivery is getting rather better. The barrel of apples has not turned up yet. I had a notice from Allans that it had been sent to West Downorth, which means that it is probably at Lavington Station, to which place I have sent a letter of inquiry, so it should turn up soon. We are gradually settling down in our new quarters. I think I told you that I am with a dairyman at Marston and take my meals at Worton. My horse is with me and [my] batman is next door. The villagers are reaping quite a harvest, the rates being as follows: single bed, 8d; 2 in bed, 6d each;

breakfast, 7½d; dinner, 1/7½; supper, 4½d; stall in barn for horse, 9d; stall in shed for horse, 6d.

The argument arises over whether a shack in Evesham is a horse barn or a cow shed. I took a slip containing the rates to each billet yesterday — one old fox I was quite ready for. So without letting him know the reason for my visit, I engaged him in conversation over the merits of an old wagon shed that some of our horses are in.

"Mr. Dewey, is that a horse barn or a cow shed?"

FLOOD FREAKS FOCUSSED: A DREADNOUGHT OF THE LAND.

Salisbury Plain has well earned its reputation as the training ground for Flanders. This picture shows a heavy traction engine ploughing its way through a flood which would make the waters of Ypres subside in impotent envy.

Daily Sketch, January 4, 1915.

"Well, it's hardly a barn, is it? No, it's more like a cow shed, isn't it!?"

"Well yes, it is, isn't it!?"

Even after that he thought he should have 9d, because "We have to live, haven't we!?"

The farm I am on is one hundred and fifty acres in extent and is owned by a couple recently married who are running a dairy. It is the best place in the village. Today they had me to dinner, and I am now sitting before their wood fire after an ample meal of roast beef, potatoes, Brussels sprouts, plums with custard, and cider. I am getting quite accustomed to the feather bed. The last two mornings they have sent tea and toast to my room, so you can see I am rapidly developing into an Englishman.

My farmer host tells me that adders abound in the hedges in summertime and are quite poisonous. I did not know that snakes existed in this part of the world — also otter — besides quantities of foxes, rabbits, stoats,[9] and badgers. One of our men shot three rabbits and a stoat yesterday, and we had rabbit last night at the mess, which saved the cost of dinner.

The country is swamped from the rains and the brooks are overflowing everywhere, which is a source of wonderment to the yokels who frequent the footpath to view the flood.

With love,
Cyrus

January 12, 1915
No. 1 H.B. Worton P.O.
Wilts

Dear Ken,

Just a few lines before dinner. I sent my batman over to Durnington

---

9   An ermine in its summer coat.

a few days ago and he brought back the parcel from Mrs. Eva — the candy was very much appreciated. There is nothing over here with the Moirs flavour. The people I am with have a fine gramophone, which is still quite a new plaything to them and we keep it working overtime in the evenings.

Sincerely,
Cyrus

January 15, 1915
Worton P.O.

Dear Ma,

Been just this minute advised apples are at Devizes. Will send for them in morning. We had a visit from a real general this morning who was on a tour of inspection of horses. He is a very affable sort of fellow and made himself generally agreeable. On leaving, he stated that our horses are the best cared for that he has yet inspected. If he had known that the usual duties had been dispensed with all morning, and grooming substituted, he might have had a solution for their appearance. They are still far from the good-looking animals they were when put on board the transports.

There is a concert advertised for tomorrow evening in the hall. Citizens 6d, soldiers free. Proceeds to go to the Red Cross Fund. The vicar is making himself active in the arrangements. He and his wife have their hands full at home also.

The captain's first consideration is always his digestive satisfaction. The rest of us make a study of his idiosyncrasies . . . and myself in particular, for I am catering for the mess. A few evenings ago he pushed his cup of tea away from him in disgust and refused to drink on account of the quantity of tea leaves in the tea. As his remarks were really addressed to me and my trusty cook, I retaliated with some remarks on the fitness for active service of a person who could not put up with a few tea leaves. This put him very much in his dignity, and he hopes for the day when he will make me take those words back: "There is no one among us who is more prepared to endure hardship [than I am] . . . " and whatnot. Later on, after the meal was over and we were gathered together, he opened up again and stated that he had never felt that he had been so stinted with his food as he had been at this meal. There was nothing to the piece of fish he had received (finnan haddie) except bone, and if he had known there was so little to eat, he would not have refused an invitation to tea that he had received at the vicarage. My reply that a person with a belly his size required a whale brought the discussion to a humorous close. The matter has not been reopened since.

He was to London some time ago on six days' leave to see "my dear wife and daughters," a trio that he married last summer and who have followed him to England. The betting among us was that he would resort to subterfuge to stretch his leave out into a longer period. Sure enough, a letter arrived written by Madam, written absolutely without her husband's knowledge, and asking "you dear duck of a major" to extend Ernie's leave. The request was ignored, but the leave was overstayed all the same. Of course we all knew that he had married a widow with two daughters, ages twenty-five and twenty-eight, say, but as I had not joined the battery until of late, I could not be supposed to be acquainted with his history.

January 18, 1915
Worton, Wilts

Dear Ken,

Just a line to let you know that the boots, etc., arrived today — they are grand — almost too much so for this climate. Thanks very much. Tell Ma I traced the apples today from Devizes Station to Poterne guard room, one mile from here, where they are in charge of Captain Pickles. I am sending a team for them tomorrow. The mails are rather slow at present. The last letters I had were dated December 31. The papers are held up unreasonably. I believe they sometimes contain unwelcome news which is considered too much for the English people to digest, such as the loss of the *Audacious*,[10] which as yet has not been reported in the English newspapers — though vague allusions to a loss have been made in speeches in the House [of Lords].

Life in billets is almost too comfortable after life on the plain. The people I am with do not have to feed me, but they insist in giving me breakfast and tea also, if I am round at the proper hour. It takes some courage to add the words "in bed" after the word "breakfast" above, but I suppose I should make a clean breast of it! And they will insist in putting a large hot water bottle every night amid the feathers.

War Is Hell!

Sincerely,
Cyrus

February 7, 1915
Worton, Wilts

Dear Ken,

The papers and magazines have been coming quite regularly of late and are much appreciated.

I am doing a lot of writing tonight answering letters that I have received lately from various parties. I would like to get up to London to see Hughie McLean but cannot do so as my application for leave has been turned down. I would also like to have a night in London with Bev Macaulay, who is always good fun — notwithstanding reports to the contrary. Saint John does not seem to be lacking in social activity but perhaps this activity predominates among those over the age limit.

I went to Devizes this morning to keep an appointment with the dentist which I made while in there yesterday afternoon — as it was six months since I had any work done, I was in a rather dubious state of mind but was much reassured morally and financially when all he could

---

10 H.M.S. *Audacious* was sunk by a mine on October 27, 1914, but the loss was not acknowledged until after the war.

discover was one small cavity for filling, which together with a cleaning he charged me half a guinea.

I purchased in Devizes yesterday a small pamphlet entitled "A Soldier's First Aid to French" which is most elementary and concise but quite helpful — this with the book you gave me should help me to make myself understood in simple matters. When Harry goes you ought to get Connie and the babies into 179 Germain. From a letter I received today from Connie I gather they would be only too pleased to receive such an invitation. I have been breaking in the boots some lately and find them OK.

Sincerely yours,
Cyrus

Chapter Three

Rough Passage to War

You cannot forget the rough passage of five days from Avonmouth to St. Nazaire, half the battery being in the Australind, *the other half on the* Mount Temple; *then came the three-day trip across France to Hazebrouck, in freight cars, bearing the now classic inscription "40 Hommes, 8 Chevaux" and the march from there to Le Peuplier, near Castre, where we had our first experience with French billets. Two weeks were devoted to battery manoeuvre before we marched south to our first position at Fleurbaix, as part of the 1st Divisional Artillery.*

February 19, 1915

Dear Ma,

The battery is now established in billets in France but until we get the correspondence regulations I will refrain from saying much. The censorship is so strict. We had quite a rough sea voyage. *La mer* has no attractions for me at all, though I weathered it better than I expected.

The evening we all left Marston and Worton I constituted myself with a rear guard and rode back to Marston to see if any of them had remained in their billets. I found two in Marston, one guarding his box of shoeing tools in Worton, and three more celebrating in the Neat Oak in Worton. We hired a team and packed the whole lot in and arrived at the station on time.

Our veterinary officer, a French Canadian, writing now at the same table with me but who came on another boat, has just given me a description of the voyage. He said, "She roll. She roll. By gosh she roll," which is very expressive. We were driven out to sea by the gale, or at least the captain steered that way to avoid side rollers, so consequently made slower time. I know that after spending the roughest day on my back I reckoned that we must be pretty nearly across. *You can imagine the state of my feelings when the chief officer announced that we had been going all day in the wrong direction.* Magee was on another boat. They had such a rough time of it that S.O.S. signals were sent out, though the passengers, if they may be termed so, were not aware of it at the time. Curiously enough, as long as I was on my back I did not feel ill but a few minutes in an upright position had a collapsible effect.

I got into a pastry shop near the place where we disembarked and bought some grub for our evening meal. I had no idea that there could be so many delicacies in the cookbook. I had a compartment in the train with an officer of the D.A.C. that I knew very well on the *Megantic*, and as he had a big hamper, well lined, I did not have hunger. At night I slept in a boxcar in blankets on a foot of straw and never had a more comfortable sleep.

I have a room in a farmhouse with Mr. Ryan and the vet. The floor is of tiles. We have straw and our sleeping kits and can keep very comfortable. I notice a difference in the types of stoves in England, here, and in Canada. I really think that our own suffer in comparison.

The lady of the farm gives us a good service — coffee at all meals — tea, an unknown quantity. However, as we are having rations, we will get the battery tea. We are to be allowed rations just like the troops and receive four shillings each day, in addition. We are paying her to cook for us and also get from her such articles as we want, which are not included in rations, e.g. milk, eggs, puddings, chicken, and whatnot. She likes to have appreciation shown for her cooking and always asks how we like each dish.

"Très excellent! Bien! Très magnifique!" and so forth are our replies.

Bonsoir avec amour,
Cyrus
No. C43221
No. 1 Heavy Battery

The First Month in the Line — Neuve Chapelle

The battery was brought into prominence almost immediately by its destruction of Fromelles Church Tower, an enemy observation point which dominated the whole divisional front, and later by a series of registrations carried out with aeroplane observation. We took part in the battle of Neuve Chapelle by shelling road corners in Illies, Aubers, Herlies, and Fournes.

Février 21, 1915
Dimanche matin

Ma Cherie Mère,
    Just a court letter avant le mail closes. Je suis having some difficulty in making myself understood but with the assistance of some French Canadians who are members of the battery, we are able to get along tout bien. I have a small book which I purchased (acheter) in Devizes for 6 pence called the "Soldier's First Aid to French" which contains a few expressions, among them . . . parlez lentement, s'il vous plaît . . . with which I preface my remarks but to no avail because of the tendency of my hearers to rattle off their answer back with lightning rapidity.
    The lady of la maison où je suis staying is a plus excellent cuillière (cook) and is overzealous in her endeavours on our behalf. Dernière nuit un bon poulet — comprenez? Hier je reçu votre letter de January 29 and

also the diary pour mon birthday pour quel accept thanks, s'il vous plaît. Tell Ken his letter of the same date and *The Daily Telegraph* arrived. Bonjour avec amour.

Votre garçon,
Cyrus F. Inches

P.S. Primroses and snowdrops in bloom here. C.F.I.

February 24, 1915

Dear Ma,

Yesterday I received from you a letter demanding votes for women and enclosing [a] Valentine and in the same mail I received eight bundles of newspapers and magazines from Ken, bringing the local news down to February 8, 1915. Ere this *you must have received my letter telling of the arrival of the apples in good condition* and my great appreciation of the same.

A curious thing about the houses here is the dog wheel to run the churn — no house seems to lack it. The windmill is also a matter of intense interest to me. I was passing one yesterday which was quite proximate to the road, and as the thing was in action and my horse was not quite sure as to what to make of it, any Don Quixotian ideas I might have had of charging into it were entirely frustrated by the action of my steed.

At the same table with us is a professor of political science from Paris who has travelled extensively, speaks excellent English, and who has written a book upon his impressions of Canada. His ideas on many questions are highly interesting to listen to as he is very well informed. I can gather from separate conversations that there is little, if any, fraternal feeling between old France and French Canada — in fact, just the other way. However, both are united against the German, which, after all, is the principal thing they have in common.

Our cook is a very thrifty lady. I imagine their staple diet here is soup, eggs, bread, beer, and coffee. She asked our veterinarian what he wanted done with what was left over from our meals. She is too honest to take it without asking, so she gets it by this hint. The coffee here is par excellence and is really the best thing she does. They do not use tea, so I supplied them with some out of our rations for my personal use. Never heard of oatmeal at all. Last evening my batman, Hall, asked the professor the French word for nutmeg. He had never heard of it and I don't think he got a clear impression from my description of it, or the grater. I don't think Valentine's Day is celebrated in these parts. The professor had heard of it, though, and was much amused over the card you sent.

With much love,
Cyrus

February 27, 1915

Dear Ma,

Madame does not like the Rochefort cheese that the veterinarian bought and which he left with her to bring to the table. In fact she considers it almost an insult on his part for bringing it into the house. When she brings it into the room she holds it away from her with the most intense look of disgust on her face. My bed, or rather sleeping bag, rests on about two inches of straw on the floor. The mice get in the straw at night and quite audibly nibble away at it. Today, after consulting a dictionary, I asked for a "trap de souris" to put in the corner and suggested to her that we have mice for tea. Up to noon, however, no game was snared and we blame Madame for using meat as bait instead of the doctor's cheese.

At the present moment she is leading the family at prayers in the adjoining room at a rate which is surprising. It must be some special service for Saturday evening because I don't remember anything like it going on before. The country around is deeply religious. At every crossroad there is a small brick chapel or a post with a box containing emblems of one sort or another. Even private houses have the chapel outside and wooden crosses by the dozen are there for the asking. I have made several inquiries as to the meaning of it all but haven't had an explanation. One man assured me that there are parts of Ireland where similar customs prevail. Wooden shoes in France are a revelation to me. I thought the custom was peculiar to Holland but find that it is not so.

By Jove but these French farmers put Godliness first and cleanliness last with a vengeance. The filth about the barnyards is nauseating, and by way of contrast, some of them have small chapels set right in the side of the stables. Pigs abound everywhere, also pubs or estaminets.[11] Some of the pubs have this sign "Écurie sans garantie,"[12] which puzzled me for some time. The professor is as much interested in farm life as we are, as he has only seen it before while on a shooting expedition. His accounts of shootings or hunts are quite funny. In some parts, he says, the hares are so scarce that they are known by name, and when a party of ten or twenty go on an expedition the neighbours say such and such a party are after "John," etc.

With love,
Cyrus F. Inches

March 11, 1915

Dear Ma,

Today is rather mild and there is a strong smell of spring in the air. The farmers are ploughing, harrowing, and seeding. It is remarkable how indifferent they seem to the firing that goes on around about. The houses near the trenches have mostly been destroyed, but those further back are inhabited by the owners and all have soldiers billeted there. The aerial

---

11 French café or cottage with barroom.
12 Meaning that horses were stabled at the responsibility of their owners.

part of the war is most spectacular. Yesterday afternoon we could see an aeroplane way off near the trench district and a considerable distance up in the air being fired at. It was surrounded by puffs of smoke and escaped injury.

We have done no work at all today, most of which I have spent in an office or strolling around the fields watching for the aeroplanes. The machines of the different countries have distinctive marks, and if one of our opponents is spotted, we take cover immediately. It is very difficult for an observer to distinguish between objects below, though if many men were together they would likely be spotted. Some of the men reported yesterday that they saw several British planes [trailing] a German and firing going on from all the planes. This is a sight I have yet to see and will not vouch for its accuracy, though I daresay it is true.

And about the telephones — it is quite unique how different parts of the battery are connected up with wires. Each battery has its telephone wagon, and several miles of wires are strung and phones installed without much difficulty.

Just at present I am acting as section officer with two of the guns, the regular man having remained for a time in London for treatment for "Salisbury Plain Throat." It is not an exciting post, as you have to be with the section all the time, ready to open fire at any minute the order is phoned down to do so. And you cannot see the results of the fire as you are miles away from the target. It is like setting off fireworks in the backyard.

I had a letter from Fraser Campbell in which he states, at last in uniform, he has just been inoculated versus typhoid. He says I would be amused to see him in kilts. He is with the 1st 8th Battalion Argyll and Sutherland Highlanders.

Under the new system of censoring, officers are allowed to seal their letters without them being read provided they sign them on the outside as a guarantee that they are not divulging anything about movements of troops, quantity and quality of food, etc.

You say that Judge Forbes has retired. Who have they appointed in his place? A Wilson was a candidate but could not resist the sheriff's job when Mr. DeForest died. It was well known that Judge of Probate Armstrong was also in the running. A judgeship in New Brunswick is a sinecure — no work, good pay. The only ones who say the contrary are the judges themselves.

With love,
Cyrus

Saturday, March 14, 1915

Dear Ma,

Today has been mild and I spent most of it in the fields watching the seeding or in my "office" reading *Munsey*.[13] My efforts to explain to the farmer that it is against the law in Canada to work on Sunday were successful in time though the moral effect was nil.

In the afternoon Harry Crerar called to see me, and we were having a quiet time over some fancy cigarettes, which I purchased in London lately through the medium of Hughie McLean, when word came to prepare for action. Our shooting lasted from half past four until five. The only result that I know of being to interfere with a football match arranged between us and another unit. They phoned us at five to come up but our sergeant, captain of the team, considered it too late and postponed the event, much to the indignation of our opponents, who made caustic remarks which provoked a message being sent back to them to take another day to practice.

Yesterday afternoon General Alderson[14] called to see how things were going. With him was a party on horseback who asked me if this was Major Magee's command, or part of it, and when he learned that it was, he said "Tell him Sir Max Aitken[15] called." And then when he found out who I was, he assured me that he will be back again to find out how his

13 *Munsey's Magazine* contained short stories and articles.
14 Lieutenant-General Edwin Alderson, commanding officer, 1st Canadian Division.
15 Later Lord Beaverbrook.

Some of Cy's gun crew in orchard.

old friends in Saint John are getting along. He and Frank were friends in the days of the adversity of both. He does not give the appearance of being very robust. I do not know just what position he holds. He was appointed official Canadian eyewitness, but I am told that such a position is not compatible with English Army ideas of censorship and that his position, as such, was short lived. Judging from the amount of news in the Canadian papers, though, eyewitnesses for the contingent must be roaming rampant in the land. I note that [barrister] Fred Taylor has gone west. I wonder if it is on business for Sir Max. I believe Fred is acting for him in several matters, including western.

Note the wax on this paper. The telephone operator just came in for a small piece of candle, and I gave him one I had burning, substituting a piece half an inch long for it, and in the relighting much grease was spilt. I just need enough to keep me going until I ride up to battery headquarters to dinner.

Our mess secretary at the present time is our interpreter, formerly referred to in my letters as the professor. He is a man of letters and I believe a very high authority on economics. He misses his literary life in Paris very much. His position in the French Army is that of sergeant. I wish you could see him in his full regimentals. He might very well have escaped from a harem. His ideas of humour are very funny. I had a great time explaining to him the Alphonse and Gaston[16] comic pictures. His impressions of the officers in the mess he keeps strictly to himself. Like all Frenchmen he can't appreciate the English Tommy's inclination for levity, their love for football in the face of trials they are undergoing. I think he will probably write a book on it all after the war.

I was very careful of my toilet this morning — breakfast in bed (synonymous for straw), hot water bath, shave, and then haircut — the first since Devizes over a month ago. One of the men is an excellent hairdresser, as I just found out, and his performance on my head and moustache was quite professional, though he assured me he is not a barber but an electrician. He says he gets his beer money by cutting the men's hair — charges half a franc. So after this there will be no excuse for shaggy.

> With love,
> Cyrus

---

16 American comic strip about a bumbling pair of Frenchmen with a penchant for politeness.

March 18, 1915

Dear Ken,

The last two days there has been an epidemic of petty offences in my section. One man planted his rifle near the gun and forgot all about it. The result — a fine growth of rust. Another fired his rifle off by mistake in the barn in which he is billeted. A third, whom I had posted in a position where he had a fine view of hostile aeroplanes, I found asleep — and a fourth, when called to come up to the loft to bed by his sergeant, was heard to remark "let him talk away" . . . or words to that effect.

Gave vent to my indignation by giving the men a lecture upon my ideas of discipline, which had such a good effect that the very next day two of them wandered away from their billet without permission and remained absent for some hours. Instead of dealing with their cases myself, I sent both up to a higher tribunal — major F.C.M. [field court martial] and they are at the present time doing "pack drill," which means they are working as prisoners under the supervision of our provost sergeant at all the fatigues.

I have gotten over my ardour for studying French — one loses the ability to study after the thirtieth milestone. But I pick up a few words here and there — "allez au diable" and so forth.

Sincerely,
Cyrus

March 21, 1915

Dear Ma,

This Sunday is a tremendously fine day, and I am spending most of it in the fields back of my billet balming in the sun and watching the aeroplanes through my glasses. The air is clear and they are flying to a great height. Frequently a small white cloud obscures the machine, which shows they are at least on a level with the clouds, if not above them. On Saturday several observation balloons were to be seen — all of which makes the scene very much like Saint John in exhibition time.

I am carrying on quite a correspondence with Mrs. H. Tilley at present. She is the moving spirit of a circle of tea friends who knit for the soldiers and I am the distributing agent. The letter is to announce that the parcel is on the way and states, "I have added to the parcel a pad and envelopes." She must have looked with askance upon the last letter paper she received from me. And you will now receive a better quality for a while also. I get lots of paper but messengers, batmen, telephonists, and whatnot do not respect the privacy of my sanction and take what they want.

With love,
Cyrus

March 28, 1915

Dear Ma,

About noon today I heard Frank mention it was Sunday and this was the first realization I had of the fact. We had a regular field day doing all our firing with regular aeroplane observation and it was most interesting. The signallers came along in a lorry specially fitted up for the purpose of carrying them and their equipment and set same up by our telephone hut. The aeroplane is fitted with a sender but no receiver and although they can send down any messages they like to us we can only reply by flashing a lamp according to an agreed code of signals. There is an electric lamp for the purpose that would appeal more to Charlie's sense of mechanics than to mine.

There was a high wind blowing but the day was bright with a coolness in the air which gave a tang of excitement to it all. The aeroplane was flying at a height of five thousand feet, but they were able to see perfectly the results of the shooting, which was quite an eye opener to them as they were not looking for much from the volunteer force. The best observer of them all is a man who goes up alone, works his machine with his feet, uses one hand for his binoculars and the other for working his wireless sender.

There was almost a riot in my section this morning over the fact that the rations had not come down for two days, and in consequence, they had been eating bully beef and biscuits — bully beef being canned beef and biscuits being a food commonly fed to animals at home. Tomorrow, however, they will have a fine feast with fresh meat, several kinds of vegetables, and tins of jam, which will put them in a happier frame of mind. As it is after 11 p.m. and I have a mile and a quarter ride ahead of me and an early rise in the morning, I'll say good night.

With love,
Cyrus

Chapter Four

The Ypres Salient

On April 1st we followed our infantry to the Ypres Salient. After resting for ten days at Steenvoorde, waiting to go into position, orders were changed *and the battery went south to Lacontre to prepare for the attack on the Aubers Ridge. The 2nd London Heavy Battery, 4.7 guns, was put into the position in the Salient originally assigned to us. When the enemy attacked with gas, these guns were captured. It was thought in Canada that we had lost our guns, and it was some time before the correction was made in the press.*

April 2, 1915
Somewhere in France

Dear Ma,

Yesterday being the first of April, many jokes were attempted with more or less success. I rode up to our headquarters and had the occasion to telephone back to my batman to tell him to deliver my logbook to a party who would call for it. After a few minutes the telephonist reported that he was playing football and they were sending for him to come to the phone. After a tedious wait of some five minutes or more and a further enquiry as to the cause of the delay, the word came back that he refused to come to the phone. He apparently has the American horror of being gulled. I forgot to ask our interpreter if the day was observed in France by the natives... [remainder of letter illegible]

April 4, 1915

Dear Ma,

After church came a loaf, then noon stables, then the painting of the guns. The guns, which are normally a green colour, are daubed with coats of several colours to make them look at a distance like anything except what they really are. So any airman looking down at ours might well mistake them for some of your flower beds in the summer.

After dinner [I] took the horses of the battery out for an exercise, 3 to 4:30 p.m. Little did I imagine when reading *Quentin Durward* and other such tales that one day I would be leading a troop of horses through Flanders. We passed by several large churches which had been set on fire and the insides burnt out — otherwise there were few signs of destruction. Just what fun the Germans saw in setting fire to these churches, which were in their path Paris-ward and back again, is hard to understand. If they were being used as observation posts there could have been some reason for it. After returning came evening stables, then supper — a pretty large day, on the whole.

The next day I walked a half a mile and called upon several of our friends in the D.A.C. An English Tommy who was at Neuve Chapelle brought a German major's brass helmet to our billet some evenings ago and offered to sell it for twenty francs, coming down to nineteen francs, but could find no buyers among the men. I might have broken my resolution if I had been there at that time.

Tomorrow morning I think I will don, for the first time, my new suit which I had made in Devizes. The one bought at Montreal is coming apart and will need some skilful needling if I am to wear it again. It also needs much drenching in gasoline to eradicate the grease spots.

I suppose you have read in the paper about the baths. The men are marched off regularly every few days for treatment, and good baths are also fitted up in common tents for officers. Our interpreter is a faithful attendant and takes great pleasure out of the visits. I have not been able to get there but don't infer from that I have forgotten how near something is to Godliness.

With love,
Cyrus

April 8, 1915

Dear Ma,

We have been in a new billet for some days, loafing. It is really the most superior billet we have been in on this side of the Channel. My batman discovered a room in the attic where I reside in clover. The building is a long brick one of two storeys, downstairs being the living rooms and upstairs the granary. The place I am in is partitioned off and from the old pictures on the walls I take it that it was once the nursery. Madame assists our cooks in getting the dinner prepared and our meals are really surprisingly good. The interpreter, who like most men never had any liking for shopping, takes much delight in pottering around in nearby towns, picking up delicacies in the way of pastry and whatnot. As he is something of an epicure, our mess does not suffer from want of attention.

This nursery, or whatever it is, is not free from mice. I have my sleeping bag stretched over some oat bags in the corner, and I can see the critters peering at me from odd crevices overhead and round about. This is not the same billet that we were in when I wrote you last Sunday (Easter). My room there was a cobbler's room — really remarkable for the amount of filth it contained. This attic is a regular Waldorf in comparison. This is the fifth billet I have been in since leaving the freight car.

The battery, at present, is a regular home for captains, the personnel being Major Magee, Captain Hall, Captain Ruffeinstein, Captain Chown (paymaster), Captain Grignon (vet), Captain Mackay, Lieutenants Ryan, Garland, Leach, and myself. I should have included the interpreter in the list. Quite a mess for him to provide for.

It is beneath a captain's dignity to do orderly officer duty, so that is the exclusive prerogative of the subalterns. My turn, therefore, comes every four days. This morning I had charge of the horse exercise and was out for a fine airing from 9:15 a.m. till nearly twelve. This is not work. I call it a luxury. We wound in and out of several small villages. On the way back we came across a fine stream of water right beside the road and watered there instead of the regular pond within the billet limits. It was good to see the thirst and its quenching. That sounds very much like a Frenchman trying to master English. The pools in the billets are frequently mere sewage holes and the horses enjoy just water.

With love,
Cyrus

Festubert, May 1915

Aubers Ridge–Festubert–Givenchy. For nearly a year the battery was with Imperial divisions. From April 15th to May 15th, 1915, we were in a position behind the village of Lacontre. It was a beautiful orchard in blossom. Nothing disturbed our serenity until the unsuccessful attack on the Aubers Ridge on May 9th when the men were called upon to fight, their guns under fire for the first time. A week later the attack was continued towards La Bassée but with little better success. The battery was shelled and was ordered to move off into another orchard at Pont du Hem, a hamlet which can aptly be described as flowing with champagne. During our sixteen days there, the only thing which occurred to break

*the monotony was a slight shelling which, happily, did no
damage.*

April 18, 1915

Dear Ma,

While leaning against one of the guns on the side of the road a few
days ago, a chaplain whom I recognized as Canon Scott[17]came along and
we recalled together the trip from the coast in the boxcar, and although
he remembered my face very well, he soon showed he was mixed [up]
as to my identity by demanding, "Where's Inches? We've got a bone to
pick with him!" It seems that at home he poses as an early riser and
had so impressed his family with his unfailing virtue that his son was
rather aghast to read in the *Saint John Globe*, over my signature, that the
father had fallen into bad habits in France — so much so that he cut the
paragraph out of the paper and sent it to the canon, who has been on the
warpath for my scalp ever since.

After a night march of the whole unit not so very long ago, we arrived
in a small town in the small hours and scrambled to find billets. I had the
unique experience of sleeping on a real bed — my first taste of French
"mattresserie." Our horses were mostly piqueted in a small square, in the
centre of which was the town pump, and as this occurred to the men as
the most reasonable source of water for the horses the pump was worked
overtime, so to speak. The result was a slight derangement of the plunger
to fix, so one of our mechanics removed the top of the pump.

My attention to the incident was called by sounds of loud laughter
and on approaching the scene of turbulence I found the men clustered
around a little grey-haired Frenchman who turned out to be the mayor
of the village [and] whose indignation at finding the pump dismantled
expressed itself in a violent torrent of native expletive. The cause of
the laughter was entirely lost on the men, who purposely refused to

---

17   Canon Frederick G. Scott, the senior chaplain of 1st Canadian Division and
     author of *The Great War as I Saw It.*

understand that the pump had anything to do with the outburst until one of the French-Canadian members of the battery appeared to act as interpreter. Then, while His Worship was repeating his tirade to the interpreter, one of the men surreptitiously replaced the top of the pump so that when the mayor turned round to point out the damage to the interpreter, to his astonishment and to the great amusement of the men, he discovered the pump in status quo — a legal expression meaning "the same old place." He got even with the men by sending his daughter (no reflection on her appearance) to affix a chain and padlock around the pump in such a manner that further action on their part, as far as getting water from it, was impossible.

We have been walking a little today and you will be pleased to hear that instead of performing upon a church steeple we have been smashing up a brewery.

Love,
Cyrus

April 23, 1915

Dear Ma,

Received your letter and Ken's papers of the eighth. Ken's papers are much appreciated not only by Frank and me but also by the Saint John boys in the battery, of whom there are about twenty. I don't suppose it is any breach of etiquette to say that at present we are not with the Canadian Division and may not see them again for some weeks. We have seen a lot of the Indian troops of late. Last evening about a dozen came along with a football and joined with our gunners in kicking it about in the field [on] the other side of our orchard fence. They were Gurkhas. I don't want to meet any of them on a dark night.

Facing page: *The Daily Telegraph*, May/June 1915.

Lieutenant Cyrus F. Inches writes of deeds which have brought honor to the Dominion — Gurkahs also in the fight with exquisite sense of humor.

Lieutenant Cyrus F. Inches, who is with the Canadian Field Artillery, under Major Frank Magee, writing his former law partner D. King Hazen, points out that the Canadians have made a fine impression with the British, and English officers have said the Canadians formed the best division in the British army. A portion of the letter follows:

"I tell you our infantry has made a wonderful name for itself and comes in for universal commendation. For some reason or other the First Contingent made a bad impression in England, which I am led to believe was shared by not a few in Canada. As one Englishman put it, their one redeeming feature was the fact they admitted their rottenness; a trait foreign to former colonial troops, which had visited England.

"I'll frankly admit that until we actually got under way over here, I thought our battery a joke. But the artillery is doing well, and as for the infantry, English officers, who looked upon them with askance, cannot say too much as to their gallantry and capacity for forging ahead. Some officers have said it is the best Division in the British army at the present time. That is, what there is left of it, for Ypres and the various engagements it has been in since, have sadly depleted the ranks.

"After Ypres and one or two other places, the infantry was put in the trenches in front of us, and our field artillery was brought down to the same place.

Canadians Lost.

"One night the Canadians were instructed to take a certain trench. The next day our field gunners were ordered to fire on a supposedly German trench, beyond the Canadians' objective of the night before. They commenced. Up went a Canadian flag to show the trench was occupied by Canadians. The artillery increased the range to a trench further along. Up went another Canadian flag. Again an increase in range to a trench still further out. For the third time the Canadian flag, and the gunners were told to desist. I was then informed that the Canadians had pushed so far ahead that they could not be found. Indeed wherever you went you heard the same inquiry, where have the Canadians gone to.

A Maze of Trenches.

"You can picture to yourself a flat country like our marsh a labyrinth of trenches, and you can appreciate, perhaps, a litle just what difficulties beset an advance. But there seems to be nothing that our infantry is loath to tackle.

"I do not know anything that makes the artillery man more aghast than the thought that he might hit his own infantry. Overlooking a mortgage in search of title produces the same feeling. Is 'search of title' a correct expression? It sounds a trifle unfamiliar

Infantry Unconcerned.

"To show you the casual attitude of our infantry, when their own safety is concerned:—Eight Canadians composing a ration fatigue, were proceeding unwisely behind the trench. A shell carried five of them off. The remaining three commenced to bemoan their hard fate in having to carry the load of eight.

"Fraser Campbell vouches for the following:—A sniper whose ammunition had run out gave himself up. He was asked why he had not gone to the German lines. and replied that he went to the nearest trench. 'Well, we can spare you a round a piece.' So they put his back to the wall and let him have it. I was under the impression he was telling this story of the Argylls, but it seems it was the Canadians. Our captain says it was too generous a donation for the Argylls.

The Indian Troops.

"There is not a jollier, merrier, lot of men than the Indian troops. They enter into the spirit of the whole show with keen enjoyment. Their sense of humor is exquisite. A few days ago a Gurkah announced that he had discovered the locus in quo—I believe of course that he used those very words—of a German sniper and obtained permission to go out and get him. He was told to bring back the helmet as a token that he had achieved success. He brought back the helmet with the head in it."

You must have had a great day at Westfield. You seem to be pouring rivers of tea recently. It is an art in which you need no instruction. I trust you will be able to get a capable cook soon. If you were near our battery, I might send you Meldrum, O'Connor, Polly, or several others on the roll of cooks.

I was enabled to see the country we are firing over the other day. No, I was not out in an aeroplane but I was out to the position to which our F.O.O. [forward observation officer] had run his wire and spent the day looking down into the trenches and the country beyond. Dwellings, churches, chateaux, breweries, and distilleries make fine targets and any structure, say two thousand yards on either side of the trenches, will require considerable repairing before the resumption of living along normal lines takes place. Such places make excellent observation stations and, when they command a view of the trenches, are good positions for snipers. And when it is discovered or conjectured that they are being used as such, some battery is directed to take a pop or two at them. Within the last two days we have had two houses assigned to us as targets and have had more or less success. A report is issued every day by the staff captain of the group of batteries with which we are associated, and the report, which is termed the progress report, tells of the work done the day before.

The airmen have a wireless connection with us and we carry on considerable firing with their observations. They are a fine lot of men and interesting to commune with.

With love,
Cyrus

April 26, 1915

Dear Ma,

Life has been so quiet the last few days that there is very little to record. We have heard rumours of severe fighting in which our infantry was engaged with much credit but have had no particulars as yet.[18] The Canadian papers seem to get everything first and even anticipate events sometimes, so that it is difficult to understand just what is going on. The medical officer for our unit, at present, is Dr. Ritchie, who is with an English brigade nearby. He says he's related to the Ritchies of Halifax and played tennis at Rothesay with Bumps about four years ago. A short, thick set fellow with fair hair.

I've been letting my old hoss run around the orchard. It is funny to watch him. If there is a discernible opening in the hedges he will find it and is off for a canter over the sown fields nearby regardless of the many signs warning parties, and particularly horsemen, off the grass and crops. The best way to capture him is to chase after him with a nose bag full of oats, which generally has the desired result.

The ditches beside the roads are full of frogs, and we spend some time each day tossing pebbles among them. They also abound in small fish, which are an endless source of amusement to the children as well as ourselves. Down the road, a short distance from here, a sentry posted on a bridge over a small stream spent his time shooting at the fish, which soon resulted in his arrest. Last night, in this connection, I noticed in daily orders that the practice of throwing bombs at the fish in the canals was strictly prohibited! The mist of the last week has practically put an end to aeroplane observation.

> With love,
> Cyrus

Friday, April 30, 1915

Dear Ma,

The last two days have been tremendously fine, and the fruit trees, in which this part of the country abounds, have been brought suddenly into bloom, making the air redolent with sweet fragrance.

---

18   The Canadians were engaged in the 2nd Battle of Ypres between April 22 and 26.

The week has been quiet and uneventful with us — notwithstanding persistent rumours to the contrary, our guns were not the four heavy ones mentioned in dispatches as having been retaken by our infantry.

This morning I am planning a trip to a town of some proportion and repute with Captain Ruffeinstein, where we expect to see the sights and have lunch before returning. Ryan sent to London for an American baseball and two catching gloves, and I have been working the winter lethargy out of my arm — a little each day.

Two days ago we mesmerized a hen. One of the men who understands poultry volunteered to catch one for us. The trick is to put its head near the floor and with a piece of chalk draw a straight line about two feet in length away from its head, moving the chalk very slowly. It becomes so interested in watching the line that it is supposed to remain dazed for some five minutes, though in this case excitement produced by a long chase and subsequent loss of feathers did not tend to make her a very fit object. Much interest is taken among the infantry in cock fighting. Each battalion, I am told, has its favourite cock.

As I write these lines I can hear a German aeroplane hovering overhead at a great height and our guns and men are all under cover to prevent our position being discovered. It is the first time for some weeks I have seen one. They are not as numerous or as active as our own in these parts. An anti-aircraft gun has recently been placed in a farm enclosure a short distance in front of ours and popped off a few shells as the machine came in range. They burst seemingly all around the machine, and the white puffs made a pretty sight against the ethereal blue of the sky. I'm feeling quite poetic this morning.

The divisional artillery has a chaplain (in reply to your inquiry) — the Reverend Almon, relation of Mrs. E.A. Smith. But the weather on Salisbury Plain was not conducive to open-air services. Don't be too severe in condemnation of the soldiers in the armoury. Most of them make good when they get away from an intemperate environment. I do think, though, the incorrigibles should be weeded out before sailing. The actions of the few misfits who were sent home from England did a lot to cast reflection on the whole contingent. To give you one instance, Dicky

Leach has relatives in Wales where he spent Christmas. His aunt was quite serious in asking him if it were true that thirty thousand Canadians had been sent back for misconduct!

On a tree outside my door I found this morning the following notice . . .

A Merry Time
An invitation has been received from the N.C.O.s
and Men of the Canadian Heavy Battery
To join them on Saturday night at a Concert
which will be held at the Billet of the _____ Batt.
Anyone who wishes to contribute to making the
event a success will give their name to
Gunner Langford. Piano & Violin
accompaniment & Stage.

There is a wealth of good entertainers in the army. At some places, Armentières for instance, there is a fine troop of follies. I have this by hearsay.

We've had another very fine, still day since the haze has cleared away. We fired a few shots at a distillery and one at what used to be a church. We spent a good part of the afternoon wasting ammunition in the endeavour to hit a house, supposed to be used by the Boches for practical purposes.

This last proceeding took place in the presence of a new chaplain, within whose diocese, so to speak, we are now embraced. He called at the mess just after lunch. We are to attend his service at 12 o'clock on Sunday together with a Scottish brigade. He visited the different billets to get in touch with the men, so you see he went about his business in true parochial style. He has resided in India and travelled considerably and thinks there is no place like England. Nor was his conviction at all shaken by a remark made by one of our officers after two weeks on Salisbury Plain, *"Is this the country we came to fight for? Personally, I'm ready to hand it over to the Germans without any parley."*

Please let Mary know I got her long letter and thank her for the cigarettes, which come regularly. [She] wants to know if she can send me anything. Tell her just to drop into Hawkers and have him put me up an ice cream soda. The water here is not drinkable unless chlorinated and even then I waive claim to any of it, unless in the form of tea, coffee, cocoa, etc.

With much love,
Cyrus

May 2, 1915

Dear Ken,

As I start these lines the London Scottish are marching past my window on their way to the trenches — perhaps you have read about them in the papers. I saw in the *Graphic* yesterday a picture of a 4.7 gun similar to the kind which it is alleged the Canadians lost and recaptured.

I am beginning to have a hunch that the guns referred to may have been attached to the Canadian Division in our place, though as to that I have no information whatsoever. Our guns are 60-pounders, so called — that is, they fire a projectile weighing sixty pounds. The bore is five inches in diameter. 4.7 is the name given to the gun having a bore of that diameter, the projectile weighing about forty-three pounds. For any further information about a 4.7 I refer you to Vassie.

With love,
Cyrus

May 2, 1915

Dear Ma,

My visit to _____ came off all right and I spent a pleasant afternoon wandering around among the winding streets. I was with Leach and Ruffeinstein. We were much pleased to see a sign, "ICE CREAM ~ ICED SEROPS," and took advantage of the opportunity to indulge in the luxury of something which was a cross between an ice cream and a sherbet, but mighty good withal. There were many signs printed in English about the shops and restaurants and estaminets, and all seemed to be doing a rushing business indeed. I think, as I pointed out before, *the towns near the trenches that are not destroyed are doing an astounding business with the troops.*

My old hoss had a thrilling or, rather, chilling experience a few days ago. It was allowed to roam at large in the orchard and overnight together with Mr. Ryan's horse, which follows her everywhere. Both escaped through the hedge, and Hall went looking for her in the morning as soon as he had discovered the disappearance. A long distance down the road he saw Mr. Ryan's horse circling around sniffing at something in the ditch and on coming up found my old hoss embedded in the black mud with only her face in view. With the assistance of a squad of Gurkhas and sentries and a rope which they got under her, she was brought to terra firma, though an officer who passed along before the final extrication wanted to shoot her and take Mr. Ryan's horse for his own unit. It is quite easy to lose an animal in these ditches. Two horses belonging to my section got into a ditch not long ago about two o'clock in the morning and I thought they were lost for sure but finally managed to get them out.

I am getting quite used to the science of getting heavy material out of the mud. Each gun weighs over five and a half tons. It is drawn by eight heavy draught horses and is not supposed to move faster than a walk. If the thing sinks a little in the mud and the horses do not feel the weight coming, they stop, back up, and pull in all kinds of directions and raise all kinds of Cain until the men man the drag ropes and help them along. Two wheels of the ammunition wagon sunk in mud ties up a whole column for some time. A horse is subject to more ailments than a chronic dyspeptic and has to have gentle treatment.

Cy

May 7, 1915

Dear Ma,

This morning I expect to reconstruct a small bridge over a ditch so that we can get our material in and out of the orchard without too great a chance of dumping it into the mire. The country has dried up and, except right after a rain, the soil is quite firm.

As I write there is an altercation going on between the proprietor of an adjoining homestead, the mayor of the nearest town, and our interpreter over some damage we did to property by taking a few old beams for firewood and a half load of bricks for filling-in purposes. We intend, of course, to pay, but the French are an excitable race and refuse to argue calmly over the matter. The dispute is drawing to a close, and I hear that twenty francs is the amount of settlement. He asked thirty for a conservative value of ten, so he did not suffer much in the settlement.

The damage to the forests and woods in this country has been great, almost irreparable . . . [next three lines illegible] . . . that would astonish an up-country lumberman in New Brunswick. I am told there are stringent regulations against the cutting down of trees. I know we tied our horses to a fine row of poplars or elms. They were in a field, all of which the owner wanted to cultivate, and it was therefore with no great concern that he saw the horses strip them of bark as far as they could nibble, for, he said, now they will be condemned and I will be able to cut them down. Of course he will not refuse compensation for the destruction.

My old hoss doesn't like the rats and squirms about in its stall so much that it has abrasions all over its head and several on its sides, so

I keep it now outdoors all night. The orchards are getting or, should I say, "are now" in full bloom. A large lilac outside my door is also about "out."

With love,
Cyrus

May 18, 1915

Dear Ma,

For some nights past we have been indulging in the novelty of night firing, loosing off a few rounds every now and then at well-selected objectives for the sole purpose, I verily believe, of keeping the Deutchers awake. So well has our policy succeeded that our opponents across the way, according to affirmations made by a batch of prisoners brought in today, have had no sleep at all for the last forty-eight hours. I find I must stop for a short time and adjourn to the apple trees to send off six rounds at two-minute intervals.

3:30 a.m. I now return to my narrative. My hours of duty for the laudable designs above outlined are 2, 3, 4, and 5 [o'clock], so my job is half-finished. Of course you must not lose sight of the fact that all these operations are not carried out without some loss of slumber to ourselves, but any slight inconvenience in this regard is amply compensated for by the elation resultant from the knowledge that the Boches are sleeping in a bed of thistles. Picture to yourself two fat old Deutchers retiring for a good old snooze among the draperies of one of these French creations termed a *couche*. Sixty pounds of lyddite[19] from one of our guns enters the window. Deutchers seek another billet.

The conglomeration of sounds prevailing during these small hours is worth analysis. I have not investigated the room overhead but am told it is a granary. The tones produced by the scurry of rats might very well

---

19 A form of high explosive used in the Boer War and First World War, made of molten and cast picric acid.

be mistaken for a titanic struggle between elephants. I occupy a small room, I think I told you before, with our right section commander. For reverberative effect his particular variety of snore can well vie with the rats above and the cannonading without. The one redeeming feature in his babel from Sousa is the twitter of the birds without, who welcome the approach of dawn with glad rejoice. Nor is their ardour at all subdued by the rain, which has been falling steadily all night.

We were notified last evening to be prepared for the aeroplane at 4 a.m. but from present indications conditions will not be favourable. These nights of uncertain rest remind me of old times in Saint John when I used to review with Connie the program for the week: Monday night, the bridge club; Tuesday, Mackay's dance; Wednesday night, choice between prayer meeting and Fred Taylor's dinner for Miss So and So. Well, there's nothing on Thursday night, thank goodness! What, the second assembly? Surely not so soon! Yes, by Jove, you're right, time passes. Friday, the inevitable bridge party succeeding an assembly; Saturday, badminton. *No, I don't know why we call a conflict between nations a strenuous life.*

I heard a cuckoo just now, the first time I think I ever heard the sound proceeding from the throat of a bird. I do not include clocks and other imitators in that category. Yesterday morning while proceeding along the road to breakfast I came across a man trying to extricate his horse from a wayside ditch. We got it out all right but the horse plus slime was an indescribable mess.

With love,
Cyrus

May 21, 1915

Dear Ma,

Time 3:15 a.m. Last evening, while passing through a nearby village on his first trip to the trenches, Fraser's column stopped. One of the men in our battery, a chap named Witherspoon, from Saint John, who had worked under Fraser at the sugar refinery, recognized him and told him where he could find me. About 5 a.m. a battalion of Highland lads came along the road and halted. Magee and I made a careful inspection of them, thinking Fraser might be with them, but they turned out to be the Gordons. They asked permission to bring two of their companies into our orchard, light fires, and cook their tea, all of which was granted, and while watching them at their bivouac, who should appear but old Fraser, who had walked in from their position behind the trenches to see me — a distance of some two miles. He had only a few minutes to stay so I lengthened it out [and] we had tea together at the mess. It appeared that only part of his battalion had gone in the night before and that he was to head his first session that evening, so I had the honour of giving him a good meal to give him confidence.

On Sunday last we fired on the first target yet that we have been able to see from our gun position. As you will note from the papers, a general engagement was on all along the line. During the afternoon our attention was called to a German observation balloon right out in front of us. They resemble small dirigibles and we call them German sausages. It was probably seven miles off but it looked nearer, and as it seems to look right down at our position, we decided to burst some shrapnel over it and wasted some thirteen rounds on it. Our line was good and to us the white puffs from our busts seemed to be just in front of it and then again, just over. But we found later from a party who had observed the shooting from a flank that we were a way short of the target. I think I would rather have cut the string on that sausage than have written Gray's *Elegy in a Country Churchyard*.

> With love,
> Cyrus

May 24, 1915

Dear Ma,

May 24 is a public holiday, etc., and the firecrackers are celebrating the day right mightily. Yesterday I received your letter and note of May 8, and I shall have to look in vain for the *Lusitania* mail.[20] Frank is not going to leave the battery. As I explained before, this battery is now associated with an English group of batteries. We are still part of the Canadian Division but have been loaned, so to speak, to another division. We are informed that Ryder left last Wednesday to join us and are sending directions to Shorncliffe[21] to him so that he can find his way here all right. The Canadian Division, both infantry and artillery, are all in our vicinity again and some of the infantry are in the trenches ahead of us. The infantry are certainly making a fine name for themselves. I have not seen recent deeds accomplished by them recorded in the papers, but you will probably be reading about them soon.[22] I am told that General Alderson and Colonel Burstall[23] have asked for our transfer back to them but do not know what action will be taken.

I was talking to an officer in the Seaforths Territorials a few days ago. He said he would be "prood" to be a Canadian. The major had a call this morning from Canon Almon. He was through the whole Ypres affair and his tales thereof were very interesting to listen to.

The billet where we have our mess is the smelliest of any that we have yet encountered. Just between the road and the house is a brick trench full of some kind of mixture fed to the cattle. It has been there all winter and is evidently some emergency ration kept for the spring. This we call the *first line of stenches*. On entering the courtyard we come to the inevitable cesspool — *the second line of stenches*. It is quite a feat to overcome both lines with unimpaired appetite.

---

20 The *Lusitania* was sunk on May 7, 1915.

21 The training camp in southern England for Canadian troops.

22 1st Canadian Division participated in the Battle of Festubert between May 15 and 21.

23 Brigadier-General H.E. Burstall was commander of the 1st Canadian Division's artillery.

There is a French interpreter just here now who came to extend an invitation to us to visit a French battery of the famous 75 pattern, and I will try to take advantage of the opportunity to see them in action. All our own guns have well-known names such as Grandmother, Mother, Amelia, Archibald, etc., which have been used so much jocularly that they are known in the official reports under these names. I have just been instructed to prepare the guns for another big show so will now close.

With love,
Cyrus

Festubert, May 1915

About June 1st we moved south again to a more advanced position at Lacontre, and took part in the Givenchy and Festubert operations, including the famous Orchard Fight. These were our days with the Meerut Division. We were on the best of terms with the Indians who flocked around in their picturesque costumes evincing an almost childish delight in watching the guns fire, while we, on the other hand took a keen enjoyment in visiting them in their quarters in the adjacent orchard. I can see them now squatting around the camp fire for their evening meal before leaving for the trenches, chattering and laughing among themselves as if on a picnic. It was with feelings of regret that we parted from our Indian friends in the middle of July and trekked north to a position near Fleurbaix which became our headquarters for two months, perhaps the most quiescent and comfortable period in the battery's history.

June 3, 1915

Dear Ma,

I have your long letter of May 17 and note the expected sailing of an early date of the D.A.C. You must have enjoyed your visit to Fredericton. Please congratulate Charlie for me on the result of his studies.

I had a letter today from the party with whom I stayed at Marston. He states he had a son a few days ago and is using the wooden chest the carpenter made me, but which I found impracticable to take with me, as a bed for the baby. He states the country is looking very pretty now but things are not growing too fast on account of the cold weather, the frost having cut the French beans and potatoes. I also had a letter today from the Malcolm McAvitys. They are at Folkestone and are trying to get a house there or in Saltwood. They saw Eva and Ronald and other Saint John people.

We have been practically loafing now for a week. At present I have a very fine tent with a table and chair borrowed from the farmer and

Officers on the Boardwalk at Folkestone.

Folkestone Beach, southern England.

under such ideal circumstances there is no excuse for me not getting up with my correspondence provided I can manufacture enough news to go round.

The vet and Mr. Garland have each invested in a second-hand motorcycle. The vet says, as to his purchase, "She not broke — but she do not go." Mr. Garland, after two days' enjoyment, has sent his into the I.O.M. [?] for repair. This afternoon my batman is in town pricing second-hand bikes — not motor ones — for me and if I can get one for a reasonable figure, I may do so. They are most useful in this flat country, which is looking wonderfully well at present with the foliage all out and the crops well advanced. Every available foot of ground is under cultivation, and it is quite remarkable the care it receives. The women, children, and men not of military attainments are in the fields most of the time hoeing away. The oats and wheat are sown in rows and, say, two inches apart, and the earth is stirred up regularly like we hoe corn and potatoes. The yield per acre, I believe, is way ahead of ours.

I sent to London for a pair of ear defenders. They are guaranteed to absolutely protect the ear from all sting and injury, temporary or otherwise, due to gunfire. At the same time, ordinary conversation, commands, etc., are distinctly audible instantly after gunfire. I find they work splendidly as far as the first guarantee is concerned but ordinary sounds are not clearly audible.

With love,
Cyrus

June 6, 1915

Dear Ma,

Yesterday I received your letters and also about a dozen packages from Ken [including] the socks from Mrs. Martin and the maple sugar. The maple sugar did not dry up in the least and was very much appreciated. The mess demolished one pound, the other I gave to Fraser Campbell, who made his second call upon me yesterday afternoon about 6:30. He stayed to dinner and until nine o'clock, when he went to his billet on the old hoss. [He] has kept it overnight and is due to return about 1 o'clock.

He tells me that he ran across Don Fisher a few days ago. The Dragoons, I believe, have been turned into infantry, much to their disgust, and Don had just been through some pretty hot fighting in which they had some casualties. Since then he has been transferred to the grenade section and is an expert bomb thrower. Fraser himself had some pretty harrowing experiences. Both [he] and I were much interested in the clipping about the tennis meeting. I am sending it on to Bumps in case he has not seen it.

We have had and are having a wonderful streak of fine weather. Today is particularly bright and warm and lazy. This position is the nicest we have been in yet. There is little work to do, and the men lie round all day basking in the sun. I will here adjourn for lunch — bully beef, boiled potatoes, lettuce, jams, tapioca pudding, bread, and tea.

While I was at lunch all four guns were called upon to silence a German battery which had opened up on something. The right section commander conducted the firing.

No horse or Fraser yet.

With love,
Cyrus

June 25, 1915

Dear Ken,

The lounge, this afternoon, is having its first real test in a heavy rain, and it's coming through with flying colours — as the rain is coming from a flank, it is possible to keep the whole front open without danger of getting wet.

Lawrence Kelly was wounded last week in a curious engagement where they sent field guns up to the trenches — not seriously. I do not know whether he is at the base or in England.

The tobacco has not yet arrived from Miss Ballentine. I met Reverend Canon Almon a few days ago. He says he has never seen his cousin Miss Smith but has corresponded with her. Please congratulate her on my behalf on that $12,000. It seems incredible that so much has been raised.

I suppose that at last the D.A.C. are upon the water.[24] They have certainly had a tiresome wait. The next thing will be getting thoroughly equipped in England — no small job, I can assure you. The first contingent was supposed to be equipped fully but much had to be added in the old country — much, I believe, to the disgust of the Canadian authorities.

This has been a quiet week. My section has not fired a round in the last five days, so there has been nothing to do but eat, write, read, and sleep. Bev Armstrong wrote to me for the history of all the Saint John men in the battery, some twenty-one in number, as he wants it for the regimental records. He wants sheets mailed to him about once a week. I intend sometime to write him a brief summary of what the battery has been doing since the middle of April — conformable to censorial regulations. But if he wants more than that, he will have to send Clarence Ward [city clerk, Saint John] or Reverend [W.O.] Raymond [historian] over with the next contingent. The engineers — next orchard — have sent over for our officers to go to dinner this evening and I have been deputed to attend.

Love to all,
Cyrus

---

24   The 2nd Divisional Ammunition Column (Lieutenant-Colonel W.H. "Harry" Harrison, officer commanding) and the 26th Battalion (Lieutenant-Colonel J.L. McAvity, officer commanding) sailed on the *Caledonia* from Saint John to England, via Halifax, on June 13, 1915.

LIEUT. KELLY IN A FINE EXPLOIT

St. John Officer Helped to Push Big Gun Up to First Trench Line

TWICE WOUNDED IN BRUSH FOLLOWING

Fired 40 Rounds Into Enemy's Lines When He Was Wounded—Stuck It Out Until Gun Was Smashed by Big Krupp and His Legs Crushed in Debris.

LIEUT. KELLY.

The following is an extract of a letter from Capt. Cyrus F. Inches to Lieut. Colonel B. R. Armstrong:—

"I feel constrained to let you know that Kelly must have a whole page in your history sheets. I heard a few days ago that the field artillery had performed a feat of arms by taking several of their guns into the front line trenches and opening up upon the enemy, who were distant but seventy yards away. The surprise of the thing caused much damage and consternation in the opposing ranks. Today Frank and I took a holiday and rode back several miles to General Burstall's headquarters, where we met Captain Wright. He told us that Kelly was one of the officers who had the honor to be sent forward with the guns and that he had been wounded in two places. The divisional staff considered that he had acted with much credit. The Chaplain, Rev. Canon Almon was loud in his praise.

"Later in the day in a nearby town we met some of the field artillery, the two Hansons, Captain Bell, Captain Crearer and others, whom we have not

seen for some weeks. They all thought Kelly had done a fine piece of work. The veterinary officer of the 1st. Brigade, a great admirer of Kelly, told me of the particulars—he managed to get off forty rounds and he was just hit in the arm, then a big Krupp came along and his gun was smashed all to pieces, and as a finishing touch, a mine exploded and the debris crushed his legs. I am glad to say that he is not seriously injured.

"With a brother officer, Craig, he is at one of the base hospitals, both are trying to stick it out, so that they will not be sent back to England, so keen are they to get back to their batteries.

Friends of Lieut. L. St. C. Kelley, formerly manager for the Royal Trust Co. here, will be interested in his exploit—one of the notable ones of the war, in which other St. John men probably also participated. He was reported wounded a few weeks ago while with the artillery in action in France.

The Daily Telegraph, July 10, 1915.

July 1, 1915

Dear Ma,

This is the day of the sports that the men have been looking forward to for some time. They are to be held at 2 p.m. near the horse lines under the patronage of Lieutenant Ryder, who is making himself quite active in the matter. We will be rather short handed at the guns but do not anticipate that much will turn up. There has been a lull in hostilities along the front.

There are four tug-of-war teams entered. The one from the battery has been practising for some days and expect to spring a surprise on the drivers, but as they have been beaten so often by the scratch teams that have been put up against them in practice, I don't anticipate that they will return in a very happy frame of mind. There are to be the usual number of runs and jumps. The only event open to outsiders is the half-mile. The officers were invited to contribute towards a fund for prizes — that is the only part I am taking in the celebrations. The battery cooks are to have a holiday also, and my batman is taking over for them the preparation of the tea.

At present we are with the 17th Brigade of the 1st Group Heavy Artillery reserve. This brigade consists of three batteries: the 13th Heavy, the 2nd London (this is the battery that lost their guns at Ypres), and ourselves. The brigade is in command of Colonel Phillips, known in the army as "Tiger" Phillips, for his initials are T.P. — a most testy old meddler who has spent most of his life in India. We get our orders from him. He gets his from group headquarters, and dear knows where the group gets theirs. By the time an order passes through these circumlocutory stages, a moving target has had loads of time to make scarce.

I have your letter of the fourteenth/ fifteenth telling of the departure [from Saint John] of the 26th and the D.A.C. I had a letter from Fraser Campbell from London written with his left hand. His right arm was injured from machine-gun fire and he does not expect to get back until August. He was hit on the shoulder, the bullet going to his ribs — two ribs broken and the shoulder bone. It is slight and he is going on well, very cheerful and full of pepper. He says that Don Fisher came back in the same hospital ship with him suffering from nervous shock and breakdown. He was raving about trenches like a madman.

Fraser says he sees Hughie almost every day (looks indeed as if the nurses must be pretty), and he looks forward to his daily appearance. *He has been showered with fruit and flowers and no one who has not been wounded and sent home to endure the never-ceasing pain of an overfull stomach can really form a correct perspective of the horrors of war.* It's something awful — a succession of fruits and candies and sweetmeats of all kinds. He says he will be laid up until October.

Apparently, Jim McAvity and his 26th Battalion have at last arrived and with it Sandy MacMillan in fine form. Maurice Fisher is engaged to K. Fawcett but I suppose that is all ancient news to Saint John people. I hope by this time you have emigrated to Westfield with both families.

<blockquote>
With love,
Cyrus
</blockquote>

July 6, 1915

Dear Ma,

The sports on Dominion Day were a huge success. The gunners won the tug-of-war contest and returned to the battery late at night in high fettle. The prizes all consisted of sums of money, some three hundred francs having been subscribed for the occasion. The pros and cons of the whole affair were the subject of a discussion which lasted long into the night and which was resumed at an early hour the next morning.

The weather is fine and warm and much appreciated by the flies, which simply swarm. On Sunday last in the house where we have our mess, Madame's son lay down on his bed for an afternoon nap. A little while later he came out of his room into our mess remarking, "Non coucher — beaucoup des mouches!"

Our interpreter has just arrived at the gun park. He has been promoted from the rank of sergeant to that of adjutant in the French Army. This entitles him to an increase in pay of two francs a day, but that, in his opinion, is not commensurate with the burden which the holding of this rank imposes upon him. He says it is the most despised rank in the French Army. When he was a private *soldat* the adjutant was always "on my back." It corresponds to our rank of sergeant major. He generally has the latest news and tells me a German warship has been destroyed in the Baltic. He says of course it is an old one. He has noted that whenever a battleship is destroyed it is always looked on with despise because of its age.

The cinema has come to town. Yesterday it was advertised in our orchard on the notice board beside the mail box:

5/7/15 — There will be a cinema show tonight and tomorrow at 8:30 p.m. at_____in black shed near the bridge. Charge for officers 1 franc, other ranks 3 shillings.

July 9, 1915

Dear Ma,

Day before yesterday I received your letter of June 22, 1915, and also some postal cards presumably sent by Charlie. I did not think the postal cards would get through to you. If you will consult any of the war maps of the Festubert region north to Ypres, the places should become apparent.

In the same mail I got a letter from Kelly in hospital in Rouen. He says his injuries do not amount to much. His left leg was crushed by the debris from a mine and a little splinter in his right arm. He did not think he would be laid up for more than a couple of days and hoped to be back in the battery within the time limit, ten days, and for that reason refused to go to England. But up to time of writing he had not been allowed out of bed, and he may even have to have an operation on his knee. I see that eyewitness Sir Max A. mentions Kelly's accident in his last message. Sir Max is a man of ubiquity, isn't he!? He must have a very powerful telescope to see all these things from his home in England.

The cherries are about over. Soon the pears will be ripe enough to pick. Already the boys are nibbling at them — such is their confidence in the brigade doctor. The ripening of the fruit is about the only progress that I can report about [in] this orchard. Things are still at a standstill, and we are having very little work to do. In fact we were all saying yesterday as we were sitting around the lounge that the daily routine has become as follows: after breakfast sit around until lunch. After lunch sit around till the mail comes. Then sit around till dinner. We likened the arrival of the mail to that of the N.B. Express in the remote districts of New Brunswick. These flies are great pests. Beaucoup des mouches.

With love,
Cyrus

July 23, 1915

Dear Ken,

I have your letter of the eighth. You seem to be very busy. Hard times do not seem to have struck Saint John except in a few spots.

For the last few days since there has loomed upon the horizon a faint possibility of leave. I have been busy digging up prizes from Deutcher shells, and it maybe I can lug some across the Channel with me. If so I will send you a consignment of junk, whittled down a little. They make excellent paper weights. It takes from ten minutes to half an hour digging them up, so far do they go into the soil, and I have acquired quite a muscle in consequence. It is a hobby with some of the men to see how many different kinds of prizes they can collect. I heard of a field gunner who had twenty-one different kinds when an order came out forbidding the accumulation of such stuff, and he had to throw them all away. I dug one curiosity up a few days ago. It turned out to be a French prize. The Deutchers are evidently using up some ammunition captured from the French. So far I have not seen that they have done any damage with it.

Though intended to burst in the air, it has mostly gone into the ground about a foot before bursting.

One of the field gunners — a captain who has seen Indian service — came into our O.P. [observation post] a few days ago and asked me to have our battery take on a "Pipsqueak" (the official name for a Deutcher high-explosive shell the same size as our 18-pounder) which he had discovered [while] firing in a hedge two miles in front. The major agreed to do it, and I went down to the captain's O.P. (the official name for which is the Leicester Lounge) to observe from there because a much better view was from there obtainable. We plotted the place out on the map, but by that time it was 1 p.m., so he said, "Will we have our little shoot after tiffin?"[25] So our shoot was postponed until he had his tiffin. The old shooting iron was in rare form, and after the expenditure of ten rounds he said, "Well, that's most satisfactory, isn't it? If there is a battery there they'll move out after dark, all right." Personally I thought the shots were a little plus, but they seemed to satisfy him and that was all I was there for.

> Sincerely,
> Cyrus

July 27, 1915

Dear Ma,

We are now comfortably ensconced in a new position where the activity along the front is not quite as noisy. I am living indoors now in a small room off the mess room. The window is low and I make that the exit into the gun park, which, as usual, is an orchard. It is really the most convenient place we have been in yet.

We are in a new brigade with three other batteries, a new colonel and all that. We are no longer with the 1st Group and I do not think that the brigade we are in now is in any group. We are not far from the first

---

25 A light meal, especially of curried dishes and fruit.

position we were in March 1 to 30, 1915. I walked over to see my old home and found it had been burnt up by Deutcher fire, as one of our successors in office had been discovered and shelled out. It is funny how attached one gets to a position. Every time we move I feel like we do when we move into town from Westfield. And then when we move into another it seems so much nicer than the one we have left.

In our last place we had been living beside a company of Meerut engineers. They moved out and we got a lot of material which the men utilized for improving their bivouacs. When we moved in here we sent three wagons back for as much of our plunder as they could carry. The lounge was taken apart and brought along and has been made into two excellent huts for the men under some pear trees near the house. There is a barn the men can use, but they take delight in camping out and guard jealously every piece of roofing, canvas, and whatnot that may be of use in making a shelter.

The aeroplanes are much more daring along this part of the line. Last evening one came over and one of ours gave chase. The Deutcher opened fire with a machine gun and ours turned back. It was strange to hear the sound of a Maxim[26] coming from on high. Then the enemy flew for home at a tremendous rate of speed. Shortly afterwards one of our large armed biplanes came up, evidently for the express purpose of engaging the foe if he thought well to return, but nothing transpired.

I hear the mail cart rumbling up. I have had no mail since before the move, so will not close until I see if there is anything to answer. There is no Canadian mail today — it comes now about once a week.

Dicky Leach got back yesterday after seven days in London. He met a lot of the officers of the Second Contingent, who are still obsessed with the idea of their great superiority — for some unknown reason — over the First. Still, we will give them the benefit of the doubt and let them prove it in due course. I know this, that the English officers openly say that no infantry could have [done] more work than our infantry has done.

With love,
Cyrus

---

26 Machine gun designed in 1884 by Hiram Maxim.

August 8, 1915

Dear Ma,

I was sincerely bombarded this afternoon by Garland and Leach. They thought they had just cause for that as I had dropped a brick into a pool of water near which they were sitting and the resultant splash had sprinkled the back of their jackets. Leach stood on guard at the door of my room with a basin of water and Garland sat by the window with a soda siphon. I was met by a steady stream as I climbed in the window but had the satisfaction of dumping a long pitcher full of water over the offender before the engagement ceased. It is a good thing the mess room floor is made of slate blocks. This is the favourite method of flooring — here and there an opening about the size of a brick is left on the wall on the floor line, and the method of cleansing adopted is to pour water on the floor and, instead of mopping up, sweeping it into one of these holes. So the situation was altogether ideal for a water fight.

We have superannuated our mess secretary and appointed in his place our right section commander, Mr. Ryan, who is something of a connoisseur of things to eat. Today under the new regime we had a departure form the usual lettuce, bread, and tea lunch by adding thereto mayonnaise, raw tomatoes, canned salmon, etc. Last evening instead of sago or rice pudding we had a deep apple pie. Tonight we waive our rights to the usual meat ration and will fall upon three chickens purchased to celebrate the change in management. We do not see any raspberries around these parts — all the land is given up to the cultivation of what the interpreter calls non-luxuries.

We have been horribly busy so far this month. My guns have fired but two shots and that was not for inimical purposes, but merely at a well-known landmark on the enemy's side of the line for the purpose of testing the accuracy of the gun. Our brigade has been grouped and we are again in a group, this time I believe, the 4th Group. Please tell Connie the B. B. magazine must be sent monthly.

> With love,
> Cyrus

August 23, 1915
Craven Hill Gardens
Lancaster Gate, W.
Tel. 5998 PADD

Dear Ken,

I enclose some shipping documents covering a small box of prizes which I sent addressed to you. They are all Deutcher prizes of shells near our different positions. The curious spiral affair is one of French manufacture captured by the Germans at supposedly Mauberge and used by them against our battery without damage one fine afternoon. Give the shell to Allan Thomas for the M Club.[27] Do what you like with the prizes. If Mr. Puddington wants one, let him have his choice. The candlestick is for Ma.

I went down to Saltwood last Saturday morning with Fraser and spent the day with Bumps and Frances. In the evening I reported at the boat at Folkestone for the return journey but was informed the trips had been cancelled for several days, pending an investigation into an alleged strewing of mines in the passage across the Channel. So I returned to Saltwood for Sunday and came up here this morning. The embarkation authorities are to wire me to this address when they want me to report. I am not sure that I shed any tears over the extension of leave.

Many thanks.

Sincerely,
Cyrus

August 25, 1915

Dear Ken,

Things are very quiet along our front at present. Fraser is looking well. He goes to a masseur every day and will probably recover the use of

---

27   A tongue-in-cheek Millionaires' Club in Saint John.

his arms in time. He has been given two more months' leave of absence. The magazines and papers come regularly.

Sincerely,
Cyrus

August 27, 1915

Dear Ma,

So, the Hon. Sham Shoes[28] is now a knight, if the clipping from the *Daily Sketch* which I enclose is correct. The English papers always seem to refer to him as "Sam" without bothering to put the word "general" before his name. Bumps said that one day last week "Sam" called all the field officers to meet him (field officers are, I think, those with the rank of major and upwards) and *told them of an interview which he had just had with Lord Kitchener which gave him the opportunity to express to the War Lord his views on the way the campaign has been mismanaged from the beginning.* He recalled the fact that he had [told] Kitchener in the early stages of the war that it was useless to attempt an advance until men and munitions were ready and expressed his pleasure in the policy the army had, at last, adopted and so on and so on.

I was somewhat disappointed that I was not asked to enlist while in London. I masqueraded around all week in civilian clothes, yet notwithstanding the robust nature of my appearance — some fifteen or twenty pounds above normal — I received no invitations, though during the same period of time Hughie's services were solicited on at least three occasions. Hughie treated me like a prince and it was certainly top hole being with him.

The personnel of those staying at Hughie's 'boarding house' in London was a little unusual: two members of the American Associated Press, a southern lady and her daughter (age forty), a naturalized German lady and her daughter (not companionable), an English lady of

---

28   Major-General Sir Sam Hughes, Canadian minister of militia and defence.

old family — once very wealthy, now living on a mere pittance — and her daughter, an actress who is commencing her career by doing small parts. The actress is at present rehearsing for a new production of Sir A. Rivero called *The Drum* which is to appear in the near future. The final boarder is Hughie. He is the life of the household and is extremely popular.

We were discussing the possibility of a small theatre party to include the actress but allowed the matter to remain in abeyance when it transpired that her evenings were reserved at present for her fiancé. Then the landlady herself is quite an entertaining subject — Mrs. Liardet, her name is, the "t" being silent like the "r" in fish. She devoted the greater part of one morning telling me some of her troubles. I say "some" because she was entirely reticent in the matter of the contemplated divorce proceedings, Liardet versus Liardet et al., in which she is plaintiff, and the other defendant, a woman, who is of such prodigal nature that she spends most of her time in writing amorous letters to the husband.

Hughie and I both heard explosions from Zeppelin bombs in the raid on London last week. Mrs. Liardet's lessor [landlord] was demanding that she insure the premises against aerial destruction, a precaution which she considered far from indispensable.

One of the journalists has had a varied experience. He was at the execution of the four gunmen in the Becker case, in the interests of the press, and was also with Harry Thaw[29] in his escape from Canada or, rather, attended the proceedings in Canada and followed him across the border.

The southern lady and the journalist had an animated discussion one evening at dinner over the real cause of the war between the north and the south. The argument was a little one-sided in that when she got thoroughly wound up she was as consistent in the continuity of her diction as an eight-day clock, and her opponent was worsted because when she

---

29   Charles Becker was a New York City police officer who was executed for the
      murder of a Manhattan gambler on July 30, 1915. Harry Thaw murdered architect
      Stanford White in 1906 (dramatized in the film, *Ragtime*) and was incarcerated in
      an asylum until he escaped to Sherbrooke, Quebec, in 1913. He was subsequently
      extradited back to the United States.

finally gasped for breath he had quite forgotten the points which he had marshalled up for her discomfiture.

I asked her if there was any antipathy towards the negro in the southern states. "Not at all," she said and to illustrate described with some minuteness a tombstone beside her grandfather's grave — "Here Lies the Faithful Servant of so and so." Then, said I, "How do you account for the refusal of Georgetown University to play the Harvard baseball team because the shortstop on the Harvard team happened to be a man of colour?" We found that we were looking on the question from different points of view, and the conversation resolved itself into a recital of family history, which, though undoubtedly a theme of much interest to students to whom the first chapter of the Gospel of St. Matthew makes a strong appeal, was anything but illuminating to a person who was not overanxious to miss the opening chorus of *Tonight's The Night*.

The last morning I was in London I ran amok among the jewellers in New Bond Street and made a couple of purchases in honour of my nieces, Patricia, Janice, and Dorothea. I trust the trinkets arrive in safety and if the fond parents feel that their daughters are too young to disport themselves so garishly, I hope they will appropriate the same to their own use until said infants are emancipated.

        With love,
        Cyrus

Chapter Five

Our Great Glory at Loos

About September 1st, 1915, the right section marched to a Fosse back of Les Brebis, north west of Bully Grenay, to prepare a position for the Loos offensive. Up to this time all our positions had been above ground, the guns in hedges or under fruit trees, but here was open country with no cover whatsoever, and to hide the guns from hostile aircraft, they were dropped into pits well roofed over with splinter-proof protection. The Fleurbaix section, after taking part in the diverting bombardment which was general along the British front, left at 8 o'clock in the evening on the 20th of September, to join up with the Loos section — a march of some 25 miles.

To enable the guns to be in the pits by daylight, fresh horses from the Loos section were in readiness at Béthune to take the last relay. After the capture of Loos, the battery moved forward into pits near Brebis. The older men will remember the tremendous exertions expended in digging and constructing these pits, and their dismay when two days later, the Germans, with probably balloon observation, turned guns of various calibres on the position, wrecking one pit and gun and badly damaging the communicating trenches.

Next day we moved into the Mazingarbe Park, getting into action in time to take part in repelling an enemy counterattack supported by gas. The park was an area exclusively allotted to French batteries so we were requested to vacate and two days later moved into pits back of Vermelles Philosophe, where we thought we would probably remain all winter, when unexpectedly orders came to march to Le Touret.

The period spent at Loos provides an interesting chapter. The battery was brigaded with 48th H.B., R.G.A., forming together what was known as Phip's Brigade, deriving its name from the O.C. of the 48th H.B. who was placed in command. When the bombardment commenced, the battery was the extreme right-hand battery of the British front where the British and French areas overlapped. We were thus enabled to see much of the French gunners, and compare with them the respective merits of British and French guns and gunnery. Here it was that we first saw to any extent the renowned 75s in action. We also made a comparative study of the British and French censorship regulations when, with much envy, we watched our allies photographing our gun position with cameras — without which a French officer always seemed to be improperly dressed.

In view of more recent experience, I often wonder just how much damage we did with our daily shoots with aeroplane observation upon the batteries behind the Liévin Hills. Fifteen to twenty rounds without subsequent fire for effect was the limit that our supply of shells in those days could stand!

Outstanding features of our work were the concentrated shoots on Bois Hugo, and our harassing fire up Hulluch way and upon Lens Railway Station. But the French showed such tender solicitude for the preservation of Lens that it was soon intimated to us that their gunners could look after that part of the front without assistance from us. Curiously enough, our great glory at Loos was the destruction of a brick wall suspected by our O.P. officer to be, as it actually was, a nest of machine gun emplacements. Though a target of no difficulty in itself, it was in *the path of the 47th Division, who showed their appreciation for services rendered in a letter of gratitude which is preserved to this day among our archives.*

September 13, 1915
[letter unaddressed and unsigned — probably to "Ma"]

This morning's German Albatross came down close to Steenwerck. From accounts received, the aeroplane was at first engaged by our anti-aircraft guns and subsequently by one of our aeroplanes, which brought it down. The machine was hit in several places — the engine petrol tank and the propeller showing shot holes but otherwise undamaged. The pilot and observer, the latter an officer, were both killed.

The machine contained cameras and a machine gun and several belts of ammunition, some rounds of which had been fired. The observer, who sat immediately behind the pilot, was provided with a revolving seat and the machine gun was in such a way fitted that it could be traversed to fire at any point on three-quarters of a circle. (This means, Ken, that if he shot ahead he would bore a hole through the pilot).

At 4:45 (13th) a mine was exploded about fifty yards from the parapet of our trench at _____. This appears to have been the signal for a German bombardment of our line, as our fire trench and communication trenches were heavily shelled for three-quarters of an hour or fifty minutes. No serious damage was done, though the parapets and parados were knocked about in parts.

As far as could be ascertained at least two batteries of field guns and one 4.2 battery bombarded our lines. What a tremendous bombardment! Enemy's shelling appeared to switch from our trenches to those further south and as soon as our batteries got going, died away.

September 18, 1915

Dear Ken,

I wrote to Ma an account of the German air machine that was brought down near our wagon lines. I enclose the report as contained in *The Times* and also the report from the intelligence summary that is sent round daily. You will also note the account of the mine explosion — a general alarm occurred in this sector and we were called to guns for a short time for defensive reasons but nothing transpired.

A few evenings ago a man from a Devon regiment in a bomb school close by came into our billet to buy a beer. All the farmers sell it. And from the noise he was making, it was quite apparent that he had called on many of them. At any rate his vision had become so impaired that he mistook our men for some of his army and expressed his opinion that that same army had a lot to learn before they could fight side by side with men like himself who had been out here nine months. In answer to his argument our men expedited his passage through the door and face downwards into the dirty, filthy, rotten muck, known as the "middens" which is the pride of every farmhouse. He retaliated by smashing every window within reach. The air became thick with his quaint vocabulary and continued so until I thought it meet to put him under arrest, but on his promise to go home if his cap was returned to him I sent him on his way down the road.

Two of my sergeants thought their judgment preferable to mine and started off with him as an escort. He attempted to prove there was still some life in him and smashed in the teeth of one of the sergeants, whereupon they pummelled him severely and then declared him under arrest and handed him over to his unit. They were sent for as witnesses next day at 12 noon and were told by the officer holding court that the man was not drunk, that their word, like that of all Canadians, was not to be relied on, that he himself had been in Canada and therefore spoke with authority, and that the Canadians out here went about in cliques causing mischief.

"Zeppelin that erstwhile inhabited the Zeppelin shed in my area — brought down in flames over England."

They came home much incensed at the treatment received and wanted me to take the matter further. But as they have their huts within earshot of my window, and as I had to be awake far into the night listening to the recital over and over again of the tortures they had inflicted on their victim before handing him over, my sympathies were entirely with the accused, and so I have let the matter drop.

Two of our men have letters from London stating that one of the Zeppelin bombs landed on a crowded motor bus in Cheapside. *Requieseat in Pace*.

Sincerely,
Cy

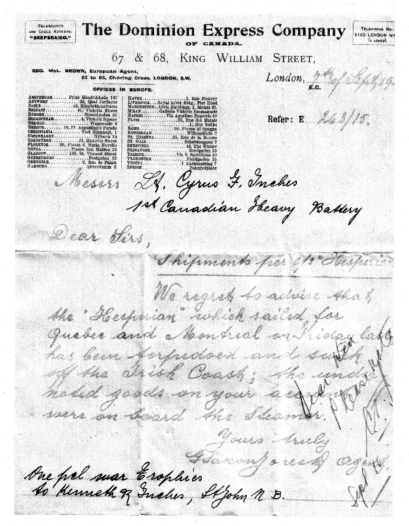

Letter to Cy about sinking of the *Hesperian*.

September 29, 1915

Dear Ma,

This letter is to take the place of the one that probably went down with the *Hesperian*.[30] Last evening, we had with us at dinner three English officers of a battery that have moved in near us but as yet have not established their mess. Two are "topping" chaps but the third — well, let it stop there. The conversation, as usual in such cases, resolved itself into a discussion of Canada, the nature of the place, and the habits of the denizens therein. Number three above named contributed just three questions during the course of the evening. 1. Is it true that all Canadians are addicted to the use of chewing gum? 2. Do not lime juice and biscuits together form a staple article and diet over there? 3. Do you have chocolates? He was asked to specify just what he meant by chocolates. Answer: Not exactly toffee — just chocolates. I really do not think he was stringing us because he had already received an intimation from his *confrères* that this particular offspring of perfidious Albion should never have been allowed to leave her shores without a nurse.

Our interpreter suggests that we establish here a small Canadian village by way of a model and charge Englishmen an admission fee of one shilling devoting the proceeds to a fund for charitable purposes. He is a man with a large range of vision and has travelled extensively in America and is conversant with the average Englishman's knowledge of colonial life. He is reminded of Voltaire's description of Canada — "so many acres of snow" — and thinks most Englishmen must be disciples of that Frenchman.

Yes, today I received three letters, one each from yourself, Bev Armstrong, and Fred Taylor, together with papers from Ken, all of which bring the Saint John news and gossip down to August 28 — a rather quick delivery. The weather for the last three days has been delightful and it augurs well for a fine September.

> With love,
> Cyrus

---

30 British passenger ship sunk by a German U-boat off the coast of Ireland on September 4, 1915.

The Winter of 1915-16 — Le Touquet

*On November 1st after spending one week at Le Touquet, we
moved to the Armentières district. The right section took over
a position near Houplines from an English battery; the left
section did likewise two miles further north, back of
Le Bizet on the River Lys. We remained in these positions
for five months, supporting the infantry in as many raids
from as far north as Messines where the front was held by the
Canadians, to as far south as the Bois Grenier, an arc of fire of
nearly 180 degrees. In March there occurred a trench raid of
some magnitude, in support of which the right section moved
out to a temporary position in front of Houplines to fire due
north upon the enemy frontline parapet at Le Touquet at a
range of some yards — probably the shortest range at which
the battery has ever fired.*

*The advanced position thus occupied could be seen from
Warneton Church. To prevent observation therefrom, one gun
of the Le Bizet section kept the church tower under a steady
fire with time shrapnel, and with apparent success, for next
day the German communiqué, in its version of the attack,
stated that "the enemy consistently shelled a church." I can
think of no other instance where the work of this battery
received special mention in any communiqué. Our other
Le Bizet gun was employed on machine-gun emplacements
in a factory south of Frelinghien.*

November 1, 1915

Dear Chacker,

The situation with this, Chacker, at present is so bizarre that I find
great difficulty in bringing the scene before your imagination. I sleep
and fight in Belgium and eat in France, where I also keep my horses.

We jocularly call ourselves Magee's brigade [because] our sections are again separated. Through a streak of good fortune my section is just near headquarters, which is called "The Chateau." The grounds are delightful. Of course the mess is in the dining room — the only place that can touch it in magnificence is the McLeans' dining room home.

The building is absolutely intact — that has a twofold meaning. It has not been reached by hostile shell and the proprietor left a good deal of furniture behind — comfortable armchairs, curtains deluxe, dishes, glasses, etc. The electric light has been cut off but a plentiful supply of bronze oil lamps proves a good substitute. We have started the furnace going and the radiators give forth a comfort. We have sent for a plumber and hope to have hot and cold water running in the bathroom soon.

My billet is right on the river, which is about as wide as the Nerepis Creek, [so] we are talking of getting a motorboat to use on the river. It will be an easy way of getting to the right section and other places that are good for observation places. It is all too good to last. Dinner is coming soon, so I'll now close.

> With love to yourself and family,
> Chacker

November 18, 1915

Dear Ken,

The football season is winding up, isn't it? It is remarkable how quickly the time seems to fly along. Fraser and Hughie are to celebrate together in London on Saturday.

Bill Vassie has been visiting us for a few days. He has had a good course at Shoebury and is in fact an excellent artilleryman, considerably above the average. It is like old times to sit in a game with him in the evenings. We restrict ourselves to a five-cent limit and have a good deal of fun out of it, as no one can really lose anything.

Battery Christmas card, 1915.

Pollard wrote Bill a few days ago and states the M Club[31] is about the only one running now — the Pokiok and LM having closed down for the war season. Harry arrived for the evening and spent the night and yesterday with us. It was quite like Saint John to have them all around again. Tell Buff that though I have been here nine months, I could easily spend nine years without accumulating a fraction of the blood-curdling tales that Bill has gathered together in eight weeks.

Sincerely,
Cyrus

---

31 Along with the Millionaires' Club, the Little Millionaires' (LM) Club and the Pokiok Club were tongue-in-cheek clubs in Saint John.

January 20, 1916

Dear Ken,

I have before me your letters of December 31, 1915, and January 3, 1916. It is getting to be a sad world when a seasoned piece of old hickory like you has to lay up for repairs. I hope that long before you receive this letter you will be round again all right. Tell Connie, please, that the box of cake, raisins, and whatnot was seen and very soon conquered. I again suggest that you eliminate the New York and Montreal papers until the football season starts again but don't forget the Saint John ones.

I had a letter from Louis McGloan yesterday. He very kindly offered to run the business[32] while King [Hazen] and I are away. He tells me that Colonel McLean has some very original Christmas cards. Fralick had a good trip to London. While there he saw many Saint John boys, including his brother and Jimmie Phillips, Weldon McLean, Jim Hazen, Jim and Bumps McAvity, and many others. He did not hear of the D.S.O. [Distinguished Service Order] decoration until just before leaving London. He was flooded with Christmas cards and just when he had about completed his acknowledgements of them, the letters of congratulations have commenced to come in, so he has to devote most of his spare time to the pen.

You may remember me speaking of Captain Peto, M.P. for a district in Wilts who was very kind to us while in Worton. He has since taken a great interest in our operations and wrote both Frank and me each as soon as he saw our names in the paper. I note his name frequently in the reports of the parliamentary proceedings.

A message has just come in from the division we were supporting asking for the names of any officers or men concerned in the operations that the O.C. considers deserving of special mention. I think you will probably see in the mentioned list pretty soon the name of two of our telephonists, Dickson and Renrod, who laid wire under ticklish circumstances. Renrod is a wide-awake young Yankee — and a good Yankee is a hard man to get ahead of. His pride is not restricted by a

---

32 The law firm of Inches and Hazen.

platitudinarian president.[33] I may be mistaken in this indictment of our friends south of the border but I have always thought upon the invasion of Belgium that the US, who to my mind had for some years been acting as the most conspicuous mediator between right and wrong, *should have been the first to render the "police" protection that even the best-regulated communities regard as the only means to maintain law and order.*

Cyrus

Here ended our first year in the line. It had its disappointments. In May we were going through as far as Don, and scarcely gained a yard. At Loos we were to end the War, and received instead the unpleasant revelation that our supply of ammunition was not large enough to keep our guns warm. In one year we had fired 13,000 rounds. Of this amount 3,500 had been expended at Loos, and in our conceit we quite fancied ourselves as expert gunners. Little did we think then that the time was coming, as it did indeed, three years later on the memorable day our infantry broke the Hindenburg Line, when, to perform the tasks allotted to us, we would have to speed up to a capacity of that number of rounds in one day. It may be instructive to note here, that during the subsequent three years we have had an expenditure of — I'm merely guessing — 80,000 rounds a year. If any of you are finance ministers and wish to figure out how much all this cost at from twenty-five to fifty dollars a round, the price, depending on the business acumen of the contractor, you may find that you have thrown away almost as much money in France as you have while on leave in London.

---

33   U.S. president Woodrow Wilson.

March 7, 1916
Mardi Gras

Dear Ma,

Clams and other Shells
Number One in short series of Lenten Meditations

You know what Courtenay Bay looks like when the tide is out —
dotted here and there and everywhere over the mud you see young and
old industriously digging away in search of clams and whatnot. If you
were here in some point of vantage commanding a view of the low-lying
flatlands, you would frequently see a similar sight. On the first occasion
you would wonder just what the critters were doing but if you had been
there a little while before and had witnessed the enemy's shells falling
in the fields, you would reason that the workers were souvenir hunters
excavating for fuses. I often speculate about what the German gunners
think they are doing and what they are shooting at for hours at a time.
The shells will fall in ploughed or burrowed ground at regular intervals,
say one every five minutes or less, with no apparent aim in life, unless it
be to pockwork the soil which the farmer has laboriously tilled.

Of course, if they fall near a communication trench or road which
shows signs of being used the explanation seems easy, but there are
times when these guides to deduction are absent and [then] it is a trifle
puzzling to come to a conclusion. When it is reasonably clear that the
storm's over, out come spades and shovels and the relic seekers do their
best to augment the damage already caused to the proprietor of the
terrain. Yet there is a lesson to us in this kind of strafing. Many of our
own projectiles which we are fond to imagine are causing trouble to our
opponents undoubtedly wander far afield into unoffending pastures,
landing perhaps unintentionally in some farmer's kitchen during meal
hour, sniping the kettles off the stove, mussing up the toast, scattering the
mangle wurtzers, and so on.

This mania for collecting souvenirs in the shape of fuses is not
peculiarly Anglo-Saxon. There is a fort within the enemy's lines in our

sector of fire — a real fort in a chain of defences built long before this war was even broached — it is too far back from the trenches to be of any present service by way of defence, but I verily believe from what I have heard that the wily Hun uses it as an ammunition depot.

There is a road nearby which is an important thoroughfare and is used by the same Hun as such, though I don't think he knows we can see as much of him as we are able to do, provided the lenses in the telescope have been properly dusted with chamois — a small piece of which every dutiful observer should carry for the purpose but doesn't.

One day not so very long ago it seemed to me that the traffic in, around, and about this blot on the landscape — the fort aforesaid — was a little too barefaced and daring to let pass by unnoticed, so we had a little shoot. I'll not make affidavit to having done any damage but it appeared through a moderately clear lens that one of the shells landed plump into the fort . . . an earthwork structure with the green grass growing all round. Result: lawn disfigured.

The inspiration for this letter came to me when, on turning my telescope in that direction some time later, my curious gaze [revealed] the sight of the Deutcher calmly (or clamly) turning up the earth in search of the fuse. The burst of the shell makes a hole in the ground, saucer shaped. The fuse generally breaks away intact and goes off on a frolic of its own into the ground making a little hole, say three inches in diameter and of considerable depth, sometimes two feet or more. By noting the direction taken by the fuse, which is revealed by the three-inch hole, it is possible to tell the exact direction from which the shell came. And if, as often happens, the fuse is set for what we call "time action," which indicates the range at which the shell is fired, we have a very fair idea of the place from whence it was fired, i.e. the guilty battery.

I am not giving away trade secrets because the Hun does the same thing and perhaps that is what the digger chappie was up to. Next subject: "Sergeant Kirby's Grenadiers."

With love,
Cyrus

Mars 8, 1916
Cendres

Dear Ma,

Sergeant Kirby's Grenadiers
Number Two in the series. (It has to do with our police system.)

I am not cognizant of the methods adopted in other units for preserving law and order, though I take it that each one has its guardroom for detention purposes and that a guard is appointed daily. In addition to these precautions we have our Sergeant Kirby, whose sole duty is to take charge of the prisoners. He always recalls to my mind the famous pirate of that name in *To Have And To Hold*, by Mary Johnston. But if unbounded enthusiasm for carrying into execution the various regulations laid down for the entertainment of defaulters sentenced to field punishment were the sole criterion to determine that an individual is gifted with piratical characteristics, I'm afraid that Kirby will never make much of a freebooter.

It comes within the province of his sphere of action to see that his Grenadiers, as we call his charges, are used for all possible fatigues. Included in this category are such pleasant occupations as mending roads, removal of garbage, burying deceased horses, and the like. For a long time the Grenadiers exhibited a decided reluctance to take Sergeant Kirby seriously and the guardroom, instead of becoming a vision of boredom, came to be regarded as a haven of rest. Crime was rampant.

When there was a particularly obnoxious fatigue to be performed it was no uncommon sight to see Kirby himself slaving away at the job with the prisoners in a circle around him humorously encouraging him along with the work at hand. This laxity on his part became so flagrant that he was given to understand he would be considered guilty of a punishable offence himself if he was found again in this undignified position. I remember that it used to amuse Mr. Siegfried immensely to see Kirby plodding away industriously with the prisoners in the role of interested spectators.

After that the burden was transferred to the proper shoulders. But I am sorry to say that still our guardroom has small terrors, notwithstanding the stringency of the penalty known as field punishment. It is provided that the offender be tied to a fixed object in view of his comrades for two hours for not more than three out of four consecutive days up to twenty-one days. He is not allowed to smoke or drink his rum ration and is prohibited from entering an estaminet. He is confined in the guardroom from 6 p.m. to 6 a.m., can have only his blankets, and must sleep on the floor. If the floor happens to be of stone, straw is provided. Automatically he descends to the bottom of the leave roster, must do pack drill for at least an hour a day, and his rations consist of tea biscuit and bully beef only. In addition to the trials above, enumerated pay is deducted for every day of field punishment awarded.

You can imagine that if these provisions were rigidly enforced the ranks of the Grenadiers would soon be depleted. Kirby is the only one that I know of who cares to attempt to do so, and his efforts in that regard make him a poor apology for a chief of police.

One of the men undergoing field punishment not long ago escaped from custody and got hopelessly intoxicated. He was remanded for court martial. He alleged that Kirby let him escape and it was nothing against a prisoner that he did get drunk because Kirby, himself, was not averse to joining the prisoners now and then in drowning their sorrows in a pint of beer and that every facility was afforded them in this respect. The man is something of a rascal, and happily for this unit got nine months in [jail] and was sent to the A.P.M. [assistant provost marshal] for the carrying out of the sentence.

I do not know just what form the next in the series will take. I'll have to meditate.

> With love,
> Cyrus

Mars 17, 1916
Vend. S. Patrice

Dear Ma,

Number Three in our lecture series will be known as *Our Neighbours* but I can't anticipate what paths I may ramble into before concluding.

I don't think I ever told you about the personnel in the nearest building to us — *Our Neighbours*. Their major is a "dugout" meaning thereby a chappie who thought he had retired from service to spend the rest of his days in ease and quietude but, owing to the exigencies of the situation, finds himself in harness once again. In such a case it takes some time to divest oneself of the barnacles — consequently, he was a trifle uncertain of himself for some time. He is fortunate in having a very able assistant in his captain, whom we had to dinner last evening for the first time and who joined us afterwards in a little session of the "Great American Endurance Contest," more commonly called poker.

One of their first miscues was their treatment of the question of "cover" or "concealment." We noticed that they had made tracks about their gun position to such a degree that no hostile scout with average eyesight would attribute such disfigurement of the soil to any other cause than the presence of guns, and were a little uneasy on that account owing to the proximity of their guns to ours.

The matter came to a head when one of our airmen reported to squadron headquarters that *the Canadians were contemplating suicide by the trouble to which they were going to draw the enemy's fire*. Human nature rebelled at once at this error of the observer. In this connection I might point out that when anything goes wrong and it is sought to place the blame on the proper shoulders, the investigation committee always asks first "Are there any Canadians in the vicinity?" and if the question is answered in the affirmative the burden of proof is cast upon them.

Two horses were illegally driven faster than a walk on the pavée road. "There go the Canadians!" It seemed a matter of small moment that at that particular time and place we had no wagon on the road. We received a file of correspondence containing the particulars of a complaint accusing our men of taking the crosses from the parish cemetery for the purpose of firewood — a charge entirely without foundation, unless it be that that is the natural way for Canadians in their native land to procure fuel. The real offenders were, without doubt, the members of a battery who chose the burying ground as a congenial spot in which to mount their guns — *Our Neighbours*.

Our Neighbours are the gunners I told you about, who on hearing our guns fire for the first time, mistook the reports for detonations of enemy shells and in a spasm of excitement spread the cheerful news that the Germans were into the Canadians. They nearly did get us into trouble on one occasion. It was during the operation described in a German communiqué in which the foe expressed such indignation at the consistent shelling of a church. The scheme required that certain batteries should continue firing until their job was completed notwithstanding the blight upon the vision of a hostile plane. *Our Neighbours* erroneously concluded that their battery was one of these and carried on directly beneath the gaze of a hostile observer who happened along at the time. They drew fire. Shells that were intended for them fell unpleasantly close to us. And then the fight was on. We proved conclusively that we had not fired at any time when our flashes were visible to those above. Finally they shouldered the responsibility. The incident was closed.

It is noteworthy the amount of prestige that three months' experience out here gives a man. Within one week *Our Neighbours* have been joined by another battery with the same type of gun. And now in their relations to their associates they carry themselves with enough *savoir faire* to impress an old campaigner.

To us . . . the most entertaining experience that *Our Neighbours* went through was their wrestling with the telephone communications. The installation of a workable telephone system is perhaps the greatest real work with which the newcomer has to contend. Nothing is more irritating than a defective instrument or wire, and it is some time before the uninitiated knows the likely places to look in his endeavour to set the matter right. Added to these difficulties, this new battery is labouring under the rather humorous disadvantage of having a sprinkling of Scotchmen of broad dialect among their telephonists and linesmen.

If there is one voice that is hard to make out over the telephone it belongs to a son of Scotland. Their line to their observation point, which is also one used by us, was not very distant the first day they fired. The telephonist which the observing officer took with him was Scotch. His efforts to make himself understood were fruitless and *the whole series was at a standstill* until one of his compatriots who could understand him was put on the battery end of the wire. The major and captain of the new battery are both Scotch, the former is a topping fine fellow, the captain is a comedy. He is a Scotch millionaire — occupation, steamship builder. Neither drinks nor smokes but uses very pretty cuss words. Has a batman who was his valet before he enlisted. He barges about in most unwieldy style, and as the room in most of the observation points can hardly be said to compare favourably with the area of a banqueting ball, the only alternative is to resolve oneself into the smallest possible space when he is about. The first question he asked when he got to our peek hole was

"Where are the German observation posts?"

As a general rule an observation post ceases to be an observation post when it becomes manifest to the enemy that it is being used as an observation post. Nevertheless I don't think the new captain's opinion of our intelligence was very flattering when we told him we could not answer his question.

With love,
Cyrus

March 20, 1916

Dear Ma,

My left arm is still a little sore as the result of an inoculation against paratyphoid which I underwent two mornings ago. It was found that the inoculation against typhoid proper was not effective in the case of a milder form of "para," so called. It affected me slightly but some of the others felt pretty seedy. A good many of the men were quite incapacitated — one man in particular, a Belgian, Duhant by name, strolled into the line-up a second time by mistake and received another injection. He was really sick for a time. This same party wrote to King Albert some time ago asking some favour in the nature of a request from the king to our major, that he be allowed to visit his brother in some town nearby because he did not think he could speak English well enough for us to understand just what he wanted.

The cinema man was brought down by the general of the Canadian Artillery a few days ago and took some reels of our left section in action — so if you see some 60-pounders thundering away in the *Imperial* [Theatre, Saint John] in a few months, you will see my old gun crews at work. I'm not with the section now as a steady job, as I am doing captain's duties, looking after stores and equipment and relieving the other officers at their jobs when they are on leave or other places. While the cinema operations were in progress I was helping with aeroplane operations with the right section, *so you won't recognize me among the actors in the play.* I understand the pictures are in a series of reels of the Canadians in Flanders.

With love,
Cyrus

March 26, 1916

Dear Ma,

A few days have slipped by somehow since I have written. Don Pidgeon,[34] who was paymaster with Harry, had a grand scheme framed up after he had been out here a couple of months. He had *accepted* a position [in] the London Pay Office and he had it all figured out that with captain's pay, field allowance, and extra London allowance of three

---

34 Half-brother to New Brunswick-born actor Walter Pidgeon.

dollars per diem, altogether he was only to receive some eight dollars and a half per diem during his incarceration. So in a moment of indiscretion he wrote a sharp letter of criticism to some political people in Canada of the way the pay department was being administered, and his attack upon his employers involved the head of the department in the London Pay Office who had agreed to take him in. As this letter of attack was forwarded from Canada to this head, this official felt it would be more peaceful for him to let Pidgeon stay in Flanders. And by way of rubbing it in, transferred him to another unit, the R.C.R. [Royal Canadian Regiment], where he not only does pay duties — which are a sinecure — but is enforced to make himself useful in looking after transport and whatnot.

Re captaincy: the H.Q. [headquarters] of the corps assure us that notice of my elevation to a more lucrative rank *may* appear in this month's orders, so I have not given up all hope yet. In the meantime I am to take over the paymaster's duties as soon as Ryan goes for a few weeks. This means seventy-five cents a day extra. I'm getting into a mercenary train of mind again so I think I'll draw these few remarks to a close.

Cyrus

March 29, 1916

Dear Ma,

The last three days have been of more than passing interest with me. Yesterday I went out in a motor with the major of the 2nd Canadian Heavy Battery over a goodly stretch or, rather, circuit of country and dined in a town — that one that Harry is so near. While at dinner we happened to pick up *The Times* of the previous day and I noted therein that my promotion has already appeared in print to date from January 22. The great virtue in this antedating is that it carries pay for the rank from that date. "Temporary" means for the duration of the war.

Yesterday received a box from Miss Thompson of Rothesay with socks, tobacco, gum, etc., which, at her request, was distributed among the "deserving poor." As a matter of fact, the men receive so much through Canadian sources it is doubtful if they really appreciate everything they get, but as these socks were of lighter variety than the usual run they come in very nicely now that warm weather is in the near prospective. Aeons ago I announced that summer had come. This was a premature conceit on my part if the weather of the last two weeks is taken into consideration....

> With love,
> Cyrus

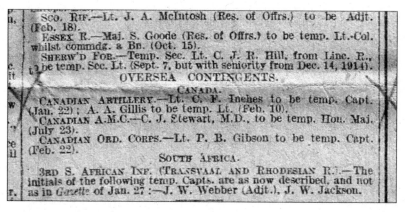

Cy's promotion to captain, *London Gazette*, March 25, 1916.

Chapter Six

The Second Battle of Ypres, 1916

*Now for some real fighting. On March 31st, the left section
marched to the Ypres Salient and was followed by the right
section three days later, relieving the 24th H.B., R.G.A., in a
position where they had been for eleven months. Two guns
were in a hedge back of the hospital, the other two in concrete
pits constructed by the 24th H.B. six hundred yards further back
than Goldfish Chateau.*

*I shall never forget my first impressions of the salient. For
many months we had listened to tales of conditions there, many
of which seemed unbelievable.* Some of those who spoke of it
did so with an awe almost akin to reverence. *It was therefore
with some trepidation of spirit that, squeezed into London buses
still bearing the familiar advertisements, we approached our
position by way of the main Vlamertinghe–Ypres Road.*

*There was something uncanny about the place; it seemed to
be alive and moving and pregnant with danger, yet there was
a fascination about it all that one could not get away from.
Do you remember, as we debussed, the reverberations from the
steady crumping[35] on our right near the Belgian Chateau? I
have a mental photograph of you standing by the roadside with
your kits waiting for the 24th Heavy men to guide you to your*

---

35 The sound of bursting bombs or shells.

quarters. I see your glances in the direction of the Chateau, and can hear the jocular remarks you made to hide whatever were your real feelings upon the prospect. To cheer you up, the men you had come to relieve told you, among other things, that the day before seven hundred and forty 5.9 shells had fallen in the rear position; this may have been good taste on their part, though I must confess that at the time I was entirely of a contra opinion, and also in regard to their unconcealed joy when they scrambled upon the buses which had brought us up. However in a few days we quite understood the eagerness of our predecessors in position to clear out. We were up against counterbattery work scientific to a degree. A day that one of our positions was not shelled was an exception.

The methodical trait in the Hun character was fully demonstrated. He appeared to keep a list of all the Salient gun positions for destructive shoot purposes, and took them on in regular rotation. We came to know that if 'X' Battery was shelled at sunrise one day, a similar fate would befall our rear section the next morning at the same hour; then the following day our forward section was due for a similar grilling. These shoots were carried out with aeroplane observation, and an early hour was chosen because at that time of day visibility on the Western front was in the enemy's favour. It was customary for the airman to range two and sometimes three 5.9 howitzer batteries in turn. When registration was completed there would come a salvo simultaneously from each battery. Until the allotment of ammunition, which varied from one hundred to four hundred rounds, was expended the sound of the incoming shells seemed like one continual whistle — not unpleasant music when listened to from a respectable distance on the side lines.

We generally knew when the shelling had really stopped and it was safe to return. The time was not yet when it was customary to expend the allotment in bursts of fire at regular intervals extending over a period of time of several hours, for the

express purposes of catching personnel who might have returned
to the guns under the impression that the shelling was over. This
adherence to unchangeable system on the enemy's part often did
us in good stead. Do you remember a part of the line we were in
later when we divined that the Hun spent Sunday in getting up
his ammunition supply for the week, shot it off on Monday, and
then remained comparatively quiet until supply day came around
again? For the first time since March [1915] we had come under
the Canadian Corps. The battery took part in the heavy fighting
in connection with the St. Eloi craters.

April 1, 1916

Dear Ma,

We had two visitors to lunch on the thirtieth in the persons of Dr.
Maclaren and Al Massie, both colonels now. They came in a car in which
they are making calls upon their Canadian acquaintances in different
parts. Dr. Maclaren made inquiries as to you and Pa and all the latest
news from Saint John.

A general man told us a good story a few days ago about the *Stars
and Stripes*. Now don't get your back up.[36] It seems an American press
representative was allowed a tour of our lines and was much interested
in the different types of shells that were falling: Pipsqueaks, Whistling
Willies, Wooly Bears, Percys, and whatnot. Finally a shell went into the
ground and did not explode. These are commonly known as "duds."
The thud can be heard for a long distance. "What's that?" inquired the
Yankee. "That's a President Wilson," replied the guide. "Why so called?"
asked the reporter. "Because it's too proud to fight," came the reply.

A "Percy" is a tremendous fellow. It is the nearest corresponding type
that the Hun has to our 60-pounder. It is a very high velocity naval gun
mounted on a railway car and is quite a terror because one does not hear
it coming before it arrives, thereby differing in its qualities from most

---

36 Cy's mother was born in Massachusetts.

guns of long distance. There are very few of the Percy family in use, which is some compensation. I have not been introduced to him yet so the above is all hearsay.

Those coming back from England say all London avers that the war will be over in June. No reasons are given for this aberration, which seems incomprehensible to the actors in the drama this side of the Channel.

With love,
Cyrus

April 5, 1916

Dear Ma,

I have seen quite a lot lately of Major Miles, O.C. of the 24th Heavy Battery . . . one of the original heavy batteries of that calibre in England in peacetime. He told me that at the beginning of the war it was considered undignified for officers and men to take cover when in danger. He (Major Miles) was walking with a colonel of the old school when a brick was knocked off a building and would have fallen on a gunner who was near the building if the man had not ducked and jumped to one side, thus avoiding the blow. The colonel immediately told the man off for his unseemly behaviour, ending up with the final injunction, "The 4th Division never duck."

April 1, 2, and 3 were very warm days and vegetation and floriculture went forward with leaps and bounds. Our ducks and rabbits are rapidly approaching the eating stage. Yesterday I invested the sum of twenty francs in a cock and four hens — my first venture in live fowl. The hens supply for the flock a total of two or three eggs a day and as eggs now cost thruppence a piece, it seems to me I'm getting fair value in the matter of interest. Thanks for the St. Patrick's Day card.

With love,
Cyrus

April 7. 1916

Dear Ma,

Re captaincy: I had a new regalia put on one coat and a few days afterwards in the dark stepped into a slimy, filthy, contaminated ditch face down, and am wearing old clothes until my Sunday-go-to-meetin' suit is ready once more. It was my own fault in that a few seconds before I had rejected the offer of a flash lamp.

Re church services: Since Easter Sunday last I think we have had two services in the unit — one in the horse lines last May and another in the horse lines in the early days at the chateau. It is difficult for the gunners to leave the guns, and as we do not get to rest billets we have to abjure some of the comforts of home. The Catholic chaplains come round a good deal and see that their adherents march off to service occasionally.

The King takes part in a good many ceremonials now. I think he has completely recovered. I have seen no women chauffeurs in France and have not heard of any. I believe there are a few in England in civilian duties, replacing men who have enlisted.

The true state of affairs in Germany is that the civilians are hungry and the troops well fed. I know of one case of a soldier in the trenches [who] sent home some of his butter in order that his father would not be deprived of his luxury. But the troops are not really as content with their rations as the Allies are. Much information along these lines is collected from the examination of prisoners and deserters and from correspondence found on captured prisoners. *Verdun is regarded as a great victory for the French.*

Did you say that Fred Crosby had sent me a pair of socks? None have arrived. If you are sure he sent them I'll put up a bluff that they arrived all right.

I have had an unusually clerical day with billeting returns, paymaster duties, and trying to keep the ammunition account straight. Colonel Phips was right — *this is indeed a stationery war*. All units were asked recently to be saving on the paper. Coming from the source it did, the advice was rather a surprise. The most natural thought was, why doesn't

H.Q. set a good example? The ammunition would set any staff of clerks crazy. A complete round consists of the shell, one cartridge, a fuse, and a T-tube. These come in separate boxes, and if one is lacking the round is incomplete. We are asked to give a strict account of everything. The amount on hand has to be counted over and over again and no two counts ever seem to agree. . . .

> With love,
> Cyrus

April 23, 1916
Pâques [Easter]

Dear Ma,

This has been a very fine day in comparison with [the] almost incessantly bad weather since I wrote you about those two pretty days at the first of the month. There was a service for our men, either Protestant or R.C. The Protestant padre called on Friday and intimated that he would rather not have a compulsory service. So on parade next morning I put the matter to a vote. Nine volunteered, so the padre decided he must confine his attention to larger congregations elsewhere. The men in our battery are not the kind who attend church in peacetime, so it is not to be wondered that they are not more eager for it under present conditions.

This afternoon I rode down to see Bumps and had tea with him and his general. The latter was stationed at Fredericton for some years and knew the Hemmings and Uncle Julius [Inches] very well. His name is Macdonell[37] and he objects strongly to spelling it any other way.

The spring is rather backward this year, and I take it the conditions in Canada must be the same for we are all in the temperate zone.

---

37 Brigadier-General A.C. Macdonell, general officer commanding, 7th Infantry Brigade.

With love,
Cyrus

P.S. I am very glad to note your steady improvement in health.

April 30, 1916

Dear Ma,

April is going out like a lamb, the weather being very fine and warm. There is still no Canadian mail but I have been getting a few letters from business houses in England about small matters of clothing, books, bank accounts, and so forth, so I feel I am still in touch with the outside world. I think we are going to lose Leach, who may go as captain to a howitzer battery. He is a classmate of Major Maurice Fisher of the new howitzer battery in New Brunswick.

I have been wrestling the last two or three days with the pay books and the monthly statement for the paymaster. The pay system is a very workable one. The men who earn a dollar a day are ordinarily allowed to draw but thirty francs a month in fortnightly payments of fifteen francs each. There are two hundred men to pay in the battery. Each man has to sign the roll on receiving his pay, and the amount is entered up also in his pay book, which he produces on getting his money. I draw money enough the day before payday from the field cashier. It is in the form of five-franc notes, a specimen of which I enclose herewith as an Easter present.

This is rather an expensive theme I've got started on. Officers are allowed to draw three hundred and seventy-five francs per month from the paymaster, for which they give their cheque — no more than one hundred and twenty-five francs. Then there are questions continually cropping up about separation allowances, assigned pay, remittances for necessitous cases at home, and a multitude of other small matters.

With love,
Cyrus

May 5, 1916

Dear Ma,

Yesterday your letter with details of your illness arrived, and I was very glad to learn that you are feeling better. It must be very trying to be obliged to keep quiet when the garden has its spring lure. Now that the warm weather is coming, and with Westfield to look forward to, I think I will soon hear that you are mending rapidly.

The box of maple sugar and socks came today — thanks very much — it is the first taste of maple sugar so far received. In the same mail there came a box of Scotch cake from Miss Puddington addressed to me by her brother, also six bundles of papers and magazines from Ken.

The Dublin affair seems to be well in hand at last.[38] I think it will turn out in the end as a matter of good like the Boer rebellion in South Africa at the beginning of the war. News of the uprising in [South Africa] came to us by wireless on board the *Megantic* [September 1914] and we were told that we would probably be sent there after getting sufficient supplies in England but it was a mere rumour as events subsequently showed.

Did you notice that the Hun has put his clocks back another hour by way of daylight saving? Where it is 8 a.m. over there, it is only 6 a.m. with us. He is certainly an ingenious old rascal. I suppose we will follow suit in some manner.

The last few days have been very warm. I am wearing slacks, i.e. long trousers, not proper dress for artillery who are supposed to be mounted but it is much freer and cooler. I am also wearing ankle boots, a pleasant change. Do you know I have never had a pair of puttees[39] on? I think I will try them out to see how they go.

The question of strawberries used to be the burning question between the two messes. The captain's mess never had any trouble getting them.

---

38 A reference to the Easter Rising (April 24-30, 1916) by Irish republicans against British rule.

39 Hindu word for a long strip of cloth wound spirally from ankle to knee for protection and support.

It is not likely the question will come up this season because right near our billets are two deserted gardens, both with strawberry patches which show signs of great promise. In our present garden I really believe I see some raspberries, the first we [have] noticed in France. It won't be long now before the blueberries will be coming in, time flies so quickly. I won't be able to send you any more postcards. The base censor has notified this battery that the practice must cease.

> With love,
> Cyrus

May 23, 1916

Dear Ma,

I had a letter from Cousin Jessie asking me to do anything I could to assist her sons getting commissions. A rotten order came out about a week ago refusing any more commissions in the artillery to men in the ranks. If they want them, they must apply for them in the New Army — English. So I don't know that I can do anything except advise her as to the situation and ask if they would like to make application on those terms.

> With love,
> Cyrus

Approaching the Somme

At the end of May we were ordered to the Somme, one section to march for five days by road, calling in at Bully Grenay on the way to take part in the attempt to recapture the lost ground at Vimy Ridge; *the other section to proceed direct to the Somme by rail two weeks later. In pursuance of this*

Canadian Corps R.A.

10th
H.A. GROUP.

B/691
15/6/16.

13th. June 1916.

The M.G. R.A. is very pleased to be able to circulate a letter received by him from Brigadier-General J.G.GEDDES, C.B. Commanding the Artillery of the 4th. Corps,-

" The 4th. Corps desire to thank the Artillery of the 2nd. Army for their very able assistance in the bombardment of the VIMY RIDGE on 1st. June and on subsequent days.

In most instances these Units marched into action the same night that they arrived in the 4th. Corps area.

They got their guns into action, prepared positions and began to register as soon as it was light.

I was much pleased with their celerity in getting into action and their accurate fire.

The tone of these batteries was thoroughly good. They worked hard and cheerfully and were only too keen to do all they possibly could for us.

The sections of the 115th. Heavy and Canadian Heavy Batteries got heavily shelled, but I am glad to say suffered no casualties. They stood up to their guns like men.

I was indeed to part with your batteries, but I hope you will let them know how much we appreciated their good work".

H.R.Roberts, Capt.R.G.A.
for B.G. to M.G.R.A.
2nd. Army.

13. 6. 16.

(2)

O/C.,
Heavy Artillery Group.

For your information.

D.L.Ryan. Capt. R.A.
Brigade Major.

16.6.16.

Official letter of thanks for a "job well done" at the attack on Vimy in May 1916.

order the left section pulled out on May 29th and for ten days occupied an extremely warm position behind a brewery in Bully Grenay. The IV Corps sent a eulogistic letter to the Canadian Corps, over the work done by us on this occasion.

The guns were registered at noon on zero day from the Lorette Ridge, upon the chimney of the General Electric Station. The balloons must have spotted the proceedings, for when the show started at 4 p.m. we were kept under heavy intermittent fire for six hours. This continued on subsequent days. To add to our anxiety, news came in of the attack upon the Canadians in the Salient, and that our personnel there were having a rough time of it, the casualties including our then O.C. who had been severely wounded. *As I was at Bully Grenay, I can only write of this attack from hearsay. The guns, being in the centre of the Salient, were exposed to fire from the north, east, and south. Hundreds of shells were rained upon the position, but the men never wavered for an instant . . . in proof whereof we have the fact that on one day, within a few hours, the two guns fired some eight hundred rounds.*

Those of you who remember the Vlamertinghe–Ypres Road in the days of normal trench warfare, when any moment harassing fire could be expected, can appreciate to some extent the miracles performed by our drivers in getting up a supply of ammunition when a show was on. But let us get out of the Salient.

June 5, 1916

Dear Ma,

News is plentiful but prohibited, as I have several times pointed out. A French paper has just come in with the cheering news that the great naval fight was not such a walkover and really a wonderful British exploit.[40] *We were just beginning to think that if the Hun got too obstreperous on the seas our communication with the New World would be cut off.*

I note that old Bumps has got his well earned D.S.O. He has turned out to be quite a marvel of strategy and tactics. I have written to him to see if he can do anything for one of the Murray boys along the lines that his mother desires but I don't think there is much possibility.

So Charles[41] has donned a uniform — bully for him! I don't see what else he could have done. *Hun dominion in Canada would be fatal to freedom of thought and justice.* You will miss him at Westfield but you must realize sooner or later that the boy is now a man. The weather is not exactly the kind that ripens the strawberries — in fact it is astonishingly cool — good way to allay the mosquito and fly nuisance.

With love,
Cyrus

June 11, 1916

Dear Ma,

It is short of writing paper I am at present so I have resorted to a few pages of Army Book 152. Every kind of book or form used in the army has a number of its own, and when one runs short of stationery, the custom is to write to the base for a supply of army form so and so. The weather has been remarkably cold of late — the strangest weather for June from time whereof the memory of man runneth not to the contrary. This morning we had a hailstorm, pieces as large as teacups.

It took me yesterday morning until 1:30 p.m. before I could get breakfast. The old woman into whose billet we had thrust ourselves would not let us have the use of her stove. Finally, after much parley, she agreed to let us have it when she was not using it. The cooking was in its initiatory stage when it suddenly occurred to her that it was necessary

---

40   A reference to the Battle of Jutland, May 31, 1916.

41   Charles Inches was Cy's youngest brother, ten years his junior.

to use the stove, and our stuff was relegated to the back benches. The inhabitants in these parts are the most contrary lot of unconscientious objectors imaginable — most of them are making so much money out of the troops that they can afford to be as independent as they please and they are.

The Russians seem to be giving the Austrians a bit of a doing these days. I suppose the central empires are beginning to feel the strain a little and will break up sooner or later. I have not heard from Frank and so do not know where to write him. My mail is wandering around somewhere but should be along soon. Many happy returns of birthdays to Mary and Connie.

With love,
Cyrus

June 15, 1916

Dear Ma,

I have your letter of the sixteenth and I am glad to hear of your improvement in health One of our men, a French Canadian, is engaged to marry a girl in Armentières, and the date for the wedding was set for May, but we have not been able to let him go to it. Result: all kinds of pathetic appeals from the men, the Mamselle, and the Maire [mayor] and all in French.

With love,
Cyrus

P.S. Thanks for the flowers.

The Somme — Opened July 1, 1916

The Bully Grenay section proceeded to Morlancourt via Lacheux and Talmas, the march from Bully Grenay to Lacheux being perhaps the longest and hardest single march ever accomplished by the battery. We were ordered to prepare a four-gun position at Vivier Mill near Méaulte, according to elaborate plans and specifications, providing for a double-decker roof with a layer of concrete, and also received a gentle hint that the work was to be completed in five days. When you consider that the men had marched from the salient to Bully Grenay, had built pits with overhead cover there, had fought a hard fight followed by three days on the road . . . you can imagine their feelings when called upon to build a position of this nature, not only for themselves, but also for the section coming down from Ypres. But they did it and in addition handled a store of six thousand rounds of ammunition.

As it turned out, this labour was extended in vain, for the only hostile shell that came near the battery in this position, splashed into the River Ancre, a deep brook which ran directly behind the guns. This incident provoked an immense amount of humour, in that one of our sergeants who was dressing on the bank was thoroughly soused. The Ypres section appeared on the scene, fagged out with their strenuous work out up north, just in time to commence the preliminary bombardment.

This lasted for six days during which time we were allotted tasks calling for a daily expenditure of 1,080 rounds. Our targets were trenches and woods around Fricourt. We were in an R.G.A. Brigade with two English 60-pounder batteries. We were an unknown quantity, and being colonials we were regarded as a joke, *so much so that while one of the*

English batteries in the brigade had been detailed for the counterbattery work and to answer all aeroplane calls, we were given the easy targets and we were not asked to fire by night!

The prolonged bombardment was a severe strain on the 60-pounder gun, as then constructed, requiring infinite care and skilled knowledge to keep them in action. After a few days when it transpired that we were the only battery in the brigade that was firing its full allotment and whose gun report showed all guns in action, the O.C. of the brigade expressed the opinion that he had been guilty of criminal negligence, as he called it, in so misjudging our capabilities, put us on night firing and gave us the counterbattery work. *We served under this officer for two months.*

When the total expenditure of the brigade had reached 30,000 rounds, half of this firing was credited to us. H.Q. noticed it and sent word to the brigade to give the other batteries more work to do, but how could they? For on one day, when only five out of twelve guns in the brigade were in action, four of them were ours.

Our work, by day was chiefly counterbattery. Scarcely a day passed that we were not standing from dawn to dusk at the beck and call of the airmen and balloon observers. Every night we had our harassing fire to get off. After our first advance and until the capture of the High Wood Ridge in September, O.P. work, from a counterbattery standpoint, was an impossibility, for there was no point from which we could see over the Ridge.

One-franc notes from
the towns of Amiens
and Bailleul.

July 27, 1916

Dear Ma,

I am enclosing for your collection of paper money two one-franc notes which I got from a person who has travelled much. The towns here issue paper money — quite an innovation, isn't it!? The awkward part of it is that Dunkirk would probably refuse to cash a Boulogne issue and vice versa. So the convenience really resolves itself into one for local shoppers.

I have some interesting postcards for you but it is now forbidden to send such material through the mail, so I must abide my time. The censor is a peculiar fellow. Some items which one would think had no interest to the enemy are strictly under ban while on the other hand a mass of material appears in the papers every day which the average person would suppress at all costs. An officer was court-martialled not long ago for giving a clue to his whereabouts by writing a seemingly commonplace sentence, but on closer scrutiny it appeared that the first letters of each word composed the name of the place.

The weather continues of an extraordinary variety — mostly cloudy, misty, and cool. Marchant is an adept tailor and keeps repairing my old

rags until they shine like new. I want to get to London and have some
new suits built — the old ones will have to do in the meantime.

With love,
Cyrus

August 2, 1916

Dear Ma,

I had a fine session yesterday with the group sergeant major —
quite an important old personage. One of our telephonists had taken a
message to him . . . and when he arrived at the S.M.'s office he found the
old fellow standing in the doorway (office in this case is a dugout in a
trench). The following conversation ensued:

Tel.: Is this the sergeant major's office?

S.M.: Get out.

Tel.: (who, by the way, is a thorough gentleman in every respect and
has just been recommended for a commission; he is the manager of a
pottery in Ontario) Who do you think you are talking to?

S.M.: I am the regimental sergeant major and I tell you to get out.

Tel.: Well, civility costs nothing. I have this message for you.

S.M.: If you don't get out, I'll have my men throw you out.

So the telephonist came away and reported the matter to me.
President Wilson (this being the name I go by at present by reason of
some lengthy correspondence between me and the colonel) immediately
wrote another note setting forth the conversation above stated, and
received a note of regret from our colonel that anyone in his department
should be guilty of such abruptness.

The sergeant major paid me a call in the afternoon and started in by
saying that my note was too strong. He had been sergeant major for many
years and in twenty-three batteries and this was the worst complaint ever
made about him. So I asked him in what respect was the note too strong.
He replied that he had not said he would order his men to throw the

telephonist out, so I asked him what he *did* say and he replied, "I told him if he did not get out I would order my man (not men) to shift him."

As the old fellow was in a most contrite mood, I told him that his explanation put a different aspect on the case, the word "shift" not being nearly as puissant as the expression "throw out," and that I would speak to the colonel and tell him that everything was a misunderstanding, whereupon he drew himself up very straight and said, "I apologize for what I said."

He told me he had applied for a commission and that any charge against him might prejudice him in the eyes of the powers that be.

The Canadian mail is overdue but is expected any day.

> With love,
> Cyrus

August 4, 1916

Dear Ma,

The jealousies that abound in the army are one of the main features of military existence. As one of the major men in this group said to me a few days ago, "Inches, I came out here to fight Huns, but I find I am spending three-quarters of my time fighting my own people."

The situation: *I think the Allies are gradually getting the upper hand and the enemy soon will be more on the defensive. The Russians seem to be the bright spot on the horizon at present for they really are doing something at last.*[42]

Are you at Westfield?

> With love,
> Cy

---

42 An offensive by the Russian Army, commanded by General Alexei Brusilov and fought between June 4 and early August 1916, inflicted heavy losses on Austria-Hungary and forced the Germans to divert troops away from Verdun.

August 6, 1916

Dear Ma,

Had a letter from Mr. Harding, my Wiltshire farmer friend. He has had three soldiers from the cyclist corps for a month helping him with the hay crop. He thinks they knew little of farm work and says he was glad to see their backs when the hay was safely stowed away for the winter. He complains bitterly of the drought in England, which has affected his water supply. I think I told you he sunk about five hundred pounds trying to get a well that would give him a better supply but failed to strike oil. I must write him again and tease him about his expenditure, which is a very sore point with him.

At the request of the orderly officer of the group, we lent our best phonograph records and box of needles to them for their entertainment. They very carefully smashed our prize record and returned the others without the box of needles, which, as all Englishmen would say, "is a bit thick."

We bought a melon a few days ago and some really good peaches. I wanted to buy some ice cream, but the only places to obtain it, apparently, were the street vendors of the town I was in and it did not seem quite the thing to go about the streets lapping away at a cone. I have heard two Englishmen say that the best ices in the world are obtainable at Fullers — they don't seem to realize that such a thing exists in America.

> With much love,
> Cyrus

August 8, 1916

Dear Ma,

I had a letter from Frank [Magee] today. He is getting tired of Lockerley Hall, Romsey, Hants, and is going to try and fool the doctors to see if he can get back about the middle of the month. Personally, I don't think he will be out for about eight weeks yet, though he says he is going to work some sort of a scheme to get here.

I also received postcards from Hugh Mackay written in Boston where he took his wife to see the ball game. When I was a kid I always vowed that the first time I got near Boston my first action would be attendance at a National League game, but as a matter of fact I did not get there until just before commencement in my third year when waiting for the results of the final examinations. All of which shows a deplorable perverseness of spirit similar to my state of mind towards Scotland at the present time. I always include a visit to the land of my father in my leave itinerary, but it never seems to come off.

Lately we have been doing some shooting by balloon observation. The "balloonaties," as we call them, ran a telephone wire to our battery position and whenever they see anything they want to take a poke at they ring us up and tell us where it is and then they correct our shots for us. They are most enthusiastic fellows and have a great time over it. The weather is now very summer-like and enjoyable.

With love,
Cyrus

P.S. [Birthday] congratulations to Errol on August 10. C.F.I.

August 9, 1916

Dear Ma,

It is good to see your writing once again. Saint John must be getting very wide awake if the girls go round the streets without shoes or stockings on. The English advocate every day strict economy in dress, but I don't remember seeing pictures quite so extreme in change of fashion as you depict in your letter.

The nation has quite assigned itself to the postponement of the usual summer holidays so that the munitions output will not suffer. The munitions workers took so many days off around Christmas time that it was alleged in the papers that a shortage had been created.

I note that cousin Jimmy is actually going to war for three weeks. That is the impression that one gets from reading the social column.

We had a famous wrestling series yesterday in my dugout which we call the "Cloth Hall" by reason of the fact that the walls and ceiling are draped with that kind of canvas you put over apple barrels, clothes baskets, etc., on the Westfield moves. Garland tackled Leach and when both were in a fair state of exhaustion, Vassie took on Garland and I busied myself with Leach. It ended up by Vassie and me coming to grips in renewal of an old feud at Saint's Rest [Beach] many years ago, in referring to which Vassie always claims he put me on my back two times out of three. Result: the Cloth Hall had to be re-draped.

With love,
Cyrus

August 12, 1916

Dear Ma,

The general of the heavy artillery came round to see us a few days ago. A general always asks the same stereotyped questions: "How are you getting on?" and "Are you comfortable?" And then passes on, very pleased with himself for having made himself so affable. If he knew our battery a little better he would never ask that second question. A condition precedent to doing anything out here is to make yourself comfortable, and I know of no occasion upon which the battery has failed in this initiatory phase of the proceedings.

The adjutant came in yesterday to see if any two of us were inclined to spend the afternoon with him touring around in the colonel's car, so Slader and I stifled any desires we might have had for sitting around reading magazines and shooing away flies and accompanied him in his travels. We had tea in a patisserie shop and some crème glacé, composed chiefly of corn starch which seemed to subdue or absorb any frost there might be in its make-up, and returned in time for dinner.

With love,
Cyrus

August 18, 1916

Dear Ma,

Fred Taylor says he has his business so arranged for a while that he can stay in Saint Andrews keeping in touch with the office by telephone. We have quite a find in Slader — he is a sketcher and draws pictures of us like Francis Walker would do. You never know just what he is going to turn out. But they are all good. He made one of Vassie doing a shoot by aeroplane which I sent to Buff, one of Ryder paying the men their fortnightly allowance, and he has one of me tucked away somewhere but he won't let me see it. I am trying to get him to sketch the kitchen, dressing rooms, and dining room. I have just retired to the Cloth Hall for an afternoon with the latest song hits from the London revues.

With love,
Cyrus

Illustrated letter from home.

August 24, 1916

Dear Ma,

Things have been quiet with us lately and there is not much to tell. The men have started a carnival of gambling which I have taken steps to confine within reasonable limits. One game, Crown and Anchor by name, is very popular. One of our drivers, LaBrache, a chap who will make trouble to get into if there is none readily available, was having a grand run with his Crown and Anchor board. He heard a voice behind him, "Whose board is that?" to which he replied without looking up, "Put your money down, old chap, you're a lucky boy. Take a chance — the board is mine." A hand was thrust down over his shoulder, and the board disappeared, and on looking up he found himself confronted by the assistant provost marshal. It seems that some of the men, not from our unit, had been conducting similar pastimes outside the Y.M.C.A. tent while service was going on inside, and this resulted in a crusade by the military police to suppress the indulgence.

With love,
Cyrus

August 25, 1916

Dear Ma,

Internal dissentions still continue.

You were told in a former letter how I had sinned in the colonel's eyes by dubbing his orderly officer [O.O.] "Horatio Bottomley." Yet Horatio he became and was often referred to as such throughout the group. We had a pre-arranged task for all guns for 7 p.m. A few minutes before that hour Horatio rang up and told me to fire on two other targets. I told him I gathered from his instructions that the program for 7 p.m. became a washout, as it was an impossibility for an ordinary mortal like me to take on the two at one time. "Oh yes you can," was the rejoinder. The most one can say for him is that his confidence in our operating powers was most flattering.

But poor Horatio came to the end of his tether at last. His proximity to the front line — only three miles distant — was so trying on his nervous system that through some frame-up with the medical officer, he is now enjoying eight weeks' leave of absence at his home in Scotland. He departed with a load of souvenirs that will satisfy the most unbelieving of his participation in a great conflict and was conveyed to the hospital in the colonel's car by the medical officer, who took good care to see that his patient went through the usual formality of going to bed. That the colonel was *particeps crimmins*[43] in these proceedings was probably due to the fact that he had an overwhelming desire to part company with his O.O.

I forgot to mention Horatio's greatest crime. When he went away he took with him a parcel of eatables which his family had sent him for the mess — an offence only equalled, to my knowledge, by our lamented Cappy Hall, who, when he left us, helped himself liberally to some extras which we had on hand on the plea that it would cost him more in England than France — and even then forgot to pay for them.

Love,
Cyrus

August 26, 1916

Dear Ma,

I have just heard from King [Hazen]. He has been on leave in London, where he says he had a fine time. He does not care much for his present job — orderly officer of sorts to Colonel Black, I think it is. He declares he is planning a shift of some kind. Molly and the baby are flourishing and Frances [King's sister] is working hard in the tea room. I have not heard from Frank since the eighth of this month. He suddenly

---

43   Partner in crime.

has convalesced so much that he is beginning to get round and enjoy things. Consequently, there is little time to write.

I hear that the new railway is starting from the Westfield end at the picnic grounds. It looks to me as if there will be few plums for Inches and Hazen from that source unless we change our politics. I don't think the electorate will stand for much more of the present provincial government. I never saw a crowd who took fewer precautions to conceal their piracy than they have done. This expression of opinion must not be published in *The Telegraph*. You will not find *The Standard* too eager to receive it.

I note in "Canada" that John Sears of Saint John, N.B., is registered in London. I take it that he is our old friend "Jack." It is hinted in the paper that Len Tilley is to command a battalion — next after Percy Guthrie. Len's recruiting efforts will prove a valuable training for leading an attack on the enemy's trenches.

Who is going to get the vacant judgeship — Supreme Court? Mr. Teed[44] is the most eligible material but as he can earn in his practice three or four times the salary that a judge gets, it is not likely he will take it no matter how much he would like to retire in comfort. It is Baxter's one ambition, I believe, to become chief justice, so I daresay he has his hooks out. Has Harry McInerney put in any claim to it?

Have blueberries put in an appearance yet? You always remark on their advent. The orchards here are not so numerous as in some parts that I am familiar with. However, we can buy plums, peaches, and melons in good quantities . . . fresh tomatoes and many other vegetables. Lime juice is a ration issue here and we get lots of it. Berries I never see for sale anywhere. There are some blackberry bushes near my apartments which will receive attention in due season. The great Crown and Anchor gaming case has reached the stage of a formal charge having been put in by the military police against the offender.

> With love,
> Cyrus

---

44   Mariner George Teed, K.C., Cyrus Inches's great-grandfather-in-law.

Canadian Corps Light Railways near the front line, from the Program for "Canadian Corps Championships, France, Dominion Day 1918."

Chapter Seven

The Somme, September 1916

*In our Bécourt Wood position we used camouflage for the first
time. In our Mametz position we received our first supply of gas
shells. I don't think any of us had any conscientious objection to
firing all we could get of them. At High Wood we laid our first
decauville railway[45] for ammunition purposes. At Bécourt Wood,
in the dark and in a heavy rain, we were ordered to fire all the
rounds we could within ten minutes on a certain wood. One gun
crew alone fired thirty-eight rounds, and when our ammunition
report for all four guns went in I was well ticked off by the
colonel, who had reckoned on an expenditure of fifteen or
twenty rounds for the whole battery.*

*This reminds me of your famous competition behind
Vermelles Philosophe with a 4.7 battery who claimed their type
of weapon could fire faster than a 60-pounder, and the six rounds
you fired in one minute to prove them mistaken. And speaking
of competitions, do you remember the champion sprinter of an
English battery who was something of an athlete in civil life
and used to run about at Fleurbaix in track regalia. The man*

---

45   Prefabricated, five-metre sections of track quickly assembled along roads or
     over smooth terrain. Small locomotives pulled short train cars through areas of
     minimum clearance and small radius curves.

you picked to beat him was never headed. They took us on in a tug-of-war next day, but we are not saying anything about that. But all this is getting far away from the Somme.

After the initial advance on July 1st, we were the first battery of the brigade to go forward, taking up a position immediately south of Bécourt Wood where we remained nearly two weeks until the capture of Mametz Wood, when, again leading the brigade, we moved to a spot between Mametz Wood and Mametz Village. In this position we spent the summer, taking part in the many attacks on High Wood and Delville Wood. In the middle of September we moved to Montauban and about October 1st to Delville Wood, proceeding after two weeks to High Wood, our last position on the Somme.

It is noteworthy that, with the possible exception of the Delville Wood position, at no time did the enemy attempt a deliberate shoot on the battery for destructive purposes. His harassing fire, however, proved very disagreeable, particularly in the Mametz, Delville and High Wood positions, but our guardian angel was with us throughout and we came through with the lightest casualties of any battery there of which I have knowledge. How it was that the bivouacs which you had to erect for living quarters in all positions, escaped being hit is one of the mysteries that will remain unsolved. When we commence to speculate on what might have happened to us on the Somme, we become frightened and direct our thoughts into other channels.

In the middle of September the battery had the novel experience of being placed under the orders of the Cavalry Corps. For the big attack in the middle of September, the cavalry were brought up in readiness to break through. Four heavy batteries — two chosen from the XV [Corps] and two from the XIV Corps — were detailed to go forward with the cavalry and to take up positions west of the line Les Boeufs–Gueudecourt for the purpose of shelling distant detraining points until the infantry and field guns arrived. This battery had the honour of being one *of the two chosen from the XV Corps. As it turned out the cavalry could not get forward and the suicide ride, as you jocularly called it, did not come off but we will never forget the exhilaration of it all, and the picture made by the Deccan Horse bivouacked all around us.*

September 14, 1916

Dear Ma,

This is a real fall day — clear air and what not — just like Bald Mountain, and the country looks very fine. Tucker's commission papers came in today and he goes off to the reserve brigade at Shorncliffe for a further course. He is immensely bucked up over it. This makes the second of our men to get commissions within a month. It is, of course, quite a loss to the brains of the battery, but it hardly seems fair to stand in their way if they want to go.

I got a box of stuff — fudge from Mrs. Vassie a few days ago, sent from the Tea Room Frances has charge of in Folkestone. The old lady is very kind and attentive. Bill gets stacks of cake and candy, sweets and magazines. Too much cake and sweets altogether, as they are not compatible with active life. So Ken has the onus of supplying the mess with U.S. magazines and Mrs. V. comes across with the English variety.

I am having a hard time getting this letter written. I started it well before lunch and now I am well into the afternoon and still pegging away in the odd seconds that I am let alone. *Old Colonel Phips was indeed right when he called this "stationery warfare."* The mass of inquiries that have to be answered, intelligence summaries digested, and reports of all kinds sent in seem to accumulate in intensity.

Patterson is indefatigable in his efforts to secure recognition as an author. His mail is full of returned manuscripts from *Punch, Pearson's,* and other magazines. I believe they pay half a crown for good ones sent in. Patterson scans the daily papers and magazines for sentences which seem to convey ambiguous meanings and sends these to *Punch* but so far they have all been returned to him. He is accumulating a mass of material which will form the foundation of a war story some day. He listens to conversations of soldiers returned from the trenches and makes notes — also puts down any colloquialisms that he hears and so forth. We are looking forward to the privilege of reading the advance sheets before they become public property. If he puts down verbatim most of the Tommy language he hears, I doubt very much if any self-respecting publisher will handle his effort.

With love,
Cyrus

September 22, 1916

Dear Ma,

We are just having a confab to decide why it is that the Princess Pats[46] have pipers, but can arrive at no satisfactory decision. Some unkind people will have it that whenever anyone is seen blowing the pipes it is a sure sign that he is undergoing field punishment.

We have installed a small stove in the Cloth Hall, which makes things very comfortable in the evenings. It is a little gem — spoil from a farmhouse that once was but is no more — has a receptacle for coal about the size of a small soup tureen and an oven one foot square by eight inches high. The wood has to be cut into lengths half a foot long and, as we have no coal at present, has to be renewed every ten or fifteen minutes. But it gives great heat.

With love,
Cyrus

---

46 Princess Patricia's Canadian Light Infantry.

September 24, 1916

Dear Ma,

It was my misfortune to run foul of the new colonel even before he actually took over. I was in the Cloth Hall with Garland, Leach, and Slader when it was announced that there was a colonel outside and he was admitted. He introduced himself as colonel going to take over Group and then a few commonplaces [were] exchanged. He [then] inquired who was responsible for the garbage pile outside behind our cookhouse, which he said should be covered with earth at least once a day. I explained that our method of proceeding was once every two days. He closed the matter by replying that there was more than two days' accumulation there. When a colonel makes a ruling like that, the argument is at an end.

Liardet, who stays on with him for a week or two until things get running smoothly, tells me the old boy is a genial character on second acquaintance but after thirty-one years of garrison life is more inclined to spend his days in bathing, smoking, and telling tales of jungle hunts than in planning the downfall of the Hun. Please understand that judgment is still reserved — first appearances have proved so erroneous in some instances of late that we are all on guard with our feelers out. And it must be taken into consideration that Liardet has just been deposed. There is already one little piece of friction.

Much love,
Cyrus

September 24, 1916

Dear Ma,

I am writing to you in the C Pip, namely the central post or dugout behind the guns which is the battery office or place where we have our phone and maps. At the same time [I'm] watching the efforts of Slader to catch a mouse which is frisking around on the floor in a tame and friendly manner. The place is infested with field mice and rats. Rat shooting is a favourite pastime of the troops, who make the bullets fly around in a sniping fashion — a little bit too freely for a sense of comfort. In some of the older dugouts the rodents are most quarrelsome and noisy, a rather disquieting circumstance in the matter of sleep for the old general and colonel — men who prefer peace and, for that very reason, patronize the best dugouts and get quite grouchy when they find they are not to occupy them alone.

I have just been called on by Vassie to settle a dispute between two sergeants over the right of ownership to a log which both want as a steadier behind their gun. One says he marked it this morning, while the other, who now has it in his possession, says he found and marked it yesterday. If the thing was animate I would rule to saw it in two . . . a reference to the precedent set down by the great judge Solomon.

Well, here comes the quartermaster sergeant with the newspaper. I'll give him this so it will catch the morning's mail.

> With love,
> Cyrus

Our Success on the Somme

It is only right that you should know that when we left the Somme, he [the O.C. of the brigade] very kindly said you were the best 60-pounder battery he had ever seen, and as soon as he afterwards became a general and later still artillery adviser at British G.H.Q. [general headquarters], we should be guilty of something worse than criminal negligence if we did not allow that he knew what he was talking about.

A largely contributing factor to our success on the Somme was [our] ability to keep our guns in action. There were weak parts that were continually snapping; spring and buffer trouble were a matter of nearly daily occurrence; spare parts were not easily obtainable from Ordinance. Our staff sergeant fitter and quartermaster sergeant [Q.M.S.] here had their chance and they took it. The former was already known in all shops from Bully Grenay to Ypres as a workman of unusual skill. He understood the gun better than anyone I ever saw, not excepting the I.O.M.s themselves, who acknowledged their indebtedness to him on several occasions for ideas, both theoretical and practical. Many a time he has repaired a gun in the battery position which should have been sent in to the shop. But his services would have been without avail if it had not been for the ever-ready supply of spare parts and material from the Q.M.S. who never rested until he got what he went after. If a part was not in stock in a shop in the corps to which we belonged, it was no uncommon thing for him to travel thirty miles in an afternoon through several corps areas until he could persuade some susceptible staff-sergeant to come across with the article desired.

Time and space will not permit me to describe the part the battery took in the many attacks which followed one another in bewildering rapidity for six months. For a list of the engagements I refer you to any history that may be written of the part played by the XV Corps and their successors, the Anzac Corps, both of which were supported by our brigade. The following names, however, now famous in history may bring back to you scenes of desperate fighting in which we participated: Acid Drop Copse, Bottom Wood, Caterpillar Wood, Bernafay Wood, Trones Wood, Guillemont, Ginchy, Pozières, Martinpuich, Courcelette, Le Sars, Butte de Warlencourt, Le Barque, Ligny-Thilloy, Thilloy, Gueudecourt, Flers, Flatiron Copse, Bazentin le Grand, Bazentin le Petit.

October and November were the muddiest months in our history. The best tribute to the good care taken of their horses *by the drivers was the report of the A.D.V.S. [assistant director of veterinary services], who pronounced our horses in the best condition of any he had inspected. You had put down brick standings so that your horses were fairly comfortable compared with horses in adjacent lines which were standing in mud a foot or more deep.*

October 5, 1916

Dear Ma,

We are having great fun in our Pullman at present. It is a dugout, forty feet long, eight feet wide and six feet high — roof of logs laid closely together with corrugated iron on top of that to keep out the rain. At least, that is what it was put there for, though an ominous trickle, when the rain gets particularly heavy, serves as a reminder that in future in building similar architectural creations, it would be well to pay more attention to correct overlapping. Three beds on each side with a small table and stove at the end for mess room purposes completes the picture. At night when each one has his candle going, reading in bed, the resemblance to a Pullman car is quite striking. And now we have to get to work and build something in the nature of a drawing room to our Pullman, for I have just been notified by Group that the major is on the way back to assume command again of his unit. Vassie, as mess secretary, [is] now devising ways and means to provide a banquet for the return of the prodigal son.

I was talking with a medical officer yesterday who had been attending a Boche prisoner. To cheer him up he showed him a picture of the kaiser, but to his surprise the Hun turned his head away with the remark "No bon."

The French have an eye to the coin with a vengeance. The British took a village and immediately thereafter a Frenchman put in a claim for apples which the Hun had appropriated.

> With love,
> Cyrus

October 11, 1916

Dear Ma,

The doctor says the Tommies were taking in five Boche prisoners a few days ago. When they arrived at the corps cage they found they had but four, so they sent back a guard to look for the missing one. They found him with a battery who said they had abducted him as the escort passed their position. They had been out here for many months and had never taken a prisoner and wanted one very much. They made a trade, giving the Tommies one hundred sandbags in exchange for the lone Hun.

I had a day off yesterday. The adjutant, the evening before, telephoned that the colonel's limousine was at our disposal for the day so the adjutant and the new M.O. [medical officer] and myself motored away back to a fine town and first of all had lunch, the *pièce de résistance* being fish called sole with some kind of yellow sauce. The most striking feature to the scene was a French general with enough medals pinned on his breast to make one think he had been through the Napoleonic Wars. I suggest, as an alternative, that he robbed some piano concern of prizes won at the Paris Exposition.

After lunch we went to the cinema hall only to discover that its operations were confined to dimanche and jeudi, a severe disappointment as I had been looking forward to the show. The M.O. put in half an hour inspecting the architectural merits of a church while the adjutant and myself, who had spent enough time there on former visits to build a replica in the dark, went shopping. The adjutant borrowed enough money from me to purchase some species of wooden ring with a red glass of sorts in it, the very latest in jewellery now that gold is so scarce — cost forty-five francs — for his "good lady." The actual worth may have been one dollar, but things are very expensive now. The prices the Tommies seem willing to pay have enhanced the value of everything, though I think the colonials have been instrumental in putting them up to top-notch rate and are accused of creating prohibitive prices.

After the shopping came tea and then a ride back in the moonlight. A culmination to a very pleasant day, though the chauffeur ran into two passing vehicles, one Tommy, and nearly incapacitated several others.

With much love,
Cyrus

October 28, 1916

Dear Ma,

My pencil has not been very busy lately, so I will try and redeem myself.

On going through my pocket book this morning I came across the [railway] ticket which I enclose and which I picked up in what was once the Ypres railway depot some months ago. The railway, needless to say, is closed at present for traffic between the points named.

November 12, 1916

Dear Ma,

Yesterday morning the report came in that Hughes[47] had won — a good deal of satisfaction was felt over old "Dry as Dust"'s defeat. In the evening we were told the result was still in doubt and now the news this evening is that Wilson has been elected.

So Charles has been a witness in a murder trial. He is getting on in law. How did he stand the cross examination? I trust he read Bardell vs. Pickwick[48] through before he went on the stand to brush up a little on the practice and procedure.

With love,
Cyrus

47 Charles E. Hughes, Republican, lost the 1916 U.S. presidential election to "Dry as Dust" Woodrow Wilson, who won a second term.
48 A fictional case in Charles Dickens's *The Pickwick Papers*.

November 19, 1916

Dear Ken,

Bill [Vassie] has developed into a most excellent and thorough shooter and takes a lot of delight out of a good strafe upon the Hun. He is also a great authority on aeroplanes and can distinguish at a glance the difference between a monoplane and a Fokker biplane. As for me, I am sad to say, they all look as much alike as the different makes of automobiles. I remember, though, that I could always tell the *May Queen*[49] at a distance from the use of coal instead of hardwood.

I hear that your nieces have all fallen captive to your winning ways. I can't think of another single, solitary thing to say, so will now close.

Sincerely,
Cyrus

P.S. Is Eddie Casey going to be as great as Eddie Mahan?[50]

November 22, 1916

Dear Ma,

I had a big mail yesterday, including letters from Burt Gerow, some Mrs. McMurray who says I don't know her, and a long one from Mary.

Bert tells a very funny one on himself. He says that Judge Armstrong[51] is already known to the profession for — well, we'll say "fussiness." It seems Burt took his client before Armstrong for the purpose of making an application in chambers. The judge took exception to Burt keeping his overcoat on, so Burt took it off and laid it on a chair. But the judge insisted on him taking it into the law library. Burt went out and thought

---

49 Riverboat on the St. John and Kennebecasis rivers in New Brunswick.
50 Eddie Casey was a halfback for the 1916 Harvard football team; Eddie Mahan was a passer, kicker, and runner for the same team.
51 Judge John Robinson Armstrong of Saint John.

his client followed him, so without looking round he said, "Did you ever see such a goddam fool?" and then to his horror he found he was speaking to the judge. Burt's chances of getting the best of a toss-up decision are nil.

With love,
Cyrus

Ypres and the Somme — Stern Realities

On December 1st, the battery was sent to Corbie near Amiens for a month's rest, a guard being left on the guns, but after being there five days, orders came to go back, pull our guns out and entrain at Bazentin le Petit for Barlin, where we again came under our own corps.

You now had two fighting seasons to your credit, and the goal seemed as far off as ever. The first summer had been a joyride. Ypres and the Somme were stern realities. You were beginning to show the results of the strain; some who were mere boys when we came to France were looking old beyond their years. Our personnel were beginning to change perceptibly, and new faces appeared among us.

While you were at Corbie you attended the movies. *One of the films showed a 60-pounder in action and you were quite startled when* you recognized on the screen your old position at Le Bizet and could identify yourselves working on the guns. *While on this propaganda theme, I might mention that photographs of the battery, taken by the official photographer at Vivier Mill and later at Mametz, appeared in the* London Illustrated *papers, and I have been told that a film of the battery in action was shown at the Scala Theatre in London in its "Battle of the Somme" pictures.*

Chapter Eight

The Winter of 1916-17

While the guns were being overhauled in the shops, the gunners as well as the drivers worked hard getting the equipment in order. The battery on December 26th took up position for the winter at Bully Grenay in front of the Fme. de Sauvage.

December 23, 1916

Dear Ma,

It is a quarter past one in the morning. Since 10 p.m. I have been busy writing a lot of letters to friends who have sent cards and remembrances of sorts. I was thinking of getting some cards of thanks printed — an original idea, don't you think? On reflection I decided it would not be in good taste.

I told you about our church service last Sunday. The senior chaplain of one of our divisions got wind of the thing somehow and called this morning and insisted that, in future, the men, if they elect to attend service, must not be subjected to an extra hour later in the day. The result is that we are having a compulsory Church of England church parade tomorrow. The complications will follow. The Methodists and Baptists will probably put in their customary plea that it is against their religious principles to attend a Church of England service and so on. As a matter of fact, the service for all denominations of Protestant is one. The Catholics, of course, go to their own.

C.F.I.

December 25, 1916
Midnight

Dear Ma,

Twenty-four hours have elapsed since I last wrote to you and our Christmas celebration is a thing of the past. I spent the day mostly in the mess writing letters. The dinner was a good one — oysters, soup, salmon, turkey, oyster scallop, potato, carrots, plum pudding, anchovies, asparagus, pie, nuts, apples, raisins, oranges, celery, coffee, and wines for those that wanted them. The turkey was the best in that line that I have had since 179 Germain [Street] and was deliciously cooked.

Since dinner the gramophone has been going steadily while some of us have indulged in a game of cards of sorts — a very pleasant evening altogether. The table decorations my sisters sent were no small part of the dinner's success. The toasts were the King, Charlie Garland (now in Ottawa), and the ladies. The civilians in the next room celebrated lustily all evening long, and as I write there is but little abatement to their joviality.

A trumpet of sorts was an ample offset to our gramophone. While we were playing cards after dinner, the young lady of the house came through the house carrying a baby about the age of Dorothea and Janice. We loaded her up with apples, oranges, and candy and it was very amusing to see her trying to make an armful of the whole lot.

With love,
Cyrus

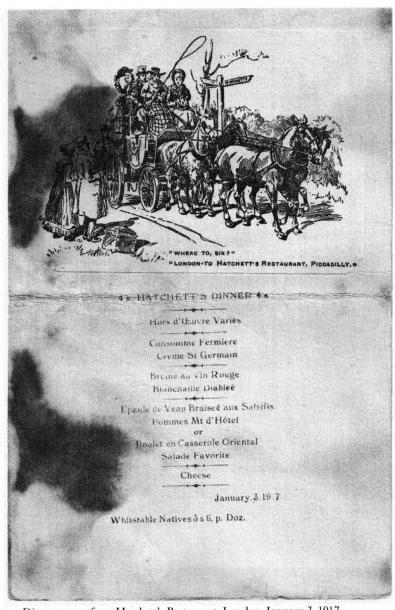

"WHERE TO, SIR?"
"LONDON-TO HATCHETT'S RESTAURANT, PICCADILLY."

4 ⚜ HATCHETT'S DINNER ⚜ 4

Hors d'Œuvre Variés

Consommé Fermière
Crème St Germain

Brème au Vin Rouge
Blanchaille Diablée

Épaule de Veau Braiseé aux Salsifis
Pommes Mt d'Hôtel
or
Poulet en Casserole Oriental
Salade Favorite

Cheese

January 3 19 7

Whitstable Natives 3 s 6. p. Doz.

Dinner menu from Hatchett's Restaurant, London, January 3, 1917.

*In January 1917 it was considered advisable to move some
batteries quickly to Belgium by way of precaution against a
rumour that was rife that the German was preparing to come
across the ice. Our right section moved south to Bouvigny
Wood into a position vacated by one of those batteries and
remained there for the balance of the winter — so once
again the battery was divided, making double work in many
respects.*

January 3, 1917
Same old quiet spot

My Dear Inches,

I looked for you on the boat on December 22 but drew a blank and
could hear nothing of Inches. We have seen the D.S.O. list and Pritchard
and Liardet and Fiske are very bucked and I believe the M.C. list is out
today but can't get hold of it. However I understand that your and Doc
Hardy's names are in it and I congratulate you most heartily, old chap,
on a very well deserved reward. It will look well when you are counting
those ten-cent bits after the collection on Sundays.

Let me know how you enjoy your new spot and is it healthy. Give my
salaams to the battery and best wishes for 1917.

Yours ever,
[Colonel] H.W. Iles

January 8, 1917
Thackeray Hotel
Great Russell Street
London

Dear Ma,

I got down to Marston yesterday, leaving Paddington at 9:20 in the morning. Mr. Harding met me at Devizes Station with his gig. The automobile is laid aside as a luxury. We got to the Manor House in ample time for dinner. Harding junior is now able to walk and is a most entertaining child. Curiously enough he cares little for toys and spends a large part of his time with a shovel — of the same pattern of our sitting room shovel — pushing cushions and other articles around the floor.

I spent all the time in the house, the weather being disagreeable. Dinner, tea, and supper seemed to follow almost on top of one another. Indeed [the first night] I ate so much that I spent a very restless night. In the morning, just as I was about to call on old Miss Chinook of the Mansion House, old Wright, the local veterinary seer, came in to see me to tell me that Miss Chinook had got wind that I was in the village and expected a call. So I immediately wended my way thither.

Her opening remarks were an assertion that she had just had twenty-eight teeth extracted. When I replied that my impression was that the average person had but twenty-four she rejoined, "Oh, Captain Inches, I think if you will look more closely into the matter, you will find it is thirty-two. And now, Captain Inches, will you have a glass of my cider — my own cider."

Though I had still a keen recollection of former poisonings, I had no course open except to comply with her request. The aftermath was so poignant internally that my figure for some time bore semblance to a jackknife. Before leaving I was reminded of my parting advice to her a year ago to forget her prejudice against Devon people and make friends with her next-door neighbour. She added with much pride that she has not even spoken to Mrs. Harding yet.

On getting to the hotel I found letters from the major, Leach, and Vassie, a note from Mrs. Vassie, and notes from Miss McInerney and Miss Canning. I had left an invitation for them for the theatre this evening but they both had other engagements. I went out and procured a seat for *Vanity Fair*, an amusing revue, taking off by way of parody scenes from a lot of other revues now running. I then went to the Cecil for dinner. The Cecil closes in the morning, having been taken over by the government.

I am going around again in the morning to see the Maclarens and to take to Margaret, who is a keen coin collector, some German coins picked up on the Somme. Harry and I were to go to dinner with Mrs. Vassie tomorrow night but she has postponed it until Thursday.

With love,
Cyrus

January 10, 1917
Thackeray Hotel
Great Russell Street
London
Confidential

Dear Ken,

Your cable received, I applied to the pay office for separation allowance for Ma. If a son is the sole support of his widowed mother, she gets separation allowance, same as a wife — thirty dollars for subaltern, forty dollars for captain. If the father is incapacitated as far as earning power is concerned, the mother is regarded as a widow. The difficulty lies in the sole support. However, each case is considered on its merits and it may be the thing will go through. I have written Mr. Hazen asking him to put in a word for me, so if you receive papers from the pay department at Ottawa, you will know what I have been up to.

Cy

January 20, 1917
Thackeray Hotel
Great Russell Street
London

Dear Ma,

This is the end of a very fine day, not from the standpoint of the weather, but socially speaking. Bumps and Frances motored up from Thursley this morning and arrived at the Thackeray about eleven o'clock. Frances had some shopping to attend to and Bumps and I assisted, down Oxford and Audley Street way. There to the Elysée for lunch — a very nice restaurant recommended by Will Vassie, who seems to know his London very well. After lunch we went to the Kingsway Theatre to see a play which Frances wanted to see called *A Kiss for Cinderella*, written by Barrie. Jackie Chipman was in the row in front of us. We asked him to tea at Rumplemeyer's in St. James's Street. He is looking very well — a trifle older. Then to Simpsons for dinner.

In the washroom I met Dr. Lunney from Saint John, who had to dinner a Saint John nurse named O'Shea, I think the name was. He has been in the Mediterranean for a year but is now stationed in a London hospital and likes the life immensely.

Then to the Gaiety Theatre to see *Theodore and Co*, conceded to be about the best thing in a musical line here at present. Bumps and wife go back by train at 2:05 tomorrow afternoon and I to Scotland in the evening. By taking a train at St. Pancras, I will be able to get a Pullman as far as Kilmarnock, which we reach about 7 in the morning. Troon is about an hour or two farther on. I wired Fraser to cut out Edinburgh, etc., and that we better spend the time at Dunmore, Tarbert, Loch Fyne, where his family seat is, as I am fed up on travelling about and sightseeing. I will go into Scotland sightseeing next summer when the weather is better. Financially, also, it is the better way, as I am fed up also on pouring out the coin. It is astonishing how it fades away. I would be afraid to tell you how much I have spent already.

I spent yesterday afternoon mostly selecting gramophone records at different stores for the mess. This is an act which requires some discriminate skill, as it is necessary to obtain, if possible, a record that will appeal to everyone. Then for a walk through the Strand, Kingsway, Aldwych, and Fleet Street to see if I could finally fix in my mind the exact lay of the land in that direction.

With love,
Cyrus

January 21, 1917
Thackeray Hotel
Great Russell Street
London

Dear Ken,

You will have read in the papers of an explosion in the suburbs two evenings ago. I was on the street at the time — *The Strand* — and saw the red glare in the sky followed by the sound of the explosion. Of course, the people were all taking cover from a supposed Zeppelin raid and many were the rumours rife all evening as to just what had happened. When I got back to the hotel about midnight, I asked the clerk if there was any authentic information and was handed a piece of paper on which were noted all the reports that they had received. There were thirteen in all and all incorrect. Of course, it was the talk of the city for hours.

Sincerely,
Cy

January 24, 1917
Marine Hotel
Troon
Ayrshire, Scotland

Dear Ma,

The weather has been very fine so far, though down to below freezing a little. We taxied over to Ayr — some six miles — this afternoon. Just outside of Troon I saw a curling match going on in a field beside the road and there were a few skaters on that part of the pond not taken up by the curlers.

We regretted very much that Fraser neglected to bring his Kodak. In the evening we called upon some people who live near the hotel, and while White — Fraser's friend — entertained the girls, to whom he seems very partial, Fraser and I took on the Ma and Pa at bridge and got beautifully done up. The wife is an inveterate gambler and wanted to keep on all night, but her husband, after playing three extra rubbers, each of which was to be the last, finally brought proceedings to a close at midnight, and here we are back in the mess for a short talk before going to bed.

With love,
Cyrus

January 28, 1917
Thackeray Hotel
Great Russell Street
London

Dear Ma,

Today, I went to dinner at Teddy's aunt's at Holland Place — very nice comfortable place and jolly people — then to call on Mrs. Vassie. Found her sick in bed with jaundice but the nurse brought word for me to go up to see her. She is very much better than she was a week ago. This evening I went with Teddy to a concert at the Palace Theatre given in aid of a canteen some English ladies are running in France for the Allied soldiers. A lot of well-known people, of whom I have read much, took part and it was a tremendous success. I go back to my unit in the morning. It has been a very satisfactory holiday — the four days in Scotland were an immense success.

With love,
Cyrus

The steady cold weather during February was about the only thing to take this period out of the usual. We had comfortable houses in Bully Grenay, a marked contrast to the life in bivouacs at Ypres and on the Somme. It has been a mystery to us why the Hun did not level Bully Grenay to the ground. It was in range of his guns and always full of troops and civilians. No other town that I know of so close to the line received such small damage. In February we had a shoot of real interest. The battery was asked to test the 60-pounder as a wire cutter. The stretch of wire picked out extended along the southern edge of the Bois-en-Hache to the foot of the Vimy Ridge. The O.P. was near the quarry, half way up the ridge. With the guns in Bully Grenay, the situation was such that the O.P. was about five hundred yards in front of the target. The ground was frozen, causing many of the shells to bounce and explode in the air. A further instructive feature was the opportunity afforded to test the longitudinal error of the gun.

February 5, 1917

Dear Ma,

The weather continues fine and cold. The infantry tell me the men prefer it to milder conditions with mud. The last newspaper we had was dated the second, so we are in complete ignorance as to what phase the submarine situation and its effect upon the U.S. is on at present. *Some say the U.S. has declared war, but we have no confirmation whatever of the rumour.*

My room is a very comfortable one. It is near the battery — large stove — plenty of fuel. Madame sends in coffee every morning.

With love,
Cyrus

February 6, 1917

Dear Ma,

Mr. Purves left us today. I am sorry his stay was not longer, as we were getting to like him very much. His seat in our mess has been taken by another Scot from the same battalion named Davidson,[52] also from the north of Scotland. Unlike Purves, he has been out here before, in the operations in 1914 when he was wounded. He seems a nice little fellow and has taken to the grub and the gramophone enthusiastically.

Fletcher, our mess sergeant, tells us that the U.S. declared war at 1:57 yesterday. Where he gets his information is always a conundrum to us. It's getting late and I'm for bed.

With love,
Cyrus

---

52 Nicknamed "Scotty."

February 7, 1917

Dear Ma,

An uneventful day . . . I have just written about five thousand notes acknowledging Christmas cards and my thinking tank is well nigh exhausted. I note that there is a provincial election on the twenty-fourth. I suppose the war news in *The Telegraph* and *Standard* for a few weeks will take the form of a short notice in an obscure corner of the paper, "The war is still going on," and the rest will all be politics.

Old Wilson[53] *seems to have been a little ambiguous in his attitude and the papers are beginning to wonder whether he is in earnest or not.*

With love,
Cyrus

February 8, 1917

Dear Ma,

I had a long walk today. It was pleasant going through the woods, for in many cases I took short cuts to avoid the dusty roads. There are about two or three inches of snow, but roads that are used to any extent are bare. The ground has been frozen since January 18, and the oldest inhabitants are in their element with their impressions as to whether such a state existed in former years, if at all. The strange part about it is the bright sunshine all day. Visibility, however, is not all that could be desired, on account of the haze which envelops everything beyond a short distance.

The Seaforth chap, Davidson, takes very kindly to the gramophone but finds it a very difficult instrument to play. He generally drops the reproducer with needle upon the records, and this evening he went so far as to put it on the wrong side of the records, making a howl from the machine that was most disconcerting.

With love,
Cyrus

---

53   U.S. president Woodrow Wilson.

February 10, 1917

Dear Ma,

It is two years ago today that we sailed from England. That was a voyage, as I remember it — five days between England and France on account of tempestuous seas and about ten berths to go around forty-five officers. And the curious thing about it was that I was not seasick as long as I remained on my back. Cappy Hall was certainly in his element. He had his sea legs and felt tremendously superior towards Leach and myself, who did not feel up to going below to look after the horses. The horse department of a transport is a lovely place if you are not a good sailor. Davidson is becoming more expert in his dealings with the gramophone. He can wind the spring now to perfection.

With love,
Cyrus

February 12, 1917

Dear Ma,

The papers of yesterday, which came this morning, announce that the *U.S. will probably "slide" into the war informally, provided of course that there is the overt act that President Wilson demands before doing anything more.* Davidson, our Scottish attaché, tells us the people of Glasgow decline to discuss the fact that Wilson's mother came from that city. This gives you some idea of the feeling in the Old Country in the matter of Wilson and his notes.

The seeming indifference of the natives [here] to what's going on is one of the features of the war. When I was in Folkestone, I went to a garage to get a taxi to take me to Muriel's house. The proprietor and wife had just moved down from London to take over the business. While waiting for the taxi to get ready I conversed with Madame, who told me they were near a Zeppelin disturbance in London and their main reason in getting away was fear of another raid. I couldn't help but contrast their attitude with that of the people here who have to be almost forcibly ejected if it is deemed best for them to seek a more salubrious clime.

I heard a couple of our telephonists the other evening recalling some old times in the battery. You may remember that I wrote you that on leaving billets in England to embark some of the men celebrated to such an extent that I, a self-constituted rearguard, deemed it advisable to hire a wagon and pile on the stragglers (one of the telephonists, by the way, mentioned that he was the bottom layer). When we got settled down over here in our first horse line, their cases were disposed of in due course and they were, among other pastimes, allotted two hours a day pack drill, meaning marching about with full kit.

The redoubtable Provost Sergeant Kirby, of course, was in charge of the squad. He was a very conscientious instructor and turned out with his own kit in full marching order and insisted on walking up and down with them for two hours. If he had bothered to make a close inspection he would have discovered that the offenders, whose haversacks and kit bags were apparently full to overflowing, were in reality stuffed with straw. Kirby is the most popular policeman I ever saw. How amused Professor Siegfried always was when he saw Kirby digging a hole to bury refuse and the prisoners standing around offering advice.

> With love,
> Cyrus

February 14, 1917

Dear Chacker,

Vassie and I are having some lively political arguments about the coming election in New Brunswick. We suppose that Walter Foster is running with premiership ambitions and I've got Bill pledged to write to him in case he does get in....

> Love,
> Cy

Pipes and Drums Band of the 236th Battalion (New Brunswick Kilties).

C.F.B. Gagetown Military Museum

February 15, 1917

Dear Ma,

The mail today brought me a letter from Judge Forbes written at Port of Spain, Trinidad, on January 4. It is a long letter telling me about the Kiltie Battalion,[54] the Patriotic Fund, political changes in England, the Saint Andrew's Church mortgage case, and church financial matters in general. [He wrote] a long description of Trinidad which herewith you will find enclosed. The working day there is apparently a sinecure.

I have done a lot of automobiling the last two days in the group car, looking the country over. I went for quite a long ride this morning with Macleod, stopping at the wagon lines for lunch and walking from there via Group back to the battery. The thaw has just set in but the roads being still icy in spots it is necessary to have caulks in the horses' shoes. It is cold but bright and pleasant. It is astonishing compared with the usual conditions in winter here. How the frosty spell keeps up. I saw ice on a pond today which was at least nine inches thick.

---

54 The 236th Overseas Battalion (New Brunswick Kilties — Sir Sam's Own) began recruiting in New Brunswick in mid-September 1916.

Yesterday I called at a factory to get a hot tub but was refused on the grounds that they only had "chaud" water, the cold-water tap not being in running order. As my French was not perfect enough to explain that, if they filled the tub entirely with hot water, I could wait until it was cool enough to take the venture. I had to depart, unwashed, after vainly endeavouring to make myself understood.

With love,
Cyrus

February 17, 1917

Dear Ma,

This evening our Scotchman picked out some Scotch records and Scottishisms which somehow had escaped his previous notice, and he leaped around the room doing the steps and yelling to his heart's content. It was extremely entertaining.

With love,
Cyrus

February 22, 1917

Dear Ma,

There was an old colonel man around a few days ago. We had been near him a year ago and he remembered seeing us — he was very communicative. "I'm a colonel," quoth he, "but I should be a brigadier-general."

It galls these fellows very much to see a man junior to them in the service put over their heads. The question of qualification for the position — speaking from the standpoint of ability to carry on — never seems to enter into their calculations. I think I mentioned some months ago that it had been published semi-officially that no officers over the rank of subaltern would be sent out here as reinforcements and expressed my doubt that the rule would be adhered to. Events lately in some places have confirmed my opinion and there is much indignation thereat.

With love,
Cyrus

February 24, 1917

Dear Ma,

Another prospective puller [gunner] has arrived on the scene — a Dr. Vipond of Montreal, a captain in the C.A.M.C. [Canadian Army Medical Corps] who is attached to one of our field brigades. I think I told you something about him. He came into tea last evening and then again this afternoon. His headquarters is not far from us, and when he hears the guns fire he makes a beeline for the position but so far has just missed his opportunity each time. He wants to pull the lanyard of every type of gun in the service. He is a capital "I" of the cousin Jimmy[55] style — even more so — runs a children's hospital in Montreal. His patients all love him. A mother brings in a crying infant, he takes it into his arms, the crying immediately ceases. Though he does not dance the Scottish dances, he has been the judge of dancing at all the Highland contests in the neighbourhood of Montreal for many decades. He is a boxer of some considerable skill. His muscles, which we all had to feel, are no small part of his anatomy. The senior officers that stand in awe of him are legion and no one can tell one off better than he can.

The Vipond Water Power Case is folklore in Montreal. If the Viponds were not men of indomitable persistency, they would not have fought corporation after corporation to the highest courts to finally establish their rights to a certain charter. He is a bachelor and the ladies fall over

---

55 Cyrus's cousin Jimmy Inches, a bumptious, loveable scoundrel, commissioner of the Detroit police force, an international big-game hunter, and confirmed bachelor.

The Canadian Corps on the Western Front, 1917-1918. Mike Bechthold

Canadian Battles

❶ Vimy Ridge – Apr 1917
❷ Hill 70 – Aug 1917
❸ Passchendaele – Oct-Nov 1917
❹ Amiens – Aug 1918
❺ Arras – Aug-Sept 1918
❻ Cambrai – Sept-Oct 1918
❼ Mons – Nov 10-11 1918

Front Lines
December 15, 1914
March 20, 1918
July 18, 1918
November 11, 1918

one another in the race to change his status. He has a photograph of one in particular that he let the other fellow take from him. A marvellous species of Munchausen altogether.

Well I suppose by this time the ballots have been counted. We do not know here even who the candidates are.

With love,
Cyrus

February 28, 1917

Dear Ma,

Just a few lines before the orderly comes to let you know that your letter of the tenth arrived yesterday, also one from Ken of the ninth. As you say, the mails are a bit irregular and when any does come it is in accumulations. I note by the paper that the Saint Andrews and the Thistles each won a match.

I also heard from Hughie McLean from Fredericton. He tells me no full battalions, as such, are to be sent over but that the draft system has been adopted, so I take it the Kilties will not take the field as a unit.[56] When a battalion is broken up into drafts in England, there is always more or less trouble over the properties of the battalion such as standards, mess equipment, and whatnot. One unit over there had a very fine silver mess service and did not know just what disposition to make of it, and you may rest assured that there are many burning disputes before a settlement is arrived at.

We have no news yet of the New Brunswick election and also no papers from home announcing that one was to be held. It may be in the English papers but as to them we have gone without for two days.

Scotty calls Dr. Vipond "Bombardier Vipond" because of his interest in artillery...and spent the evening with him last night listening to a series of "cousin-Jimmy-type" anecdotes. *How Jimmy and Vipond would hate one another!*

> With love,
> Cyrus

---

56 Major Hugh McLean was second-in-command of the 236th Battalion. The battalion was indeed broken up in March 1918 after proceeding to England.

Andrew Bonar Law. PANB P194-17

Walter Foster was leader of New Brunswick's Liberal party. Although the Liberals won the 1917 provincial election, Foster was defeated in Saint John County. Later in the year he was elected to the Assembly in a by-election in Victoria County and served as premier until 1923. PANB P37-334

Chapter Nine

Vimy Ridge, April 1917

On March 13th we moved south to a position we had prepared under the Thirteen Trees at Berthonval Farm, east of Mont St. Eloi. Soon commenced the long bombardment preliminary to the capture of Vimy Ridge. The 2nd Brigade C.G.A. [Canadian Garrison Artillery] headquarters came out from England. We became a battery of that brigade and ceased to be an independent unit.

March 9, 1917

Dear Ma,

Yesterday's papers which came in this evening have write-ups on Lord Beaverbrook in connection with his second instalment recording the life of the Canadians out here. I have heard it whispered that he does not write a word of it himself, but I suppose we have to take our hats off to him, more or less. He has a remarkable knack of getting along and his relations with Bonar Law[57] are a distinct asset in his favour. The last papers we had in re provincial election contain Walter Foster's acceptance of the onerous duty of leading the Opposition.

With love,

Cyrus

---

57 Andrew Bonar Law, who was born in Rexton, N.B., was chancellor of the exchequer in British prime minister David Lloyd George's cabinet.

March 13, 1917

Dear Ma,

Scotty said goodbye to us yesterday. He was very loath to go and we, on our part, were sorry to part with him, for his humour made a very lively mess. He said he had not laughed as much during his life as he had during the six weeks he was with us.

A copy of the English magazine *Canada* came in today and the mess notes with mingled feelings of joy and regret that *the [New Brunswick] government went down to defeat*. The new crowd will have a hard time forming a cabinet, but that is very small consolation to the defeated! It will be a very interesting Houseful.

I am glad to see that J. Ray Campbell won his first election, though he will have to appear in the role of oppositionist. We thought at first that when we got news that Walter Foster had been defeated that his party had been beaten also. It was rather tough on him, wasn't it, but it has a very salutary effect here in that it prevents Vassie from crowing too much over us.

> With love,
> Cyrus

March 14, 1917

Dear Ma,

The wall of our mess room sagged in today, the wet weather having loosened up the foundation a little, and while it is being repaired I have betaken to the kitchen to write this letter and have been followed by Vassie, Macleod, and Slader, also Hopper, who are standing around making inane remarks, which is not conducive to a coherent relation of events on my part.

The major has not yet returned to France, and our colonel told me today that he must be lost because they seem to have lost track of him. These things come very slowly.

Vassie received some pickles today from home. They are homemade pickles, and we are going to try them out with mutton at dinner in a few minutes. As I'm making a nuisance from the standpoint of the cook, whose movements are restricted by the presence of so much extra company, I'll clear out.

With love,
Cyrus

March 16, 1917

Dear Ma,

Met Bea Sturdee yesterday. He is now with some infantry battalions out at rest, acting as camp commandant with three camps under him, glad to be out of the trenches for a while. Sandy MacMillan and the battalion he is with will be near us soon, and I am looking forward to seeing them all again — also Harry with his D.A.C. No word from the major yesterday. Major Cook, my old friend of D.A.C. days, told Slader he had seen in the *Gazette* that Magee is a colonel, so I gather that the thing has really gone through. However, until we have official notice we have as a matter of form to still show him on the strength and report him absent on leave. The people here seem to have lost all trace of him.

Norman Macleod was talking to Colonel MacKenzie about the election. MacKenzie is a keen supporter of the losing side and if home would probably have been a candidate. He had a lot of particulars which he had acquired in odd places and which supplemented what little we have had to date. Vassie received the weekly edition of *Canada* today. It says that another seat will be found immediately for Walter Foster so that he can sit in the House as premier.

With love,
Cyrus

March 21, 1917

Dear Ma,

Among the newspapers before me I have a notification from the sergeant major that the unit is minus one horse, which strayed from the lines, and he has given me a minute description of its imperfections as well as its perfect qualities in order that an advertisement can be inserted in the weekly orders in due form of law. But word had just come in that the beastie has been found in a neighbour's lines, so that is one item that it will not be necessary to worry about — a good thing, too, because by the time the notice appears in the orders a horse has time to be found and lost again and change hands several times. We had a very successful dinner party last evening, Jack Fairweather and Ray Ring being the guests.

> With love,
> Cyrus

March 24, 1917

Dear Ma,

At last some mail from Canada has come in and with it your letter of the fifth, also some Easter cards. When is Easter? Has it come or is it something still in the future? The cards are extremely pretty. Thanks very much.

The ration wagon which generally brings the battery mail reports [that] it could not [bring] mail today because the postman who had just brought in a cartload said it would take two hours to sort it, so we will have to wait until the horse line orderly comes up in the morning on his regular trip. We opine here that some goodish bundles of mail received hard treatment when the *Laconia* and another steamer fell victims to the submarine campaign. I note that Mrs. Rankine has sent some socks and whether they came or not I'll send her a note telling her what comfortable goods she can produce.

They tell me that out of the twenty-eight government members in the House at Fredericton, eighteen are Roman Catholic, and out of these, fourteen are French and that the French are going to demand a French premier. While some say that W. Foster is going to run again in Madawaska, where there is such a swamping majority of French that he will get in without doubt. There will be interesting times (no sour grapes in this) when the R.C.s get a grip on things. Lionel Teed came to dinner last evening, staying late. His battery is a very short distance from ours. The lad has grown a lot since I saw him last.

With love,
Cyrus

On April 1st the new section arrived and from that time we have been a six-gun battery. I remember asking the officer who brought the new men out how they measured up. He replied, "You will find them all of the best," and as it turned out he was absolutely right in his prediction. For a while the older men regarded them much as a veteran cowboy looks upon a tenderfoot; very soon they were taken into the family circle on terms of equality. Certainly no reinforcements we ever had received such a rude introduction into the rigours of warfare. The weather was vile, the mud conditions appalling, the bombardment on, in its full intensity, and the battery position was getting its full share of the shelling in that vicinity. They acted, to a man, with the best traditions of the battery.

April 6, 1917

Dear Ma,

Your good letters of the thirteenth, fifteenth, sixteenth came this evening, also a *Saturday Evening Post*. Always welcome . . . *doubly so, now that the country from whence it comes has thrown down the gauntlet to the enemy of mankind. Tears!* Also an Easter box from the Misses Maclaren containing one of Stewarts' cakes and a box of Yorkshire toffee. Also a receipt from my tailors for payment for a suit I purchased while on leave. They sent me a bill with the clothes with the charming intimation that they would deduct 19/6 for cash. I had heard that "cash" to the English mind means payment within three months of delivery and acted on that assumption by sending a cheque which was accepted with the expression of many thanks. It was a swanky-looking suit at one time but I can't say that it has improved much in appearance during the last two months. Overalls would be better in this season of the year.

> With love,
> Cyrus

April 6, 1917

Dear Ma,

It's a real fine day — first one in the last decade. I have just come from Group, where the battery commanders are meeting their new colonel — Magee. I thought we were not to be in his group. I find I am in error. Ryder is to remain with him until the machine gets running smoothly. At the present time they are all living in one room, but if I know the colonel, he at least will soon have a mansion of his own. He showed me yesterday's purchases for his mess — crockery ware galore. But what he prizes most in his collection are two small toast racks which he had sent out here when he was in England. He gave me a cake that his mother sent me, one of those Rankine kind in an Estabrooks tin box.

It's a grand advertisement for Estabrooks and Red Rose tea. It is difficult to see what notoriety Rankine gets out of the arrangement.

With love,
Cyrus

April 8, 1917

Dear Ma,

Easter Sunday and the first spring day to date — and a very busy one with us, too — quite unlike the millinery and floral displays which always seemed part and parcel of the day in childhood times. I wandered around for a goodish bit all day, stopping in at 8 o'clock in the evening for dinner with the colonel. I congratulated him on the changed order of things. When I was there before he came out they had hardly anything to offer one except bully beef and biscuits, but of course all that is now different and the meal provided was civilized and good. He stole our wagon lines cook from me, much to Leach's annoyance, and Leach was obliged to share the sergeant's cook, but among a few reinforcements from England there was a cook of no mean ability whose services were promptly requisitioned to fill the vacancy. A large box of chocolates arrived today — an Easter gift from Mrs. Vassie.

Cyrus

After Zero Day [the attack on Vimy Ridge on April 9], we
moved forward a thousand yards over open fields. The ground
was so bad that in some cases sixteen horses were used to
move a gun, and the ammunition supply became a problem
of difficulty. A few days later we went further forward to a
position south of Cabaret Rouge, near Souchez. Hardly had
we conveyed our decauville railway from Berthonval Farm

and laid it from the Béthune–Arras road to this position
than we received orders to go south to the Twin Craters on
the way from Neuville St. Vaast to La Folie Farm. A brush
road which the engineers were constructing had reached the
craters, but to make a position for the guns you were obliged
to build a road for a distance of a hundred yards through the
shell holes, a work of formidable difficulty, but which you
accomplished with surprising celerity.

We were in action there less than a week when we were
called upon to go forward another six hundred yards to a
position at the end of the brush road, immediately behind La
Folie Farm, preparatory to an attack which was expected to
advance the line far enough to enable the artillery to move
down to the plain in front of the ridge. There were targets just
out of our range at the Twin Craters which could be reached
by going a little forward, and though the position selected was
practically on top of the ridge, from which our smoke by day
and flash by night could be seen for miles around, we felt we
could stick it for the four days intervening before the attack
came off.

Again, you were obliged to build a road, the material for
which you carried from La Folie Wood, and move guns and
ammunition forward. I can hear over again your remarks
when you looked back and saw an English 60-pounder
battery calmly moving into position upon which you had
spent so much toil and had just vacated. It was your own
fault, however, for if you had not earned for yourselves
the reputation of super-men, you would have had the easy
pickings.

The attack did not materialize and the battery was
withdrawn, but not before it had all four guns knocked out. It
was a most spectacular shelling. The initial salvoes caught
two wagons of ammunition in process of being unloaded. It is
to the great credit of those in charge of the horses that they got

them away with slight loss. The heavy shelling at intervals of eight hours with the ammunition constantly exploding made the greatest pyrotechnic display in the history of the battery.

April 12, 1917

Dear Ma,

It so happened that all the officers, wagon lines and battery, turned up today at the battery mess for lunch and ate up everything in sight. Luckily the mess sergeant, who was back at the canteens for supplies, got back just in time for tea, for the colonel and his signalling officer made his first visit to the battery since assuming his new command. We had nothing to satisfy his request for a cup of tea except the liquid itself, until the ration wagon appeared at the psychological moment and we were able to supplement it with some cake. Our officers now are Vassie, Macleod, Hopper, Patterson, Slader, Leach, Skelton, MacLachlan, and Ryder. The latter does general superintendent's duty at Group with the others sitting around watching him.

Lou Barker's brother was slightly wounded a few days ago [at Vimy], and when coming back stopped at a dressing station a short distance from Barker's battery. I suppose the papers are full of new pushes on the Western Front — old

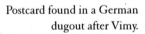

Postcard found in a German dugout after Vimy.

Hindenburg must be thinking seriously these days. No Canadian mail has come in for some days, so I take it there will be some along soon . . . *a good plan would be to turn the U.S. Navy into mail carriers.*

Cy

April 14, 1917

Dear Ma,

Just a few lines to enclose you some Hun postcards. I found these in one of their old dugouts [after Vimy].

With love,
Cyrus

April 15, 1917

Dear Ma,

It has taken me a full half-hour to write the above as I am having a bad attack of hooliganism. We have been living for six weeks in some fine huts erected by ourselves out of materials provided for the purpose. Slader and Vassie in one, Patterson and Hopper in the next, and Macleod and myself in the third. The huts are identical in structure, like brick buildings in a mining village. Each one has a stove and all are equally comfortable but for some reason everyone seems to have a partiality for the hut inhabited by Macleod and myself. It gets Macleod sometimes, and he fires them all out, calling them hooligans. Macleod is on duty at

"My house. Myself and Macleod. . . . "

the guns this afternoon, consequently hooliganism reigns supreme and my theme is disconnected and incoherent.

About fifty yards back of the guns we always build our Glory Hole. This is the name for the central post [C.P.] which is a room for the map board and instruments and for the telephone operators. We make it large enough to contain a bunk for the officer on duty so that he can be comfortable at night. But why called Glory Hole? I have an instinct that I told you all this before, but in case I didn't, the original Glory Hole was the name given to the cabin set apart for the bellboys on the good ship in which I sailed from Boston to Yarmouth and where I finally got accommodation for the small sum of three dollars. We had a position back of High Wood in the fall, and the central post was so small and it reminded me so much of the Glory Hole that all C.P.s in future became known as the Glory Hole. Our present GH is very cushy — one built under the superintendence of our man MacLachlan, who was on trial, so to speak, and made a good job of it.

Love,
Cy

April 16, 1917

Dear Ma,

This is the end of a partly perfect day. The perfection occurring between the hours of sunrise and 10 a.m., after which it clouded over and by five in the afternoon the rain returned again. The weather always seems to come contrariwise just as we seem to be getting the old Hun on the run.

I called at Group this morning and found the colonel with the quack (as he calls his M.O.) off for a joyride in the new car and Ryder away — consequently there was no one on the premises that could give much information about anything. Then I called on Major Stanley for lunch. He took me over to Prowse's battery, where I spent the afternoon.

Stanley is a haberdasher at Charlottetown in civvy life — Prowse Dry Goods [is] next to Stanley. Their headquarters are across the road from one another.

We have just had a caucus (more like a circus) in my room on the Irish question, with MacLachlan supporting Home Rule and the rest of us [supporting] all sorts of bizarre alternatives which have one feature in common — *isolation for six months from the rest of the world and let them scrap it out among themselves!*

With love,
Cyrus

April 19, 1917

Dear Ma,

The colonel gave a dinner party last evening. It was a very enjoyable affair. Mrs. Vassie writes Bill that King Hazen has a job with the War Office and that he and family have taken a place in London in which to live. She also said that Ronald McAvity was to have a position there and that Bumps's wife is at Folkestone again in the tea room. Mrs. Vassie, by the way, is staying in Folkestone at present. I had a note from Bumps today asking where I am. I must look him up as I find he is only about fifteen minutes' walk away. . . .

With love,
Cyrus

April 21, 1917

Dear Ma,

We had Bumps to dinner last evening. He is employed by the division as an intelligence officer. I walked over to his quarters with him after dinner and spent a while with him. He is not more than a mile away. A mile seems considerably shorter in this country than it did formerly. I reckon I walked some fifteen to twenty miles today, and it did not seem anything very stupendous.

There is an article in one of the London papers — *a summary of an interview by the reporter with Honourable J.D. Hazen,*[58] *who expressed himself as extremely pleased at the result of the Canadian effort at Vimy Ridge. The Hun got a bad smack there and now the news of the French advance is quite encouraging.*

Sir J.D. Hazen.

PANB P106-46

I had Marchant cut nine inches off my great coat. The bottom got so weighted with mud that it made travelling difficult. Now it looks like quite a stylish British warm. Major Stanley to tea this afternoon with us.

> With love,
> Cyrus

April 23, 1917

Dear Ma,

I have two other letters to write this evening, one to Barbara Cash, who wants to know why it is her husband has not had leave for seventeen months, and the other to May Kerrick, who inquires why it is that she has not heard from her man since March 3. So I suppose my diary will have to be sidetracked until tomorrow. I can't tell Madame Cash that the real reason for her husband not getting his leave is that he was a naughty boy and in consequence goes to the foot of the leave list, pursuant to an army order to that effect, but I can tell her that I have put his name at the top of the list now, and if leave is opened he will get away. As far as May Kerrick [is concerned], she will have to be satisfied with the answer that

---

58 M.P. for Saint John and minister of marine and fisheries and the naval service.

Jim is in his usual robust health and that it is not my fault if he does not love her enough to drop her a line once in a while.

> With love,
> Cyrus

April 26, 1917

Dear Ma,

Bea Sturdee came in while I was dressing a few mornings ago. He is the camp commandant of the area in which we have our wagon lines, a position of some importance. He lives by himself in a tent. He will not join any of the messes in the vicinity because he does not want to be on too friendly terms with anyone. The result of this diplomacy being that he can give everyone hell — in other words, strafe them to his heart's content. He took down the numbers of men and horses we have and also the number of tents, and in regard to the tents stated that if we moved from the area we would leave the tents behind us. I told him I understood him perfectly but omitted to add that these tents were issued to us by the corps artillery, that they were corps property, that we brought them into the area, and that when we leave we will all take our mansions with us. I do not remember having seen him since Valcartier, possibly Salisbury Plain. He is looking very well.

A not uncommon sight is the burning up of a captive balloon by an airman. They use, I believe, explosive bullets which set fire to the balloon. Generally, the occupants come down safely by parachute. The number of air fights that go on these days is astonishing. *Terra firma* for your humble servant. No Canuck mail for many days.

> With love,
> Cyrus

P.S. "Scotty" was wounded. C.F.I.

May 6, 1917

Dear Ma,

It is now one o'clock in the morning and bright moonlight. We had several days of warm weather, which brought out foliage along at a tremendous stride. [And] just as we were congratulating ourselves that the backbone of winter had snapped with a crack . . . the wind veered around a trifle, and fine and cool is the proper entry for any well-conducted diary. The woodlands abound in spring flowers. Are daffodils a wildflower in France? There are spots that are covered with them like dandelions. The spot I have in mind is a neglected farm, and it may be that the hand of man had something to do with the seeding. Then there are other varieties flourishing which you could probably give name to in English, French, and Latin, but which in that respect are unknown to me, though I have a sense of appreciation enough to recognize their beauty.

With love,
Cyrus

May 9, 1917

Dear Ma,

We are living in a room now in a locality infested by rats, large, medium, and small. Vassie, who has an intense dislike of the pests, is lying on his back in his bed looking out the door, where they are scampering up and down in battalion formation, and turning his flash lamp on them whenever they show any inclination to force an entry. I must say they don't bother me very much once I get to sleep. We have a cat which voluntarily attached herself to our mess, and I think we will make her do sentry duty. It is an animal that seems accustomed to Englishmen and answers to the call of "Pussy." My last view of Bill on blowing out my candles at one in the morning was seeing him still guarding the entrance to our apartment with his flash lamp. I asked him this morning if he stayed on the job all night, but he assures me he went to sleep shortly after I did.

Thank you very much for the parcel containing honey and other Easter gifts, all of which are much appreciated and very useful. The maple sugar is very fresh and nice.

With love,
Cyrus

May 12, 1917

Dear Ma,

This afternoon I went to the wagon lines on business. The particular business was to indulge in a hot water bath which has been established for the use of officers — the locus in quo being within a stone's throw of wagon lines aforesaid. It was an exhilarating experience and I have commended it to the use of all our officers. In fact I am seriously thinking of making it compulsory.

Do I snore? Whether I do or not, I see where I change my apartment tomorrow. Just at present the plan of the beds is as follows:

door	Vassie	Hopper X	MacLachlan X
	Inches	Slader	Paterson X

The heavy snorers are marked X — as Vassie, who is busy reading in the opposite bed, remarks, "There is rather a complicated barrage going on, isn't there?"

From the time when Patterson and Hopper joined up with us last June, I have ingeniously manoeuvred the matter of billets in such a way that your humble servant has been out of earshot of the sonorous rumblings above described. Regrettably, the exigencies of the campaign have thrown us all together for a few nights. As Vassie further remarks, "There is this comforting phase to it — no rat will dare shove his nose in the door way with this bombardment going on."

I have Frank in a furor these days. It is in the matter of a clipping from a Saint John paper with his photo and describing some invention which it is alleged he submitted to the War Office and suggested its acceptance. I think it further says England looks on him as the greatest artillery expert in Great Britain, etc., etc.

With love,
Cyrus

May 13, 1917

Dear Ma,

The *Gazette* today contains a notice that King Hazen has been taken on the staff and Ronald McAvity has gone to the Q.M.G. [quartermaster-general] staff H.Q. Cushy appointments, aren't they!?

Tell Ken that the *Courier* with the article on Walter Foster came today and that I am having no end of fun with Bill over it. In fact a political argument developed at dinner tonight and one thing led to another until Bill very heatedly tried to prove that the First Contingent was politically not a volunteer movement but that the government had simply carried out an order received from the Imperial Parliament to send one contingent. MacLachlan, who had been neutral during the debate, could not follow this proposition and came over to my side. MacLachlan asserts that Canada and Ireland are the only countries to which a man can go with a happy conscience after the war, in that their contributions to the cause are wholly voluntary without the taint of conscription. I replied that I could very happily proceed to Ireland after the war, but I would prefer to take with us the two thousand machine guns to combat Sinn

Fein.[59] As this promised to prolong the debate indefinitely, the discussion came to an abrupt end.

With love,
Cyrus

May 15, 1917

Dear Ma,

This morning I went to the wagon lines to examine some equipment which needed repairing, also to hold office. This latter is a disagreeable business altogether and is more befitting the functions of a magisterial court. This morning, for instance, there were three offenders — one charged with kicking a horse, another late for parade, and a third drunk in his billet. A peculiar thing is that the defence put in by a man who kicks a horse is that the horse kicked him first or stepped on his foot. It is one of the offences in this unit that we seldom let a man get away with.

I wrote a long letter to H.Q. today asking for seniority over all battery commanders who came out *subsequent* to June 1 last. It will cause a good laugh but we may as well get some fun out of it.

With love,
Cyrus

May 16, 1917

Dear Ma,

Just finished another big evening in the way of official correspondence.

My longest letter was to the deputy director of medical services, whoever he may be, telling him a few things....

---

59 The political wing of the Irish Republican Army.

We brought to France with us — attached from the C.A.M.C. — a man named Beezley, from up Oak Point Bay [New Brunswick] I think, whose special duties were to make water tests and chlorinate the water. For some unexplainable reason about three months ago we were sent another man in his place and ordered to send Beezley back to the Medical Corps. One look at the newcomer was enough to convince even a casual observer that the word "sanitary" did not befit his composition. I put him through an examination: (1) How much compound would you put in a water cart full of water? Answer: One scoop. (2) How much would you put in a gallon of water? Answer: I don't know. A lovely subject to rely upon for an uncontaminated water supply. So I have, after giving him a fair trial, put these facts up to the powers that be with the request that our sanitary detail be given a job that is more suited to his parts.

With love,
Cyrus

May 17, 1917

Dear Ma,
    We did a shoot yesterday with ground observation. An observing officer of another battery who discovered the target did the observing for us, we being connected with him by a phone wire through devious channels. Today I was told the observer was Errol Starr.
    The football and baseball fever is at its height at the wagon lines region. Our battery received a challenge from a team representing the third section of the 3rd D.A.C. I did not see the game and what I write is hearsay. The opposing team had many — some say forty-four — straight victories to its credit. They appeared on the field in uniform, white running breeches and whatnot. Our team, mostly wagon lines but reinforced by two of the best players from the guns, who were given a special dispensation to allow them to take part, won five goals to nil. They say that after the first goal the other sections of the same D.A.C.,

who have no particular love for the third section, made quite merry at the expense of their representatives. "Turn those trousers back into stores!" and similar remarks were made. Since the game our team has been flooded with challenges from many sources. We have a vast amount of good athletic material if a chance would only offer to develop it properly.

Bands are quite the thing these days. This evening a band played near our mess about dinner time, proceeding from one unit to another over a considerable area. I remember that last summer I received quite a surprise. I was nosing about in some territory about halfway between our battery and the front line. Hearing some music, I ascended a small crest and over on the other side was a band in full operation with infantry lying around on the grass, enjoying it immensely.

> With love,
> Cyrus

May 18, 1917

Dear Ma,

This is Loyalist Day, isn't it? I suppose there will be some kind of a commemorative demonstration — proceeds to patriotic purposes, etc., in the old burg.

This has been a quiet day for me — have hardly stirred out of my room, which means I have done a powerful amount of reading and writing. The documentary stuff one has to wade through is getting beyond the pale of simplicity. Some weeks ago, when we were to move at any day into another group some miles distant, about midnight I was called to the phone. The new group had managed to get phone connections with us somewhere and the message read, "How many pairs of gumboots have you? Reply at once." Now the information required was peculiarly within the knowledge of the wagon lines, who were six miles back and had no telephone communication with them. So without more ado I yelled back, "The answer is twenty!" . . . and that is all I have heard about it. I suppose I am charged up with twenty pairs, though as it transpires, if it came to a showdown, I don't think I could produce more than seven.

There must be a Canuck mail somewhere on the road — it is now some days since one came in. The last I heard of the river [St. John] was that huge cakes [of ice] were running past Gagetown. The "one-scoop" man I told you about has got to go, and the parties who unloaded him upon us have been ordered to send a "good man" in his place.

Love,
Cyrus

May 20, 1917

Dear Ma,

This being Sunday there is a church service on the side of a hill nearby. The band is playing the choir music while our guns are chiming in by way of accompaniment. The off-duty crews are not at the service, they are down at the wagon lines watching our football team playing the mobile veterinary section, and our baseball team is trying conclusions with a field battery. Later, I heard the baseball team lost. The football fellows won seven to nothing. One of our goals was made by Taylor, a well-known Montreal player, kicking the ball over his head with his back to the goalpost. MacLachlan, I find, is a National rugby man in Ireland, substituted in a game against [the] All Blacks.

With love,
Cyrus

May 22, 1917

Dear Ma,

MacLachlan has started a war on rats. One chewed up his newspaper, ate his soap, and knocked a cigarette case off a shelf onto his head the other night, and he thinks it is time to take offensive measures. He is certainly the living embodiment of the stories of a wild Irishman. He talks like one and says "Divil a bit" in a manner that would warm the heart of a writer of fiction, and when he gets mixed up in his speech he makes some typical Irish bulls that cause much merriment. He is a very fine capable fellow. I hope you will be able to go to Westfield soon and will pick up in the weather there, which is the best kind of a doctor.

With love,
Cyrus

May 24, 1917
...and a public holiday

Dear Ma,

I suppose another May 24 sees you in Saint John instead of Westfield spending the day, but you must surely try to get up there by July 1.

A Jock officer of a B.C. Scottish battalion who is living near our battery came in today to borrow something. He said he has been living alone for some time on a detached job, so I asked him to come to dinner this evening. Evidently his cooking has not been successful for he jumped at an offer I made to him to join our mess. His name is Clarke and he comes from Vancouver. During dinner he mentioned he was born in Saint John and is a cousin of Gershan Mayes and other west end people. We have duly established him as a member of our mess as long as he is here or until we trek away somewhere else.

The days are getting very long — dawn commences at 3 a.m. and it remains light until nearly ten in the evening.

With love,
Cyrus

May 30, 1917

Dear Ma,

This has been a gala day at the battery. The general in command of the Corps Heavy Artillery sent word that he would be at the battery at 4:30 to present a military medal to our Marsden, the battery cook, who performed a gallant act some weeks ago. Colonel Magee and Colonel Ray of Quebec . . . happened along at the time. The general made a speech explaining that he had not the medal with him but only the ribbon — he remembered he had forgotten to bring it. In his talk to the men the *general mentioned incidentally that he has received word this morning that Slader has been awarded a trench decoration, the Croix de Guerre.* Slader is in Paris so I have sent him a wire which may get through to him telling him of the honour conferred upon him in order that he can get the colours up in the French capital, where some attention may be paid to him.

With love,
Cyrus

Alpine Warfare on Hill 145

We moved north again to the Zouave Valley near Souchez, taking up three positions of two guns each on the side of the ridge back on Hill 145. The track up the hill being too steep and tortuous for horses, the drivers came up from the wagon lines to help the gunners manhandle the guns up the incline. Probably no other 60-pounder battery has been in a similar position on the Western Front. It was Alpine Warfare with a vengeance. *There we remained for most of the summer. At one time when it was thought the enemy were withdrawing from Lens, we rushed two guns forward to the brick stacks near Bois Hirondelle, but they were soon withdrawn. When we were called upon to make this move, it was suggested that we had more than our share of the moving among the 60-pounder batteries, but the general did not make a change in the orders, saying he wanted a battery for the job in which he had the utmost confidence. This will give you an idea of how you were regarded at headquarters at the time.*

July 31, 1917

Dear Ken,

You have been going through a great trial lately and must feel about all in. I wish I was there to help you share the burden. The only word I have had of Mother's death yet is Connie's cable to Harry which arrived on the July 28, the contents of which were immediately communicated to me. Friends here have been very kind and sympathetic. Harry came up and spent an afternoon with me.

I take it you were all able to be with Mother at the end. It is a great consolation that she did not suffer and that the end came peacefully. Life must seem all upside down with you at present. My own plans for the future were to settle down as before and try to be of some real service to the family but now they seem all out of adjustment. Harry is urging upon me to apply for three months' leave to Canada but I can't quite see my way clear to do so at the present time. The temptation is great though, as I would dearly love to see you all again. Would you kindly put the enclosed in your own bank account as a slight reimbursement for what you have been spending on my account towards running expenses and say no more about it.

Cyrus

Hill 70, August 1917

In preparation for the Hill 70 show, we prepared and occupied for a short time positions at Liévin, north of Cité de Rollencourt, and also in Cité des Cornailles, but both proving to be untenable, we finally settled down on the banks of the Souchez River immediately back of Cité de Caumont, laying a decauville railway from the main road to the river for our ammunition. Here one of our guns blew up with disastrous consequences to the gun crew. After the capture of Hill 70 we went to a position on the railway cutting north of the Cité de Rollencourt. Three of our guns had been condemned for wear and, owing to an alleged shortage of 60-pounder pieces, were not replaced. So we never had more than three guns in that position, and quite fortunately, too, for it was not a good six-gun position.

Hard work and much firing were the principal features of the Vimy and Hill 70 operations. Our firing was not of an interesting nature, being confined to counterbattery work without observation, and harassing fire. For the first two years we had done a great deal of shooting with aeroplane observation. Since the start of the Vimy operations all that work had been given to the howitzers. Of course we answered many N.F. calls from the air, and did some shoots with the balloons, but there was little real pleasure in it. In a way you had an enjoyable summer. Nearly all the men spent ten days at the Artillery Rest Camp at Divion and many got down to the Army Rest Camp at Boulogne. There was an excellent baseball diamond at the wagon lines, where the C.G.A. league games were played, in which our team were runners up.

August 15, 1917

Dear Ken,

I have been pretty busy lately with one thing and another and have not had much chance to write. It's now 2 a.m. of the sixteenth, and I am dashing off these few lines before going over to transfer a gun from one pit to a new one, and I expect to get no sleep tonight — the first all-night session I have had for a long time and I'm not used to it.

I understand Fred Taylor's engagement was quite an item in society. I heard it from Doug White before it was generally known here, but it did not remain a secret long after I had heard of it. I believe King Hazen is over here as a town major and Mack Mackay as an assistant R.T.O. [railway transport officer].

Yours, etc.,
Cyrus

September 6, 1917

Dear Chacker,

Slader was back today to see Major John McGowan. What job do you suppose he has at present? Nothing more or less than O.C. of a Hun prisoner cage — examines the prisoners and all that sort of thing.

Clancy wrote a letter to one of the New York papers claiming to be the man who carried the Stars and Stripes at Vimy. Since then he has been deluged with letters of congratulations from all kinds of Yankee patriotic associations, including the Daughters of the Revolution, and he also receives from them parcels galore. When asked by McGowan to explain how it was he carried the flag in question, he rolled up his sleeve and exhibited to John's curious gaze a marvellous bit of tattooing about his wrist in the form of the Stars and Stripes. I think he is the same chap who came to me once with a very knotty legal problem.

There are two men of his surname in the battery, but I think he is the one that for a long time could not make up his mind whether he would marry the girl in Canada or a French woman to whom he was paying some marked attention. Finally, as the best way out of the difficulty, [he] obtained my consent — a consent, by the way, which has never yet been withheld to marry — and did marry a girl in England with much formality, publication of bans, and whatnot.

I went to the beach with the M.O. and lolled around on the sand. In the afternoon he took me to the Canadian hospital, where we had a lot of fun with some nurses who were old friends of his. I'm going to try and get a Paris and Nice trip with the doc in the winter — no use in going to Petrograd also because from present appearances it looks as if the Boche is trying to transfer the capital of his empire from Berlin to the Russian metropolis....

With love,
Chacker

September 16, 1917

Dear Ken,

Times are as usual. Wherever there are any Canadians around there is a general unrest.

At present I am short-handed. It is the policy not to sacrifice pleasure for business, and if there is any leave going round we get our hooks into it if possible. MacLachlan's leave came through sooner than expected and he was whisked off to the northeast in the Group car this morning in a wild state of excitement. There is some house party going on at his country seat on the west coast of Ireland in County Clare, and he is looking forward to getting in some good tennis. That's a pleasant-sounding prospect, isn't it!?

The English papers publish daily the results of the National, American, and International Sports Leagues! And I note that there is to be an account of each game in the World Series — a thousand words, I

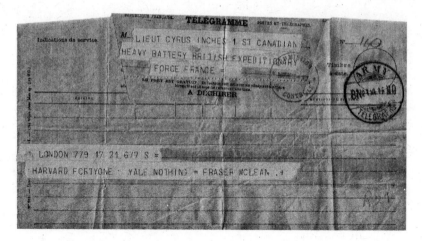

Telegram from Fraser Maclean.

think, have been arranged for. I take it that there will be no Harvard/Yale game this year. That will be a great disappointment to many followers of the sport over here. I am now counting on getting away in about a week's time for ten days in England. I will send a cable to let you know when I arrive there.

> Yours,
> Cyrus

September 30, 1917
The Royal Overseas Officers Club at the R.A.C.
Pall Mall, London SW1

Dear Ken,

Thanks for your cable in answer to mine announcing my arrival here. I have not met many Saint John people yet…. The moonlit nights are seemingly the times for air raids, which are not growing in popularity. I have seen some Americans about. *Great things are looked for from them in the spring. I trust they will move quicker than they did in getting into the fight.* Cudlip tells me Percy Wetmore now has the rank of lieutenant-colonel — surely that can't be true.

Sincerely,
Cyrus

October 5, 1917
E.F.C. — Officers' Rest House and Mess

Dear Ken,

I am waiting here until the train leaves for railhead. None of my friends had motor cars, so instead of two and a half hours elapsing between boat and battery, I am in for eighteen hours of boredom. I'm sorry I did not go up to Scotland instead of poking about London.

The air raids are of course the thing of absorbing interest in London. It is quite a problem. The better class of people are calm but the alien element has the wind up. Reprisals seem to be the only solution — after all, the damage done is really negligible. Statistics show there are more casualties from traffic accidents. The worst feature of it all is the moral effect.

Yours and etc.,
Cy

October 9, 1917

Dear Ken,

I don't think that suggestion that Kipper Wetmore will be given a battery has any element of truth. There would be a revolution in the C.G.A. if any game like that is put through. He will be lucky if he got a captaincy in the next six months. Magee, Major Wright, the M.O., and

Lieutenant Napier have just come back from Paris. They went down in Magee's car and spent three or four days there which they say were very jovial.

I had a letter from General McLean last night — he says he is going to support the party that is for conscription.

So cousin Jimmy is ordered into khaki. He is almost as much advertised as Ty Cobb, that other Detroit specialist. I hear that Chicago won the first two games in the World Series — the accounts of the games are being published in the *Continental Daily Mail.*

Yours and etc.,
Cyrus

Chapter Ten

Passchendaele, November 1917

The "third battle of Ypres"

On October 21, 1917, we left for the Ypres Salient for the Passchendaele operations, taking over the guns and position of an English battery. It is impossible to do justice to the description of this position. It was a swamp back of the Frezenberg Ridge, and about five hundred yards from the Potijze Road. The English battery had moved in while the ground was hard. Subsequent rains had made the place a veritable quagmire. The light railway ran two hundred yards in front of the guns, to which it was connected by a decauville [railway]. In this way we got our ammunition. The battery we took over from had three guns in position and three in their wagon lines. We immediately got orders to put these latter in action. To do so we obtained the services of a gun-carrying tank and loaded it with one gun which was duly delivered at the battery position. As the tank was crawling away for another load, it was hit by a shell and put hors de combat. *No other tank being available, we found a two-gun position to the right front of the battery beside the light railway, loaded the guns on trucks and ran them in.*

When our infantry had taken their second objective, we were ordered forward. The only guns available for this move were the ones beside the light railway. These were transported on trucks to a position east of Wieltje, an area allotted to the 2nd C.H.B. [Canadian Heavy Battery]. The O.C. of this battery kindly allowed us to come in beside him and also supplied us with a goodly share of his ammunition, which enabled us to take part in the operation next morning. No horses could get within a thousand yards of the location. Guns were placed all along the line which so ear-marked our positions, that about all the Hun had to do if he wished to get a gun was to range on the railway.

The next problem was to get our four remaining guns out of the swamp. To do this it was necessary to take them to pieces and to take each part by decauville to the light railway; an arduous job for the decauville would sink out of sight in the mud, upsetting the truck, and to add to these difficulties, the harassing fire in these parts was disconcerting in the extreme. Your morale at Passchendaele was wonderful. You were exposed to heavy fire every day and night, but did not seem to mind it, notwithstanding the casualties. The saving grace was the softness of the ground, which minimized the effect of the burst. In our last position we had the misfortune to blow up another gun; this time, however, the casualties were very slight.

At Passchendaele we were given a supply of the new shell, 8 c.r.h. [calibre radius head], which added several thousand more yards to our range. For the first time we had planes over in daylight, dropping bombs around the battery. In neither position could the ration wagon approach the battery; you had to carry the rations in from the road. So after all, though a harrowing experience from start to finish, the six weeks we spent there provided some novelties of more or less interest.

October 21, 1917

Dear Chacker,

The moonlit nights are beginning again, which means that the good London people will have visitors again from Hunland.

[On leave last week] I ran into a raid on landing in Folkestone and there was one every night for five nights in London. I went to one theatre and after the first act got fed up on the show and started across the street to another but found the door guarded — no one being allowed out during the raid. But while the doorkeeper was wrangling with a crowd at the door, I slipped out through another and was able to get some more enjoyment for the balance of the evening. Though on second reflection I must admit the show was rotten, and it was like getting out of the frying pan into the fire.

On arriving in Folkestone the first night, I took a taxi to go to Sandgate, where I thought Frances was staying. I stopped at a barber's for a haircut and told the taxi to wait. The raid started in the middle of the haircut. I'm glad it was a haircut and not a shave, as the cutter jumped a mile in the air every time a motor car rushed by. When I got out the streets were dark and deserted, the taxi with my bag and belongings being included in the desertion! I went back to the pavilion where I got the taxi in the first instance, on the off chance he had gone back there, and after much parley and a wait of fifteen minutes they unlocked the garage and gave me my property.

I have just been called to the phone to be told that three or four Zepps have been brought down in eastern France — quite a bag, isn't it?! Love to the Shenanigans and to yourself.

Chacker

October 27, 1917

Dear Chacker,

   I got a nice letter from you yesterday all about Westfield. This is a funny war, isn't it? Just when we think the Dagos have it all their own way, along come the Huns and Austrians and smash 'em all to pieces.[60] But against this is the cheering news that the French have come back amazingly strong.

   I committed an awful crime in London — I had my picture taken. They sent me four proofs and as I couldn't make up my mind which was the ugliest, I told them to print three of each and send the whole works to you (that's the latest slang Chack — whenever you want to say "everything" it is proper to express it as "the whole works").

                    With love,
                    Chacker

November 23, 1917

Dear Ken,

   One of our bombardiers was awarded the D.C.M. [Distinguished Conduct Medal] not long ago for carrying some wounded men, belonging to another battery who got into trouble, away from the shelled area. It was a pretty stout piece of work, though in recommending him I did not think he would get more than a Military Medal [M.M.]. I thought if he were recommended for the latter, he would not get anything, so made a bold stab for the D.C.M. *This system of honours beats anything in the way of a lottery or gambling transaction from start to finish.*

   Fraser Campbell came to France again on October 15 — [he] got fed up with staff college life. He was sent right to the trenches in command of a company in his old battalion and is now very near me if I am not

---

60 The Italian Army suffered a severe defeat at Caporetto beginning on October 24, 1917.

mistaken. *We have no definite reports from the push near Cambrai yet. Apparently, Cambrai still remains Boche.*[61]

Sincerely,

Cyrus

Letter from the sister of Ernest A. Snelling, a member of Cy's battery who was killed on November 6, 1917.

(continuation of the above letter)

My poor mother is distracted for he was her bright star. She thinks, had she been there, she could have done something for him, knowing that brandy, for instance, will start the working of the heart, if it is almost stopped. Would it have been possible? She only wants to come to France and die on his grave.

Why did God want our boy? Surely such as he are needed in this world

---

61 The Battle of Cambrai began on November 20, 1917.

in these terrible times. He was so full of the joy of living (even though some of his letters were a little despondent lately) was an ardent lover of nature, and amongst his papers sent home is a blotting book with pressed specimens of wild flowers and leaves he has collected from time to time and which I expect he was going to show us when home on leave and now he is sleeping his last long sleep.

I'm sure, if you knew him well, you must have loved him, even as we did and if hearts ever break, ours are breaking now. To you he was a man but to us he never grew up. He was always mother's boy and our darling baby brother, though he was more kind and thoughtful than an elder one. We should very much like to know where he is buried and can you let me know if he had a coffin? If not, could he be put into one even now, at our expense? Also, would it be possible for us to have him brought home? If you could let us know these details and tell me to whom to apply in respect of same, I shall be deeply indebted to you.

Trusting you will be able to understand this incoherent letter and will make all excuses, knowing the cause and with again our grateful thanks

I am Sincerely Yours,
(Miss) Eda Snelling

December 2, 1917

Dear Ken,

I am a deputy presiding officer for this unit in the elections. Voting is open from December 1 to 17, and we expect to make it an auspicious occasion. I am getting enough election materials and papers to run a daily newspaper for a long time. I think the big vote will be for the government, though one can never tell, as "local" politics at home seem to follow a good many over here. For instance, there is a rabid Tory from Carleton County who avers he would not vote for [Frank] Carvell under any circumstances, while I know of a neighbouring battery commander, a life-long Grit, who today cast his vote for Laurier on the ground that conscription will be a farce anyway.

We did not let Saint Andrew's Nicht go by unnoticed — a Haggis which arrived in the mess the day before served to uphold the old traditions. It was not very ripe and therefore quite palatable.

Someone has started a rumour that the battery will be out for a rest about Christmas time and I trust it turns out to be true, then the men will get the full benefit of Harold's eighteen quid when it comes wafting in. We certainly have had no real breathing spell since the middle of March, and it seems almost too good to be a fact.

Sincerely,
Cyrus

The Winter of 1917-18

No one showed any great regret when we received orders to march to Gouy Servins, preparatory to taking up positions again in the Vimy Ridge region where the Canadian Corps were to spend the winter. The march down, which took five days, was made in easy stages by way of Merris, Merville, and Béthune. At Merville the poll was opened for the Canadian elections. Voting was proceeded with for two days after we reached Gouy Servins.

Christmas time found us back in the line again, with the battery split up, three guns back of Petit Vimy, and three near Liévin Church, back of Bois de Riaumont. These remained our positions for nearly five months, during which time your powers of endurance were tested to the utmost.

Four miles in a direct line separated the half batteries, which in many respects had to be run as separate units, the Vimy section being under the 1st Brigade for tactical purposes. This necessitated the running of two sets of orderlies, signallers, clerks, to say nothing of two ration wagons and water carts. But we had come to take a situation like this as

a matter of course. Just reflect here on the number of times the
battery had been split up: the Fleurbaix–Loos positions, when
the sections were twenty-five miles apart, for three weeks; the
Le Bizet–Houplines positions, three miles, for five months;
Houplines–Ypres, twenty miles, for three days; Ypres–Bully
Grenay, forty miles, for ten days; Ypres–Vivier Mill, one
hundred miles, for five days; Bully Grenay–Bouvigny Wood,
four miles, for two months; and now Vimy–Liévin, four
miles, for five months.

I always watched with pleasurable interest the reunions
you had after these separations. There was so much to be told
on each side, and of course, each side tried to prove they had
been through the biggest fights.

December 13, 1917

Dear Chacker,

We are out for a rest, and as the battery and wagon lines are all together I am holding the long-deferred election. The vote is almost solid for the government. It takes an hour to poll twenty votes, and as we have over three hundred to record the process is a tedious one and the papers that have to be made out . . . take a lot of time.

While the column was resting for the afternoon in a small town, I hired a sitting room for ten francs (equals two dollars) and polled fifty-seven votes. Today we got through a hundred and one, and in the meantime we are pestered with inquiries as to why we have not voted long ago. They are keeping close tabs on us to see that all are polled before the seventeenth.

Macleod has just come in from the Canadian Corps Heavy Artillery H.Q. and tells me that the staff captain says I'm to go to England on the fifteenth to take a short senior officers' course. I'm trying to get it postponed until after Crissus, as I don't want to spend the rest period working in England, and I want to be in the mess on Christmas Day.

Thank you for the olives, cherries, peanuts, butter, and Oxo, which makes an excellent soup.

Love,
Cy

December 15, 1917
The Royal Overseas Officers' Club
R.A.C., Pall Mall, London SW1

Dear Ken,

I left the mess this morning at 9:30, jumped into a motor car, and reached London at 5:30 p.m., coming straight here. Just as I was going to dinner I met Sandy MacMillan, who was spending his last day of his leave. We had dinner together. The theatres were generally booked up, being the Christmas season and Saturday night, but by chance I was able to get an odd seat at the Palace, where Lily Elsie is the chief attraction. Tomorrow morning I leave Waterloo for Winchester, where I have been detailed to attend a battery commanders' course of two weeks, or a month — opinion is divided on the subject — and I have a sanction in my pocket for two weeks' leave after the course is over, provided I am not recalled.

Yours sincerely,
Cyrus

December 26, 1917

Dear Ken,

I have just got back to Winchester, where I found your cable on the letter rack. The election results are a little surprising. I was told by an

Major-General Hugh
Havelock McLean, M.P.

officer in London that General McLean[62] had been defeated but do not credit the report. If he is, I think the soldiers' votes may help him some.

I went down yesterday to Hindhead in Surrey and had dinner with Colonel and Mrs. Ritchie, Frances, Mrs. H. Clinch, and the babies. It was a very pleasant gathering. I got back to London at midnight and came down here this afternoon. I am the first one in but thought it better travelling in daylight than waiting later or getting up for the 5:10 train in the morning. The camp is four miles from Winchester Station. On Sunday we all go to Salisbury. We will be conveyed in lorries each day to the plain. Quite a long trip I believe.

Sincerely,
Cyrus

With our main wagon lines at Gouy Servins, and advanced lines at Bully Grenay and Neuville St. Vaast, anyone who wished to make a visit to all departments of the unit was obliged to travel at least twenty miles. The establishment of a 60-pounder battery does not provide adequately for such contingencies. Up to this time, however, by making strong representations to the base from whom we received our reinforcements, we were generally able to be from fifteen to twenty men over strength. But when the Heavy Artillery Reinforcements Camp was inaugurated the privileges of this nature came to an end, and from that time the battery has

---

62 Hugh Havelock McLean, M.P. for Royal, was elected to the Unionist government.

never had even its full complement of men actually available for duty. To show you the disadvantages under which you have been labouring, I ask you to compare our establishment with that of a 6-inch howitzer [battery]. When we are about up to strength we can run a gun crew of twelve men divided into two crews of six each, so that the men, except in cases of great emergency, are on active duty every alternate twenty-four hours. The 6-inch howitzer, on the other hand, has at least twenty men per gun, yet among those who know both types of armament who will say that a 6-inch howitzer is harder to manipulate than a 60-pounder? Then, of course, they had their motor transport, and no horses to look after. It wasn't fair, was it?

Vimy and Liévin were ticklish positions: both were unusually close to the front line for 60-pounders, within reach of all calibres of guns, and both received constant attention from the Hun. It is a matter of debate among you gunners to this day which possessed the fewer attractions. To add to your discomfort you were obliged to drill and fire with box respirators adjusted and also [to] wear them for hours at a time when "Gas Alert" was necessary. While thus engaged in combat with the foe in front, you were suddenly called upon to cope with conditions in the rear. A wave of "Spit and Polish" had hit the army with overwhelming force, and we were soon engulfed in it up to our necks.

We had always been proud of the serviceable condition of our horses, harness, and other equipment, but now we were asked to compete in a steel work burnishing competition with an R.G.A. brigade of 60-pounders which had been resting in reserve for many weeks in the vicinity of our wagon lines with nothing whatever to do except to keep their horses and equipment in condition. With a third of our personnel absent through illness, leave, or on command, leaving one man to three horses in the battery lines and one man to five horses *in the ammunition column, you entered the contest, jingled chains right merrily from dawn until dusk for many a long day, and soon showed that you were as formidable in peace as you were in war. I am sure you would all like to forget this phase of last year's campaign, but as it became so very largely a part of our daily routine, I feel my narrative would be incomplete indeed if I did not refer to it.*

January 16, 1918
The Royal Club for Officers Beyond the Seas
Royal Automobile Club
Pall Mall, London SW1

Dear Ken,

Yours of December 16 received. I am meeting a lot of old faces. Spent the last two evenings with Harry. The first evening we dined at the Savoy, and I attached to the party young Billy Beaver, one of our gunners who got a commission in the R.F.C. [Royal Flying Corps]. He was a little boy when we left Canada and was the baby or mascot of the battery until he left for England for his course a year ago. He has brought down five planes during the short time he has been in France, three of them in flames. He tells of his experiences in the most boyish unassuming manner and asserts he feels much safer in the air than on terra firma. Last evening we had Colonel Massie with us and went to see Lily Elsie. Harry says he and Connie saw her in *The Count of Luxembourg* when they were over and that she is as charming as ever.

Re fire in Halifax.[63] *How did our cousins make out? Are they all safe?* I am going to Edinburgh Friday morning by day train — berths at a premium, besides I want to see country.

> Sincerely,
> Cy

---

63 A reference to the Halifax Explosion on December 6, 1917.

January 20, 1918
School of Gunnery
Witley

Dear Ken,

How is Charlie? I was very sorry to hear he was laid up. He works too hard, that lad. Several cadets taking this course worked in Cy's battery or know him [Cy]. *They all swear by him and would do anything for him but they don't seem to display the same enthusiasm for Magee.*

Yours,
Peter

January 28, 1918
Royal Automobile Club
Pall Mall, London SW1

Dear Ken,

I leave at 7:35 a.m. from Victoria. I met Semi Mackay at 6 p.m., dined with him, and took him to the theatre for a final windup.

As I write the guns are booming away as there has been a raid on all evening more or less. Some bombs from the sound must have dropped pretty close. I hear a large Canadian mail came in today so I should get some letters at the battery when I arrive tomorrow evening.

Sincerely,
Cyrus

In February the gunners were relieved for two or three weeks by the gunners from one of the English batteries in reserve. [They] went to the wagon lines where they listened to lectures on esprit de corps and whatnot, by a lieutenant-colonel of the R.G.A., and did standing gun drill. For this you employed the full gun crew of ten men as laid down in the handbook.

As you had been carrying on for years in actual firing with not more than six men, frequently with four or five, and sometimes with only two or three, the practice of crouching around a gun ten strong, and going through the pretence of ramming home an imaginary shell, was a little awkward at first, and perhaps a trifle irksome; be it to your credit that you survived the ordeal. And then you went back to your guns again in light railway cars.

One of the scenes that is indelibly stamped upon my memory is the separation at Lens Junction near Ablain St. Lazare, when two cars turned south with the men for Vimy and the other two continued on their way north to Liévin. You kept calling to each other until out of earshot and then resorted to waving at each other until the cars for the south curved round into the Zouave Valley. We knew hard times were ahead of us, and as it turned out, some of you were indeed parted forever.

I have forgotten something. We planted potatoes. In fact the whole British Army was planting potatoes. Our athletic field at the wagon lines, the only space in the village, available for recreation purposes, was given up by you for this laudable purpose, and in addition we supplied our quota of men and horses to help people who had the enthusiasm, but lacked the wherewithal, to plant likewise.

February 2, 1918

Dear Ken,

Thanks very much for the boots, you are too generous altogether. I trust they will be the last I will require. *Taylor writes me that good authorities are counting on the war ending soon. I have heard a lot of such talk and am hoping, against my better judgment, that it will turn out that way.*

Cy

February 9, 1918

Dear Ken,

I just received your cablegram of the third. Has Charlie been sent over for service or is he in command of a draft like Atwood Bridges? If he is sent to Witley for duty, Jack Fairweather will be there to show him the ropes. I'll drop Jack a line to be on the lookout for him. If Charlie is only to be in England for a few days and is to go back to Canada, it is just possible I'll be allowed to run over to see him. I'll make a strong bid for it anyway.

Sincerely,
Cyrus

February 16, 1918

Dear Chacker,

We have been having some training lately; for that purpose we are under an English colonel for a couple of weeks. I feel very much like a friend of mine whom I met a year ago, who was taken to task by his colonel just after pulling his battery out of some awful mud and who remarked when told that his equipment was in a filthy, muddy state, "The horrors of peace are much worse than the horrors of war."

I got in bad with him from the very start for he alleges that on his initial visit to the battery a few days ago he met one of our men who kept a cigarette in his mouth, did not salute him, and did not get off the duckboard to let him past.

On the fourteenth I went with Frank to the dinner for the original officers of the 1st Canadian Division who landed in France, February 1915. Nine generals and Prince Arthur of Connaught made speeches and there were songs in between. One was a familiar singing voice at the end of the table and it turned out to be Fred McKean.

They have the most wonderful shows over here. Each division has its theatrical company and many smaller units have them also. Some people say they like them better than the shows in London. In the better companies the principal "girl" is so much like a real woman that it is difficult to see the difference, and if he has a good voice the illusion is almost perfect. Most of them are of the revue type with some sort of plot running through them. A great deal of the music is of a catchy style from the latest London successes. . . .

                        With love,
                        Cyrus

February 19, 1918

Dear Ken,

I've just finished writing about fifteen letters and so am a mental and physical wreck. *I have been holding a reception for Saint John people in the wagon lines.*

Went to a divisional theatre show last evening. The theatre, by the way, is about two hundred yards from our mess in the wagon lines and there met Steeves, who was on his way into the front line. Today a member of the theatre troop came in to borrow eleven blankets to supplement their bedding for the night. I consented formally, for I thought I saw a chance of never seeing our goods again, but as they had been very good to our men, I thought I could hardly do anything else. Just as he was leaving he asked me where Charlie was, so I asked him his name and told him to take anything he wanted.

This afternoon Ward Pittfield came in for tea. He looks a little older but otherwise military discipline has affected him but slightly. Harry is to make his lines near here in a few days, so we are looking forward to having some parties. Have had no word from Charlie yet.

                        Sincerely,
                        Cyrus

Chapter Eleven

The Second Wave of 1918

The second wave of the year took the form of a terrific enemy onslaught on the Fifth Army. At any moment he was expected to attack the ridge. We all felt [that] if he did come over quickly the guns, situated as they were, were doomed. Every battery on the plain — except ourselves, one of our siege batteries near us, and the odd field gun or two — was withdrawn behind the crest of the ridge. We took precautions in both positions. Our establishment in rifles was increased to six per gun. Lewis guns were given to us; *our gunners trained in their use; and emplacements built for them. Extensive schemes for barbed wire protection were drawn up. We built a series of reserve positions extending back as far as Villers au Bois. We made as perfect as possible our anti-gas measures.* But throughout it all we had a feeling of supreme confidence. Our infantry had declared they would never retreat and that was enough for us.

When the attack was made on the Third Army south of Arras, our Vimy guns came in for a tremendous gruelling. Never before had the soil of any position of ours been so ploughed up. Note here that this was the second and last time in our career that we were up against a genuine enemy offensive. The first one was the experience of the two guns in the Salient in June 1916.

It is a matter of great good fortune that we never took part in a retreat, otherwise some of us might recently have gone through the process of repatriation. Not one of us has been made a prisoner. *It is one of those things which is not done in the C.G.A. But we captured one, though we can't prove it. One of our men last fall found a Heinie wandering about some miles behind our frontline looking for someone to whom to give himself up. He escorted him to the nearest prisoners' cage, handed him over and then came to the battery to report his exploit. We sent him back immediately to the cage to procure a receipt that we might have something to place among our records to show for him, but without avail.*

March 20, 1918

Dear Chacker,

Bumps got back from leave two days ago — says the baby can talk all right now. He is at least eight miles from me, and I can sit at my tables in my cellar and talk to him over the phone, quite natural-like. Can't say much, for only business is allowed to be talked. You should see my telephone system. I have one in my room. The telephone exchange with the "telephone girls" is in the cellar next door and we have wires running to each gun, with one of the gun crew on the phone to each gun pit. We are connected up to brigade and the O.P. When we go to the O.P. we take a telephonist and a phone. By various exchanges we can get the wagon lines, where we have another phone. We are also able to get through to the balloon. The observer there has a phone up in his basket, and I can sit here and get his observations direct from him.

Then, of course, we have our wireless station, and he phones in anything that affects us just as he receives it. Write me some more Pat and Jan stuff.

> With love,
> Cyrus

April 15, 1918

Dear Ken,
   Rumour has it that there is a large Canadian mail in the back country. I sincerely hope that it does not come up the wrong railway route.
   Did I tell you I have two new officers, Underhill and Woodward of Vancouver? I have them in the other section with MacLachlan so that British Columbia ties can make them work together well. So the roll is now Vassie, MacLachlan, Hawkins, Sinclair, Underhill, Woodward, and self, with Hopper and Tovey attached. Hawkins, Sinclair, Underhill, and Woodward all being siege officers, they are at a loss to know why they were sent to heavies. Of the lot, five never saw a 60-pounder working before. It is like a new toy to them. They are used to a 6-inch howitzer, the trail of which can be easily traversed by one man, while it takes four, under good conditions, to swing ours around. Harry Pike of West Saint John holds the proud distinction of being the only gunner in the battery who has been able to lift the trail of our gun unassisted. I was not there when he did it, so I accept the statement without comment.
   The English girls are proving a great attraction to the Canadian force. During the last six months, I have signed numerous consents to marry. Unless a gunner gets his O.C.'s consent, he does not get separation allowance. I have never refused to give my consent yet, for which, *God forgive me, I always find myself allied with Cupid.*
   I am running three canteens (beer) now — one at each position and one in the wagon lines. I appointed Vassie "O.C. Canteens" and "auditor-in-chief of the accounts." The letters we exchange daily over the same are really very amusing. I enclose the last one I received. I'm damned if I know quite how to measure the quantity in the barrel unless I pour it out and I have always been told that it does not improve the quality of beer to expose it too much to the air.

                    Yours and etc.,
                    Cy

Portrait collage of officers in 3rd New Brunswick Regiment, Canadian Garrison Artillery, 1918. Among the photos are Cyrus Inches and "Bill" Vassie, as well as many other officers named in Cy's letters, including Harry Harrison, Frank Magee, King Hazen, Colin "Semi" Mackay, Jack Fairweather, and Charles Inches.

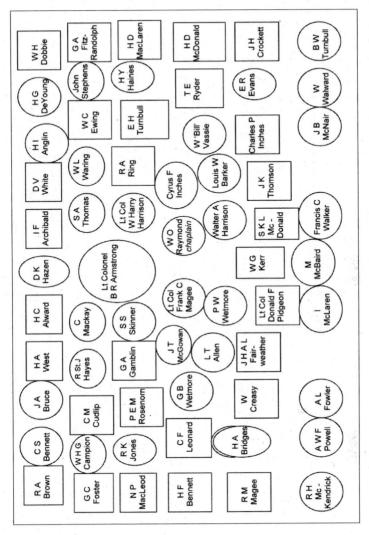

Photo Key.

May 2, 1918

Dear Ken,

Sunday last we had a church service in the battery at 9 a.m. which was well attended for us. It came at an hour when the crews had changed for the day, and as no one had turned up at the appointed time and place I broke a rule, which I have tried to hold to, rightly or wrongly, not to make those things compulsory. I made a tour of the dugouts and hauled all I could find of the men who had just come off twenty-four hours on the guns away from their shaving mugs into an old gun pit, which accounts for the large attendance aforesaid.

Ward Pittfield came in for tea and took me back to his battery for dinner. Their O.C. is Major Craig, Kelly's friend. You will remember them as the men who took the guns into the front trenches in the summer of 1915. Tuesday, a rotten, vile, rainy day.

Wednesday, did some real work in that I physically and mentally built an O.P. in the loft of a souvenir of a house which has a good commanding view of a bit of scenery which we have been ordered to violate.

Sincerely,
Cy

May 21, 1918

Dear Ken,

I am going to dinner tonight to the Tramway Company's mess, which is not far from here at a place called Whiz Bang Corner. George Adams is host. He called to see me last night but I was over at Cobbett's battery to dinner with Doug White. Beautiful weather here — too warm, if anything.

Cy

After holding the line for sixty days our corps, excepting the C.G.A., were sent back for a rest, and we were left behind with the 8th Corps, with whom we remained until the middle of May when we said good-bye to good old Vimy and Liévin forever joined up with our wagon lines, and then proceeded with them to the Bois de Hazois, near Divion, for a three weeks' rest — or as near to a rest as a unit with 230 horses to look after daily, can have. Fine weather was the order of the day. You took part in the brigade sports in the eliminations for the corps championships and loafed about to your hearts' content.

May 26, 1918

Dear Ken,

This is 9 p.m. and the advance guard of rooters have just drifted in from the ball game. It is the first game we have played in the Brigade League. (I kept shop at the guns with a mere handful of gunners and a telephonist or two.) The team with associates armed with megaphones, gas alarm rattles, and whatnot went down on George Adams's Tramway Special at 2:30 p.m. to Group headquarters where the diamond is laid out, some three miles away. A special lorry was detailed to pick up a "fatigue party," so called, from the southern position, and the wagon lines contingent rolled up on foot, on horseback, and in G.S. [general service] wagons.

My batman is the first one to return. His remarks are so incoherent through excitement that I am not quite clear as to just what happened but I have been able to get from him a general idea of the way in which we won the match. My batman sized up the proceedings in a way which I hardly think does our team justice, for given a little opportunity to practice we will round out into a really good nine. Said he, "I'd rather have a bum team with good rooters, than a good team with bum rooters."

He was a rooter.

To make a long story short, our opponents played a formidable game, so much so that when we went to bat in the last half of the ninth inning the score stood thirteen to seven in their favour. A judicious use of megaphones and rattles soon reduced this lead by five runs, making it thirteen to twelve with men on second and third and two out. Gunner Earl, who was the next batter on the list, was wending his way towards the plate. His work throughout the afternoon had not stamped him as a "contact patrol" of skill sufficient to write home about and his approach was not hailed by the men behind the rattles with any great degree of enthusiasm. Seemingly, our baseball captain, Corporal C.P. Ingraham of Saint John, held the same views, for suddenly and with a quickness of decision which quite vindicated the trust we had in him, he turned to Gunner Earl Douglas, our crack second baseman and said, "Earl, you bat."

Earl did not show much alacrity in carrying out the order. In fact he waited until he had two strikes to his credit, then he obeyed . . . and from all accounts the ball must be still going — the two runs were all that were needed. The two teams are coming back to their batteries on the first ammunition train up this way and I trust there will be no improper use of the explosives and that the protest will be decided by disinterested parties. It will be another bogus "Earl" case all over again.

Sincerely yours,
Cy

The Liévin men for two nights immediately preceding the departure from Liévin had gone through a deluge of mustard gas. The whole area had become so affected that for forty-eight hours you had lived in a reeking pestilence. Every man was more or less afflicted with blindness and loss of voice. The holiday came in the nick of time. The worst cases went to hospital; the lighter cases recuperated in the wood. This was the first real rest the battery had ever had. *I remember calling the corps headquarters during the previous winter. An officer there, who that day had been compiling statistics, drew my attention to the fact that we had been steadier in the line without rest than any other Canadian unit. It rather bucked me up because it showed that these things were really noticed by our higher command, whether the remedy was forthcoming or not.*

June 6, 1918

Dear Ken,

These are great tournament days — something on all day long. Yesterday our officers played 2nd Siege at indoor baseball. I stayed in camp guarding the fort and so anything I can tell you about it would be hearsay. The final score was twenty-one to twenty in our favour, fifteen of our runs being made in the second inning. Vassie distinguished himself in the outfield by catching the same fly three times before he finally made secure of the ball.

I was playing a game in the brigade bridge tournament in my tent when the first reports of the ball game were brought in. Caldow was given the credit for winning it by contributing a three bagger, clearing the bases, when he was sent in as a pinch hitter in the last of the ninth. Others also claimed the honour, and there was a lively argument in progress when in strolled old Hop [Hopper] with the announcement, "Major, I won the game."

His voice is negligible at present, owing to a slight whiff of gas. He had acted as chief coach. He thought his efforts to make himself heard so disconcerted the opposing pitcher that our batters could hit him at will. Our baseball team is practically *hors de combat* as far as further effective work in the league series is concerned — our catcher, both pitchers, second baseman, and two others of the best are *all evacuated*, "gas," and we are doing our best to build up a new team. The weather continues delightful and we are having a wonderful holiday.

> Sincerely,
> Cy

June 8, 1918

Dear Ken,

Vassie, MacLachlan, and Hopper are going for a ride to Rouen tomorrow to bring back the paymaster — Fraser took him down. They say it is the best place in France outside of Paris. Don Skinner lives there. He and Fraser used to room together at McGill. He was able to give them a real time — lots of W.A.A.C.s [Women's Auxiliary Army Corps], American nurses, and so forth predominate there. They say an order was published there forbidding officers and coloured troops walking or

Battery officers (from left to right): Budge (Veterinary officer, R.C.H.A.), Inches, Roseburgh, Underhill, Beecroft (5th C.S.B.), MacLachlan, Jones, Hawkins, unidentified ladies.

talking with W.A.A.C.s. Three officers were court-martialled for speaking to them in the streets.

We lost the league game yesterday. All our good players are in hospital and we were in bad straits. The great bridge tournament is in full swing — lots of interest in it.

Training begins on Monday 8 a.m. to noon each day — musketry, machine gun, and etc. — so it looks as if we would have to do a little work after all. I believe the theory is that, notwithstanding how stale or played out [the] men may be, they lose their efficiency if allowed more than four days' complete rest. Don't believe in it myself, but I am supposed to have quaint ideas of my own as to military discipline and life — so much so that I would not be a bit surprised any day if I was transferred to another sphere of activity. All we can guarantee is a fighting unit but that is only a small fraction of what is required.

Sincerely,
Cy

June 15, 1918

Dear Ken,

Just been having a rubber of bridge and a game of ring toss before starting in the Group car for the scene of conflict: 1st Brigade Officers Indoor Ball Team versus the 2nd or 3rd. We have to go about fifteen miles. They have me down for third base but I don't star in any position west of second base and, as in indoor ball, a good deal of the play is a bunt down the third base line. I see where I'm for it, alright.

We have a good chance to win with the 135-lb wrestling in the corps show. Our entry is a French Canuck who has some brutal holds — "half nelsons," I think they are called. They seem to have the effect of making his opponents yell for mercy.

I was invited to a dance by the colonel a few evenings ago but sent MacLachlan in my place to look things over. Now everyone is keen to entertain the nurses here at tea, but I don't suppose the affair will be pulled off. One of our divisional artilleries is having a gymkhana [series of athletic activities] on our sports field on Tuesday — we will probably see a lot of old friends. They put up marquees for entertainment purposes, jumps for horses, and all of the knick-knacks. Caldow and Woodward rode to an up-to-date military centre last night — saw badminton, tennis, and whatnot and took in the show *Way Down East. Regular Coney Island country about here now.*

C.F.I.

June 19, 1918

Dear Ken,

. . . trying to make a clean-up of my table before lunch as I want the last afternoon in camp for frivolity. The order cutting our holiday short came unexpectedly as we were looking forward to six weeks of it. This battery needs three months, but the needs of individual units do not receive much consideration. It is all a matter of luck. For instance, the battery that relieved us had only had one month in the line this year and that was an easy one.

Sincerely,
Cyrus

The Third Wave of 1918

The Spanish Influenza — On our way back to the line we stopped for two days at Petit Servins; and here it was that the last of the three waves into which I divide the first six months of the year nearly put us out of business. Almost every man went down suddenly with the Spanish influenza. I was unsuccessful in my attempt to have the battery quarantined, and we were ordered into position. We had to move the

column in relays. The available drivers took some of the
horses to our new wagon lines at Madagascar Corner and
then came back by lorry for the remainder. We went into
position at the Nine Elms, back of Thélus. We were still with
the 8th Corps. In a few days we were ordered to move three
guns forward a thousand yards to enable us to reach some
distant targets that we could not get from the Nine Elms. The
move [was] to take place at night, and after the firing was
over the guns [were] to be brought back to the main position.
It was pointed out on our behalf that a battery further north
could reach our targets and that we could reach theirs, and
a swap of targets was suggested, but this game did not go
through, and we went forward. I consider this one of the
finest things you ever did. *You made the move with a mere*
handful of men, some of these even groggy with influenza.
One man per gun was left behind to work the three guns in
the main battery position in case of emergency!

June 25, 1918

Dear Ken,

Our medical officer [Doc Campbell], who has been such a good
friend to me, has been recalled to Canada. His successor, Captain Stovey,
is a friend of Dr. Skinner, who is now working in a base hospital in
Boulogne. I expect to get a ride down to Boulogne when Doc Campbell
leaves and will try to see him. Stovey tells me that Skinner had quite a
thick time of it — went through the Retreat[64] — pretty rough sledding
for an old fellow.

I think the three-day fever is going to pass me by. MacLachlan,
Woodward, Underhill, Hawkins, and Rosburgh have had it but old salts
like Vassie, Hopper, Caldow, and self only get drowsy for a day or two.
The doctor sent a preventative gargle — half a teaspoon to be used in

---

64 A reference to the Allied retreat carried out in the face of the German offensives.

water. Caldow took a mouthful out of the bottle and his teeth went black for a time. The doctor makes a good story out of it.

Paris leave is open. Ten days does not count on the English leave roster. Old Hop went crazy when he heard of it and wanted to go right off. I said we would draw for it, so we put the names in a hat. Hop drew them out, Caldow recorded. I drew first, Caldow second. Hop's face got longer and longer. There was one slip left in the hat and it was for him. Caldow took pity on him and changed places. Underhill goes in my place as I don't want to go at present.

Sincerely,
Cyrus

June 29, 1918

Dear Ken,

Woodward and Underhill, "Woody and Undy," have left for Paris this morning. Woody was dressed up in Hop's spurs, Hawkins's boots, his own pants, Caldow's coat, and wanted Hop's hat but Hop told him it would slip on too easily, it was so greasy, so he didn't get it.

I want to go to Paris, in fact in our drawing for place, [I] was first on the list, but it is absolutely impossible for me to get away for some weeks. Vassie is in a similar boat. There is tremendous indignation in the C.G.A.

The battery Semi came out with and two or three others which came out recently were given the second rest period. We have had none. I note that the Spaghettis have chased the Austrians over the Piave.[65] This is not bad news.

Sincerely,
Cyrus

---

65   In mid-June 1918, the Italian army launched major offensives at Asiago and across the Piave River, pushing back the Austro-Hungarian army.

July 2, 1918

Dear Mary,

I got down to the Canadian Corps sports yesterday — it was a wonderful scene. On arriving there the first thing that caught my eye was Bumps in the centre of the field playing in the tennis doubles. . . . Harry was there but I somehow missed him.

There were only about twenty thousand there and it was impossible to find every one in the different grandstands and pavilions. The Duke of Connaught and Borden[66] were there and it was a tremendous and unique event altogether. The big event of the day was the ball game in the evening, which went twelve innings. After the game we went thirty miles nearer the sea and had dinner.

Jack Fairweather is to go to a siege battery as captain. He tells me Charlie is grinding away hard and turning out very high marks. Reay [McKay] told me the latest joke on the Yankees. *Two of them were walking in a trench when they came to a dugout. One said to the other, "I reckon there is whiskey and a Victrola down there." His friend replied, "I'll wager you're right; the deeper the dugout the higher the rank."*

Main arena, Canadian Corps Championships, Dominion Day 1918.

---

66   Sir Robert Borden, prime minister of Canada.

The clowns afforded a lot of amusement. One went up to the moving picture machine and pretending it was a telephone, asked for long distance, expressing a desire to speak to the 7th Division. Atwood Bridges came in third in the hundred-yard dash — a very creditable performance. Bumps and old Johnny Foulkes, the former Canadian champion, started in to play the [tennis] singles finals but stopped after each had won a set. The court was poor, the bands were playing, all kinds of events were going on around them, and an aeroplane overhead was executing some thrilling manoeuvres, so they decided to play off under circumstances more conducive to real tennis.

With love,
Cyrus

July 7, 1918

Dear Ken,

   This life is like living in the suburbs and going to business to the city, my duties at Brigade being simply to sleep there at night in the absence of the colonel, who lives near the divisional commander. It is a good three miles to the battery. There is generally motor transport available.

   Oh yes, there is some news after all. The general visited the battery position and found a bully beef tin and an empty cigarette box lying around. There has been a tremendous furor over it, and the colonel *has been ordered to submit a report on me in two weeks' time as to my fitness to command a battery* — same old story. When there is any real work going on we are the ones to be picked for the heavy part — come a quiet period and all this is forgotten and the axe falls. An interesting circular came in from the staff captain a few days ago (by the way, I may not have mentioned that we have been with an English corps for some time) stating that the corps commander would inspect my horse lines and Leach's in a few days and giving us the tip that the general is particular on certain points, the first one of which I remember is *that officers' cookhouses must be whitewashed* and then followed about fifteen more points of a similar nature. There is not the slightest doubt in my mind that the person who conceived of this brilliant idea has already, or will soon receive, a D.S.O. for it.

I take it that there will be a mail in very shortly.... Young Beaver of the air force has several more planes to his credit. Most of the old fellows who left for three months in Canada — fourteen, I think there were — are now back in England. *Only two or three are fit for anything. I never thought for a moment they would be allowed out of Canada again.*

Sincerely,
Cy

July 10, 1918

Dear Ken,

I'm beginning to think of leave again as there seems to be quite a lot of it going around. I'm about twelfth on the brigade list of sixty-one officers so I don't suppose I'll have to wait more than six weeks. In the meantime Leach wants me to take ten days in Paris with him but it's a little difficult to get away at present.

The English general is on the warpath and the old antagonism, R.G.A. versus C.G.A., is burning again fiercely. My name is absolutely mud. I thought I had more powers than were really delegated to me as Colonel Magee's assistant, and the other evening when a report was demanded immediately by the general upon a certain proposed scheme, I unwisely wrote it myself and told them in plain Canadian what I thought of it. The next morning the colonel received a curt injunction in writing that Major Inches was under no conditions to sign any papers emanating from Colonel Magee's office. That was about a week ago. Up to date, no orders have been received to carry out the scheme. *It's a funny life; I'm laughing so I can hardly sign my name.*

C.F.I.

Monchy-le-Preux

One month later we sidestepped further south to Roclincourt,
coming under the 17th Corps, and here we remained until
the Canadians came up from Amiens, when we commenced
to prepare for the capture of Monchy. Your spirits revived, the
period of frightfulness was over; you were at last going to be
on the offensive.

August 18, 1918

Dear Ken,

There seems to be another lull on the Western Front. If the Hun is going
to get to Paris this year, he has to wiggle before the rains come.

Sincerely,
Cyrus

August 25, 1918

Dear Ken,

We follow the papers very closely, watching the progress of the various
offensives. I note with interest the attitude of the American papers —
they will certainly do big things but I don't imagine they have been used
in strength as yet. When they are, the turf is bound to burn.

Yours and etc.,
Cyrus

The Hindenburg Line

*After the capture of Monchy [August 26, 1918], we moved
forward to Athies, just north of the Scarpe. We were only there
a few days when we were called upon to find a position from
which we could reach distant bridgeheads on the Scarpe near
Corbenham, Brebières, and Vitry en Artois in the direction
of Douai. Shelling these bridges was to be our task when the
attack was made on the Hindenburg Line. We chose the area
beside the Roeux Chemical Works in front of Fampoux for
three guns. The other three we put four hundred yards further
back. This position was the record one in the history of the
battery. You were within twelve hundred yards of the front
line, much in advance of the nearest field guns. Some part
of the area was almost always under fire from the enemy day
and night. On the day of the big show you fired nearly three
thousand rounds and could have fired more if ordered.*

*One night the gas bombardment of the area was terrific.
Some of the field batteries to our rear lost most of their
personnel. Twenty of our men were obliged to go to hospital
from it, notwithstanding [that] they had worn their
respirators for eight hours. This finished our stay there. We
were in the 22nd Corps. The field batteries complained that
it was our guns that drew the fire upon the area, and we were
ordered out. We merely sidestepped six hundred yards to
the south into the town of Roeux, which we had entirely
to ourselves, remaining the most forward battery in the corps.*

September 7, 1918

Dear Ken,

Lively times at present but old battery still going strong. Haven't had
a chance to get back to see Charlie but will do so at first opportunity. *All*

the old stomping ground of earlier days is being reclaimed. It was at Merville that I opened the poll for the first time for the holding of the elections last fall. We still have to get back Fleurbaix, which was the locus in quo of our first position in France. Lacontre, now recaptured, was the second.

Cy

Bourlon Wood

In September . . . much to our delight, we received orders to rejoin the Canadian Corps, and exchanged guns with an English battery at Cagnicourt, a position from which we could look over at the treetops of Bourlon Wood. This turned out to be a position of comfort, for while the other batteries about had a thick time of it, we were left alone.

We felt severely the absence of our gas casualties and were further handicapped by the promotion of seven N.C.O.s [non-commissioned officers] to the new batteries training in England. To fill these vacancies gunners were made corporals, and bombardiers were elevated to the rank of sergeants. In this crippled condition we commenced preparations for the crossing of the Canal du Nord. We were allotted an area north of Inchy. (By the way, if you can stand for an awfully rotten pun at my expense, a facetious member of our mess on the Somme used to say that if we could only take Inchy, the war would end. He wasn't far wrong.)

The spot was not far behind the front line, and being under observation, could only be approached by night. We brought our guns up and dropped them into the covered pits of a reserve gun position built by the enemy. All our batteries moved up gradually. No one was allowed to show himself by day. The enemy must have had an awful surprise when at zero hour, all this heavy stuff opened up on him, from close

*behind the front line in a locality where no sane person would
ever think of looking for artillery.*

September 17, 1918

Dear Ken,

Yesterday I went to Boulogne with Harry and Lou Barker. Harry
was going on leave. We only had a half-hour there as it was late in the
afternoon when we arrived, and owing to the poor roads at this end of
the journey, we wanted to get back early. Does one good to get a breath of
sea air once in a while. We were fixing up a puncture when a lorry passed
by with Andy Rainnie gesticulating wildly at us from the front seat.

*I see that the Yanks have come through with some real stuff at last —
pity the Hun had not anticipated it and we would have had the whole sixty
thousand.*

Sincerely,
Cy

September 21, 1918

Dear Chack,

You will have heard that I found Charlie and spent a few hours with
him. I am trying to get him transferred to the siege, where most of his
friends are and so he will feel more at home. It was delightful meeting
him again. I saw him walking across the parade ground some distance
off and did not know it was he at first. I am planning to see him again
soon.

I also spent a day in a car with Harry. We went to Boulogne together
and I saw him established in the officers' rest house, a very nice place,
before leaving. Tell Ken I just have his weekend cablegram. What branch

of the service is Ummer[67] taking up? It's none of my business I suppose, but I think there are lots that should have been drafted before him.

One of the N.C.O.s in the wagon lines has just received the Military Medal for salving some ammunition from a tight corner. *First time the wagon lines have been honoured in decorations.* They do a lot of hard work and drudgery and perhaps it is my fault for not looking after them in the line of awards.

There are going to be some drastic changes in the C.G.A. soon. The position of brigade major is to be filled by a Canadian, I think, and I could have a try at it if I wanted to, but I let them know the other day that I have not the qualifications, but made myself very clear on the point that if I did not get a chance for the [promotion] I would feel anything but flattered. There are majors who are ahead of me on the list, but I had the courage to point out that I had seen much more service than any of them, which I thought should count for something. I further pointed out that I had been so long on the job I was losing my efficiency, though I can't say I was entirely pleased when this was about the only part of my speech with which my auditor seemed entirely in accord.

I passed up my leave a few days ago until circumstances seem a little more propitious. When I get away I think I'll go through to Loch Fyne [Scotland] where Fraser will be all October and get some real air into my system. *It has been a long pull this year without much exhilaration, i.e. such as the fun of the Amiens show and we feel peeved that we were not in it.*[68]

With love,
Cyrus

Cambrai

We had no trouble in getting across the canal and in taking up a position north of Bourlon. From high ground nearby

---

67 Ummer (or Errol), another younger brother of Cyrus's.

68 The Battle of Amiens, fought between August 8 and 11, 1918.

we could now look down upon Cambrai. In a few days we moved to Haynecourt, where we were when Cambrai fell [October 9, 1918]. A disagreeable feature of this position was the heavy bombing at night. The Hun was now on the run.

We followed quickly by going into action at Blécourt; Hem Lenglet for a night; Marquette, for two hours; Escaudain, where we did not fire; Bellaing, where we fired for two days; and Raismes, where we were hung up for several days while the enemy made his stand at Valenciennes. From Blécourt onwards the towns were full of inhabitants who gave us an enthusiastic welcome.

October 3, 1918

Dear Ken,
    Stirring times.
    New officer to replace Hopper, viz. Keltie Jones. MacLachlan left today on leave so this leaves me practically on my own hook. No Vassie. No Hopper. No MacLachlan to fall back on. Don't know what I'd do without Caldow to look after the horses and get up our ammunition supply.
    Captured the other day in a dugout what appeared to be a Hun gramophone and set of records and sent it to wagon lines and boasted for two days of my souvenir. Caldow reports it to be an inferior French make with some worn-out French records. However, I've a wonderful Hun automatic pistol out of some dugout where we lived like sardines for three days until we moved forward again. Three more Military Medals for recent operations.

                    C.F.I.

October 23, 1918
The Royal Club for Officers Beyond the Seas
Royal Automobile Club
Pall Mall, London SW1

Dear Ken,

I spent last evening with Bumps and Frances at Cambridge, where they have taken a house for three months while Bumps attends Staff College. Their boy is a splendid specimen of young manhood and gives promise of developing into a great athlete. Charlie is at the I.O.D.E. [Imperial Order of the Daughters of the Empire] Hospital, well situated on Hyde Park and is enjoying himself immensely. The O.C. is a fine chap who has been very kind to me at different times and is looking after Charles well. I am meeting many Saint John people, mostly officers on leave, among them Don Malcolm, Cudlip, Ewing, Alward, Crocket, and others.

Sincerely,
Cy

October 30, 1918

Dear Ken,

I arrived back at the battery last evening, having left Boulogne at 11 o'clock. I found the unit miles farther ahead than they were when I went on leave. The men are enjoying themselves immensely. It is something new to move forward into a town full of civilians and have them greet you with flags and other tokens of enthusiasm, including therein beaucoup osculation. It is pleasant living in houses once more without having to provide shelter of the corrugated iron and tarpaulin variety. The civilians have an intense loathing of the Hun, who seemingly treated them without much consideration.

In one house where the officers' mess was established the people of the house thought our discipline was very lax because they noted that whenever one of the officers entered the kitchen for a moment the cook did not click his heels and come to attention. It is also noteworthy the way the French kids come to attention and salute — the Hun had them well trained.

In one house where some of our officers spent the night the old lady came to one of us and asked when it would be convenient for her to use the kitchen stove. It was a great contrast to the first billet we were in on the Somme, where we had to get an interpreter in to cajole the woman of the house to let us cook a meal and it was only after a bribe and waiting until well into the afternoon that we were allowed to make use of it. It is quite late so I will hie away to bed.

As ever,
Cy

November 1, 1918

Dear Ken,

I have your letter of September 24 with enclosures, towit the clipping re: your marriage and snapshot of May.

We got word last night that both Austria and Turkey had thrown [in] the sponge, which will all tend to make the issue simpler for awhile, though it will be an awful difficult job to get Europe fixed up again on any well-defined lines which will please everybody. When one reads of the Czechoslovaks, Jugoslavs, Croatians, Romanes, Ruthenes, Magyars, and whatnot, it makes the head ache to follow or to attempt to follow all their claims for recognition.

The houses we are living in have been vacated by their owners so we have kitchen utensils and fuel galore.

Sincerely,
Cy

November 2, 1918

Dear Ken,

I note that Errol will not cross over until spring. At that rate it looks like he will not see an awful lot of the war. I've again come to the conclusion that the nearer one is to the front line, the less one knows what is going on. We have to wait for the English papers to get any real news. Before the advance we got *The Times* the day after publication, now it takes three days to come and correspondence is also prolonged by two days.

I don't think Semi got special leave to be married. I was told it was a rest consequent upon some rough work he had been through.

We have some decent living quarters in a mansion of some pretensions, with facilities for real civilized living. The guns are outside and nearly shake the house to pieces but we are impervious to sound

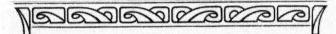

Canadian War Record

YPRES	April 1915
FESTUBERT	May 1915
ST. ELOI	April 1916
SANCTUARY WOOD (Mount Sorel)	June 1916
SOMME	Sept. 1916
VIMY RIDGE	April 1917
HILL 70	Aug. 1917
PASSCHENDAELE	Nov. 1917
AMIENS	Aug. 1918
ARRAS	Sept. 1918
BOURLON WOOD	Sept. 1918
CAMBRAI	Oct. 1918
VALENCIENNES	Nov. 1918
MONS	Nov. 11, 1918

Canadian battle honours.

by this time. I wrote Harry from London to let him know Charlie was doing well.

There is a feeling in the air tonight that the Hun has gone back a bit — certainly there has been no liveliness in our immediate vicinity, which is some evidence; however, we will know for sure in the morning. I wish you could see the job he makes of the railway. He does not rest content with blowing up the bridges and culverts but cuts a bit about a foot long out of every rail — this you can well imagine makes operating rather difficult for some time.

Just been able to get a bushel of good apples which prove very appetizing.

As ever,
Cy

The Final Rounds of the Great War

After the capture of Valenciennes we marched through the city to St. Saulve, where we went into action, for two days; from there to Onnaing, where we took up a position in the Square; one day there, and then to Quiévrain, where we fired our last round in the war.

The Last Shot in the C.G.A.

Between 8 am until noon on November 9 last, we fired one hundred and twenty rounds harassing fire at crossroads on the Hautrage–Tertre road. This was the last firing done by the C.G.A.

Chapter Twelve

Armistice

We were at Hainin ready to fire when the Armistice was declared
We spent a few days there getting our equipment in order, and
then moved nearer to Mons, finding billets in Jemappes, from
which place we started our march to the Rhine. But this march,
the life in Bonn, and the withdrawal by train to Sclayn and
Namêche near Namur, are so fresh in your memory that I will
not impose any further on your good nature by dwelling upon
them.

November 17, 1918

Dear Chack,

We are still at Hainin working hard, trying to make our equipment look new when a good deal of it isn't. But from this moment on, everything has to be up to barrack-room order. The G.O.C., H.A., who is Colonel [A.G.L.] McNaughton, soon to be General McNaughton, is to inspect us tomorrow afternoon. Horses and wagons are looking clean but the harness is not up to much. It takes at least two weeks to get harness looking anything like passable.

I don't know when we start to march to Germany, probably in a few days.

Francis Walker called to see me a few evenings ago. He is with the 11th Siege Battery in the next village. He looks well and is enjoying life immensely and is looking forward to a possible job of interpreter as he has some knowledge of the "nicht, verboten" stuff. The C.C.H.A. [Canadian Corps Heavy Artillery], who are in Mons, are having a delightful time, going to dances and etc. Stairs of Halifax was in to lunch today. He tells me the Belgian girls were just learning the one-step at the beginning of the war and have not progressed any since.

Love,
Cy

November 22, 1918

Dear Chacker,

Recounting the last few days . . . On Wednesday got up at 5 a.m. and moved the battery to Jemappes, just west of Mons. Chose positions for horses beside the Chateau Sports Royal, at the same time commandeering the chateau for the mess and sleeping quarters. Went to dinner with Captain Hart.

This morning, Barker came along with the car at 8:30 and we ran up to Brussels, some thirty-odd miles away, and spent the day there. We arrived there at 10 o'clock, just in time to find a vantage point from which we could view the entry of the King and Queen of the Belgians. The shops and hotels were closed until after the procession and the streetcars did not run until 4 o'clock. We had a spin around the town in the afternoon and met Walter Harrison at the Pala Hotel. He has asked us to go to the divisional show in Mons tomorrow afternoon and then to a dance. The staff officers in Mons are having a wonderful whirl with the Belgian girls!

First the colonel commanding the brigade, Johnny Angus MacDonald, then Major Cook (both old, wet, fatter friends) and officers here and there all along the line would call out and ask about Charlie. He is quite

Entry of Canadians into Mons, November 1918.

a famous man with them on account of the way in which he took his wound. The story, which I told you before, had become quite a classic in the brigade. These gas-shell fragments always carry infection and heal slowly. I know Charlie would like very much to be out here now. As for myself, they can't send me home any too quickly. I have my doubts if many [officers] outside a curious few have any desire to go farther forward.

With love,
Cyrus

November 27, 1918
Perkins Bull Hospital for Convalescent Canadian Officers
Putney Heath
London SW15

Dear Nona [Connie],

Cy and I had a great time while he was here on leave. He took me to lunches and shows several times, and it was really awfully good of him to take five days out of fourteen days leave to come to Plymouth to see me.

There is a most welcome change in London since the Armistice was signed. The paint has been scraped off the street lamps, and the streets are quite bright in the evenings, even with the reduced number of lamps. People no longer have to curtain all windows at night. Electric signs are beginning to reappear.

Last Saturday there was a great demonstration in Hyde Park. The King held a review of fifteen thousand discharged men. There were vast crowds all about as usual, and I tried to get where I could see something but could see nothing till late in the afternoon, when the crowd started to break up and I managed to get a very good view of all the big bugs. I think I will be going before a medical board in a few days and will be finished with hospital by the end of next week.

Regards to all,
Charlie

December 7, 1918
Deidenberg, near Amel,
near St. Vith
Germany[69]

Dear Ken,

Today I received a letter from Charlie dated December 2 enclosing your two cables of November 30 about father. I am very glad to know that he is able to be up again and hope that the improvement continues and that he is his old self again. I am looking forward to seeing you all again in the early spring if my plans work out all right.

In a few days I expect to go to the south of France for an extended leave. The general today very kindly offered to send me away [to Canada and his dying father] at once, but I want a bottle of Rhine water as a souvenir before I go. *The M.O. assures me a short stay in the dry air will rid me of a slight bronchial infection, which has bothered me ever since I inhaled a little too much mustard [gas] last May.*

While at Hamoir on December 6 a big football match took place between our gunners and drivers, which the former won at a cost of ten francs to me. The civilians challenged us to a game, but as the match had already been arranged between battery sections, it was decided to take them on next day. However we spent the next day *en marche*, spending the night at Chevron — a day's march with us means reveille at 5 a.m., lunch, water, and feed in some village midday. We consider ourselves extremely lucky if we get to our destination in time to get the horses fed before dark. These are very short days. The weather has been wonderful, which has proved the saving grace.

Last night we spent at a small place, Ville au Bois, seven kilometres from the frontier, which we crossed this morning. The road we took was through woodland mostly, with the odd farmhouse here and there. Deidenberg is a very small place, just a comfortable size for the battery. The people are very docile and seemingly inoffensive. I am living with two others in the burgomaster's house where we have our mess. It is a

---

69   Now part of Belgium.

nice place, piano, fine furniture, and crockery. The women are kindness itself. The men obey the order to doff their hats. They were not inclined to do so at first, I am told, but after a few had been knocked off and trampled in the gutter they soon conformed to the order.

In this house the family seems to have had a lot of relatives in the war, judging from the photographs about. One of the sons, a very sturdy type, arrived home a few days ago. He seems particularly anxious to fraternize with the batmen, though most of the men one meets are sullen enough. Notwithstanding the unspeakable crimes they [the Germans] have committed in Belgium and the rotten way they fought, it is hard somehow to keep these things in mind. The people feel that they are better off than those on the other side of the Rhine and seem quite reconciled to the British occupation.

By the way, I have not yet noticed the slightest indication of the starvation which we were always led to believe was rampant in Germany. These people say they have all they want, though they are told it is bad in some of the large towns. If I spend any length of time in Nice I won't make any determined effort to come back to the battery. *I am fed up on military matters, and it will only be sentiment which will impel me to do so and once away I trust any sentiment I may have in the [battery] will vaporize.*

Well, we were looking forward to a day's rest but it seems that that is not to be, for the movement orders have just come in for the morning.

> Sincerely,
> Cy

December 14, 1918
Dünstekoven
Germany

Dear Ken,

Two days ago I received from Mackay's Liverpool your cable of December 4 notifying me that Father's condition was less satisfactory. This took nearly ten days to reach me from Liverpool and, as it was, came a day later than their letter of confirmation of sending. I await with anxiety further news.

I think I wrote you last from Hellenthal. Our march in Germany has been as follows: ninth, arrived Deidenberg; tenth, Hünningen; eleventh, Hellenthal; stayed there on the twelfth; thirteenth, Strempt; fourteenth at 3 p.m., the column is just pulling in here. We are now a day's march from either Bonn or Cologne. I do not know yet our destination. The people continue friendly. There are a few sullen ones who can't help showing their true feelings, but their military training does them in good stead and they have great deference for higher authority. Speculation is rife this afternoon as to our destination. Our brigade H.Q. is in Cologne. They report the civilians are giving them a most wonderful time. Caldow, I think I told you, is back from leave. He tells us he got married but that is all we can get out of him.

                    Sincerely,
                    Cyrus

December 21, 1918
Bonn

Dear Ken,

Now that the train service is better the letters are not so long delayed.

The railway from Arras to Mons was completely destroyed and had to be repaired. This was done by the Canadian railway people, who are the adepts out here for that sort of thing, as well as forestry.

We are making preparations for the celebration of Christmas. We ordered turkeys for the men, but it looks as if they might not come. The mess is deluged with parcels from Canada with all kinds of eatables. I never had such a surfeit of sweets in my life. Tomorrow I am quite determined to make my visit to Cologne. I ought to be shot, I know, for not going sooner but sightseeing never appealed to me to any great degree, though I suppose it has educational value.

I had a humorous letter today from Colonel Iles who is home for Christmas. He has had five days shopping in London with his wife and declares that he considers wives a luxury and that Bonar Law should tax them as such.

Sincerely,
Cy

January 20, 1919
The Royal Club for Officers Beyond the Seas
Royal Automobile Club
Pall Mall, London SW1

Dear Ken,

Was sent to Borden Camp on the eighteenth to await sailing orders. In the meantime I am up here until my papers — such as medical history sheet, casualty report, and whatnot — come from France. Until they do I cannot get my clearance. Charlie was dismissed from hospital as fit on the seventh. He has been wandering around Scotland. I find he arrived today in London and is here somewhere.

As ever,
Cy

January 22, 1919
Tavistock Hotel
Covent Garden
London, WC

Dear Ken,

Charlie went down to Borden yesterday morning and was assured his name would be given preference for the next sailing — probably very early in February. He came back today to clean up a few things and found your cable from Mackays at the N.B. office. I think he should have no trouble to get away [to Canada]. I am hourly awaiting a wire that my papers have arrived and ordering me to report for examination. After that I will be put first on the C.G.A. list to go. It may be that we will go by the same boat. I trust we will not be too late [to see Father alive].

As ever,
Cy

February 4, 1919

Dear Ken,

Charles and I occupy a room together in the concentration camp at Rhyl in Wales, near Liverpool. He has been warned to sail on the eighth but I am not so sure of getting away so soon by reason of the fact that the allotment for senior officers is limited and there are several who have been a long time in camp awaiting shipment. The sailings are not being carried out according to schedule, and many have been cancelled at the last minute.

Cy

February 14, 1919
The Royal Club for Officers Beyond the Seas
Royal Automobile Club
Pall Mall, London SW1

Dear Ken,

Charlie and I were to sail on the eighth. The sailing was postponed until the fifteenth. I received permission to reside in Liverpool until the boat sailed. On the twelfth I received the cable with the *news of Father's death* so returned to Kinmel Park and saw Charlie. He had not heard from the N.B. office but had before him your previous cable to me, so he was prepared for the worst. He took the news of Pa's death very bravely but it hurt him a lot. They were such great pals.

He found that his place on the boat had been given over to a repatriated prisoner, but the A.A. and Q.M.G. [assistant adjutant and quartermaster-general] assures me that Charles will get away about the fifteenth.

I came up here last night and interviewed Argyll House today about *going back to the battery* and have just been notified by them to hold myself in readiness to proceed there on further instructions. My application to go to Canada was made on compassionate grounds, and those not now existing, I will return to my unit to be demobilized with it in due course. I will cable you as to my movements so you will know where to address me.

I am very sorry I could not get home in time. The O.C. at Borden did everything to expedite things for both Charles and myself — so also the A.A. & Q.M.G. at Kinmel, Colonel Thackeray, who was a sub with me on Salisbury Plain. But the matter of getting papers straightened out took considerable time. At present I have a bed at the Savoy in the suite occupied by Elkin and Thomas, who sail next Wednesday on *The Scotian*.

Sincerely yours,
Cy

February 19, 1919
London

Dear Ken,

I expect to return to France about the twentieth. Charlie will sail on the *Empress of Britain* on February 22.

Sincerely,
Cyrus

February 25, 1919
Church Army Recreation Hut
On Active Service With The British Expeditionary Force
Namur

Dear Ken,

I left Victoria Station by the staff train yesterday and by good luck evaded a stay of several days in Boulogne and caught the Cologne Express at 7:30 p.m. I arrived here about 6:30 this evening, the train being some eight hours late according to schedule time. They count on the Express, which is a converted hospital train, making the trip in thirty-six hours, Boulogne to Cologne, but it is rarely less than forty-eight and sometimes takes three days.

I was struck off strength of the battery on January 15 and am therefore joining as a reinforcement. As such I had to report at the military landing officer's office at Boulogne, and as he had received no instructions regarding me, he was going to hold me there until he had sent official messages all over the country but finally changed his mind and let me go right through.

The battery, I believe, is some eight miles from here at a place called Sclayn on the Meuse. My intention is to jump a lorry in the morning. I trust you received my cable.

Cy

March 4, 1919
Belgium

Dear Ken,
   The battery was delighted to have the O.C. [Inches] back again.
He looks pretty fit and cheerful, as usual. *I guess he wants to take his old
battery back to Canada and certainly the men are keen for him.*

Sincerely,
Peter

March 18, 1919

Dear Ken,
   We are in beautiful surroundings here. Sclayn, where we are living, is
a small town on the banks of the Meuse about eight miles from Namur.
The mess is in a fine house on one side of the Meuse — our billets on
the other. The river is about as wide as the St. John at Edmundston, only
much deeper. All day long the barge traffic is considerable. On one side
of the river is the double-line railway, the chief line through Belgium for
the army of occupation. I never saw such a continuous run of trains both
ways. The cars are mostly Boche.
   We are now down to fifty horses and are getting rid of our wagons
and equipment and guns, so there will be nothing to do except mount
guard in our turn on some river barges containing stores captured from
the Hun. Woodward leaves in the morning for England, having been
recalled to Canada. Captain Hart expects to go in a few days to England
as he is to travel by the married peoples' boat, and it is possible Caldow
will leave soon. MacLachlan is still in England trying to get a job in the
Malay Straits. Underhill has been evacuated sick, so it's probable I'll find
myself shorthanded very soon.
   Our orders to move on the twenty-fifth have come in! It is, I am told,
a three days' journey to Le Havre, in boxcars — then a few days there,

then Witley via Southampton. Don't like the idea of eight hours' trip across the Channel, never travelled that route before.

Colonel Magee is back from a trip to Brussels. He says he met Harry there, who told him they were busy turning their horses, which means their move will come during April. That riot at Rhyl, though deplorable of course, seems to have started things moving more quickly at Liverpool.[70] The redistribution of officers that will take place in England has been made. I won't take any of the present officers to Montreal. Hawkins goes to the 4th Siege (Barker) and Keltie Jones to the 6th Siege and both go to Saint John. Caldow and Hart go over on the married people's boat with their wives and Rosborough goes with the 5th to British Columbia. We send all our married men to England tomorrow, these include our mess provider and cook, but I think I'll be able to scratch along.

Had a letter from Francis Campbell today. He is on his way to Cambrai to see if he can locate his brother's grave. I expect mail from you any day now.

As ever,
Cy

P.S. I am glad to note that Charlie arrived home in good health.

March 23, 1919
Namêche

Dear Ken,

I am told the other day that we are to be in Canada by the first week in May at the latest. Possible that is so, barring complications arising through strikes,[71] we may make it. Things are moving more quickly than was thought possible. The moving of the 3rd Division was somewhat

---

70   A dozen riots or disturbances involving Canadian troops waiting to return home took place, the most serious occurring at Kinmel Park, Rhyl, on March 4–5, 1919.
71   Dock strikes in England.

lengthy owing to the fact that redistribution took place in England and it could only be accomplished when the whole division got over. Now this matter is attended to here, which saves a lot of time.

Beecroft, who rejoined his own unit some time ago, spent last night with us. He is in charge of a football team which has come up from Mons to take part in the preliminaries of the corps championships. He told me a rather remarkable story. Apparently his brother, a captain in the machine gunners during the Somme, had his guns and men wiped out and nothing has been heard of him since. Beecroft, who was in England at the time, made all sorts of inquiries, but his brother was reported missing. While in Folkestone shortly afterwards, Beecroft attended an exhibition of war photographs, one of which showed a wounded man on a stretcher. He recognized him as his brother and tracing the thing up, found the photograph had been taken subsequent to the fight. He also got in touch with the stretcher bearers and a man walking beside his brother. All they could tell him was that the man on the stretcher was not badly wounded and was talking of being in Blighty soon. Nothing has been heard of him since. Beecroft is going down to the Somme to see if he can find out anything but doesn't expect to, for his brother had no identity disc. The corps sports took place at Brussels yesterday. We planned to go up but quite cold at the last moment.

Sincerely yours,
Cy

Our Position in the C.G.A.

As you are probably aware, at the time of the Armistice, there were fourteen batteries in the C.G.A. divided up into three brigades. It is interesting to examine the gradual growth of the C.G.A. and the part played therein by this unit. The history of the C.G.A. for the first seven months after the First Division came to France is the history of this battery. Then the 2nd

Heavies appeared on the scene. We were alongside each other at Ypres in May 1916. During the Somme the siege batteries received their baptism of fire. The 1st and 2nd Siege were in close proximity to us throughout, and the 3rd and 4th much further north. During the winter of 1916-17 the 1st Brigade was formed. In March the 2nd Brigade H.Q. arrived. By the end of the summer, nine siege batteries were in France. In January 1918, three more siege batteries commenced to train in England, and came out by degrees during the summer, forming the 3rd Brigade. At the time of the Armistice two new 60-pounder batteries were in training in England. Seven of their N.C.O.s were promoted from this unit. Ten officers of this unit have served as captains in the C.G.A.; six of these received their majority; and our original O.C. was promoted to lieutenant-colonel. The C.G.A. had received the benefit of the experience in warfare which these officers acquired while in this unit.

The C.G.A did not get from the home authorities the same recognition that was lavished with a free hand upon other branches of the Service. I have often felt that we were nobody's children. In the first place it was with great reluctance that consent was given to the creation of even the small number of batteries we have today. Secondly, the headquarters staff of the Canadian Corps' Heavy Artillery was, up to last fall, composed entirely of R.G.A. personnel whose attention was given solely to the fighting end of the game. Being Imperials, they could not possibly have the ambition to develop and exploit a C.G.A. that would be regarded by ourselves and other branches of the Service as a real and potent part of our own corps. When last fall we did get a purely Canadian H.Q. matters began to move; two new 60-pounder batteries were authorized, and if the war had lasted for another year I think we would have had several more, because others had commenced to see, what had always been known to us, that the 60-pounder gun was the most effective artillery weapon in the Service. You won't be far wrong if you say to all comers that the 60-pounders won the war.

Commissions

We sent thirteen men to England for commissions in the artillery and twelve for the R.A.F. One of these has twelve planes and five balloons to his credit. Most of his work was at Passchendaele. Do you remember how he used to circle over our positions and wagon lines?

Our Battle Record

The battery has taken part in more engagements than any other unit in the Canadian forces.

Honours

I regret that many men have not received the recognition in this respect that they deserved. Most of our honours came from the Imperial Corps, on the principle, I suppose, that a prophet is without honour, etc. etc. The total is 45, divided as follows: 1 D.S.O.; 8 M.C.; 1 Croix de Guerre; 1 Medal of St. George (Russian); 3 M.S.M.; 4 D.C.M. [Distinguished Conduct Medal]; 26 M.M.; 1 Croix de Guerre (Belgian).
In addition to the above there have been 7 Mentions.

Our Establishment

*This consists of 7 officers, a sergeant-major, quartermaster-
sergeant, staff-sergeant fitter, 9 sergeants, 8 corporals, 10
bombardiers, 18 acting bombardiers, a farrier sergeant,
corporal shoeing smith, 4 shoeing smiths, 2 wheelers, 3
saddlers, 2 fitter smiths, and 222 gunners and drivers,
including 4 drivers A.S.C.[Army Service Corps]*

The Old Originals

*The battery came to France two hundred strong. When the
Armistice was signed, fifty of those men were still with us,
fifteen on the guns, thirty-five in the wagon lines. If any other
60-pounder battery, with our length of service, can show such
a record, let them produce the proofs. I venture to say it can't
be done. Some of the men who fired the first round took part
in our last series. We have a few men who acted as gunners
steadily throughout our stay in France, without a turn in
the wagon lines. In February 1918, when the married men
of the first contingent, who had not seen their families since
August 1914, were sent to Canada, thirteen of our men were
able to take advantage of the privilege. Only two of these men
returned to us. Hopes were held that the single men would
soon follow but were abandoned when the enemy offensive
began in March.*

*The determination of the old originals to see the thing
through was a great factor in keeping up the morale in the
unit. We have the case of one man who was a physical wreck
after the Somme, and went to hospital for an operation. The
doctors wished to send him to Canada. He refused to go and
was allowed to come back to us. He went back on the guns
and, though ill enough at times to go back to the hospital,*

he remained steadily on duty for two years — until the armistice. On the way to the Rhine, he caught influenza with complications. The nurses tell us that he was one of eight in the ward. The seven others died, but he kept saying to himself he was going to see the Rhine, and his willpower pulled him through. He rejoined the unit at Bonn.

Casualties

The experience of the battery in this respect has been pronounced by experts as phenomenal in its nature. Over and over again, when we were in a tight hole and losses appeared inevitable, we came through without a scratch. Our records show a record of 160 battle casualties. Something more than half of these were from gas, mostly very slight, in fact, but one death resulted therefrom. I refer to the gas shell which somehow got to the bottom of a dugout, penetrated the gas curtain, and burst inside. Only eight men have been killed by or died of wounds from enemy shellfire. Four men died as a result from injuries in the gun pits, and there were two deaths from illness. Many of the casualties, classed as wounded, were so slight that it was difficult for the men to believe that they had genuine Blighties,[72] entitling them to put up a gold bar.

You may have noticed a tendency in some people to make much capital out of the large number of casualties they have suffered. I can't understand exactly what their object is in doing so, unless it is an endeavour on their part to convince others, as well as themselves, that their units have been deciding factors in the war. I don't know what you think about it, but my proudest boast is that we have come through nearly four years of fighting with so few.

I remember that we served at one time under a lieutenant-

72 Army slang for a wound serious enough to be evacuated to Blighty (England).

colonel in the R.G.A. who made frequent visits to the battery, when his first question used invariably to be "How many casualties?" If the answer was in the negative he would show immediate disapproval. He held a theory that casualties were good for a battery and that a battery that was not having any, was not doing its bit. I hope I am not guilty of lèse *majesté if I say I entirely disagree. A battery which is put into such an exposed position that its personnel is wiped out may win undying glory, but what benefit does the infantry ahead of it receive from its support, for a battery permanently neutralized is a battery useless.*

Effectiveness depends on good morale and having had but light casualties, your morale was such that you were one of the most effective batteries on the British front. When the supreme tests came, your nerves were in such good condition that never once did you fail in support of your infantry. If you wish instances, I will quote again as outstanding examples: Ypres, Bully Grenay, Delville Wood, Liévin, Vimy, Chemical Works, and Haynecourt.

E. Sub

A striking fact is the complete absence of casualties of any kind among our signallers; the more remarkable when one looks back over the O.P.s they have manned, the miles of wire laid, and the deeds of daring performed by them in keeping up communications.

I won't enumerate in detail all the O.P.s used by us but will refer briefly to a few of the more interesting ones. Some of you will remember our first O.P., the haystack on the Rue Petillon, where we always thought we were being sniped at; then there was the well-known Ritz on the old Rue du Bois near Richebourg, a building a short distance from the front line,

which said building dwindled away day by day with constant
strafing. The steel tower at Maroc, used by us at Loos, was
only accessible at night. The water tower at Armentières and
the church tower at Le Bizet were chilly places. The tall
chimney in the factory at Ypres was, fortunately, knocked
down at a time when we were not up it. We used the Lorette
Ridge for the 1916 show, and also during the winter of
1916-17. The only decent O.P. after our first advance on
the Somme, was Switch Trench, to the right of High Wood,
from which we first saw Bapaume. A task of danger was the
running of the line to Hill 145 in the Vimy show. Later we
had the expedition to establish communications in the Hill
70 operation. The four days in the cellar in the front line at
Passchendaele was a most trying time. The panoramic views
from Vimy Ridge, Bois de Riaumont, and Bois Hirondelle
will live long in our memory.

Then there was the work of keeping up communication
between the battery and brigade headquarters, which in times
like the second battle of Ypres and the Liévin, Vimy, and
Fampoux positions, became arduous in the extreme. E. Sub's
fondness for piano, good grub, and the best billets became
notorious; I wish I had time to tell of their exploits, but to do
so I would have to write a whole book. Here's to the best
signalling party on the Western Front!

Finale

When I started this ramble, in retrospect, my intention was
to be very brief. Incidents kept recurring to me, however, and
I could not resist the temptation to jot them down. I have
written without access to the battery diaries and maps. If,
therefore, you find some errors, put it down to faulty memory.
I hope that someday a full history of the battery will be

written. Steps are being taken now, I believe, to provide some means of keeping a 1st C.H.B. institution of sorts in being after we get home. And now I say farewell. If any of you can reciprocate, to even a small degree, the kindly feelings which I have for you, and will drop me a line occasionally, nothing will give me greater pleasure than its receipt. My address is Saint John, N.B. If you can't think of anything to say, drop me a postcard with your signature, and I'll know what it means. If you are ever in Saint John come in and have a chat over the days gone by.

Good luck.

CYRUS F. INCHES   *London*
Major, C.G.A.   *April 8, 1919*
O.C., 1st Canadian Heavy Battery

April 8, 1919
Hotel Russell
Russell Square
London WC1

Dear Ken,

    I arrived in London today. The battery went to Rhyl from Witley, I believe yesterday morning, and will sail near the end of the month for Canada. I expect to be in London for a couple of days before going to Rhyl. After that I take it my eight days' leave will come in due course. I suppose you are getting fed up with hearing of my continual round of leaves and holidays but *I have lost all interest in this war game and have become the greatest malingerer of them all.*

                 Sincerely,
                 Cy

April 11, 1919
Westminster Hotel
Rhyl, North Wales

Dear Ken,

   The whole battery started yesterday . . . on eight days' leave. They will be shipped to Canada soon after their return.

                              As ever,
                              Cy

April 28, 1919
Westminster Hotel
Rhyl, North Wales

Dear Ken,

   We expected to sail by the *Mauritania* from Southampton on the twenty-sixth — it was postponed until the twenty-ninth. There is a possibility that we go on that date but it is so remote that it is hardly worthwhile mentioning it. From all accounts there has been a further postponement until May 2.

   The situation is peculiar. The C.G.A. was shipped up to Rhyl to make room at Witley for the 2nd Division. The rule at Rhyl is first come, first served. The *Cedric* and *Orduna* are at Liverpool waiting for those ahead of us at Rhyl but the [dock] strikes are holding them up. The Rhyl authorities say that if we are sent off by the *Mauritania* ahead of those who were here before us, they will not be responsible for any riots that may occur. They have a pronounced attack of "wind up."

   Here's hoping we get away on May 2.

                              Yours and etc.,
                              Cy

Our Honoured Dead

Sgt. Duggan, died of heart failure, 1st March 1915

Gr. A. Cobham, killed, 30th July 1916

Gr. W.L. Hunter, died of wounds, 31st July 1916

Gr. L. Nailon, died of wounds, 15th March 1917

Gr. G.J. Wilkins, died of wounds, 15th June 1917

Gr. H.S. James, died of meningitis, 16th June 1917

Br. R.S. Beal, died of wounds, 9th August 1917

Gr. W.J. Bunclark, died of wounds, 9th August 1917

Gr. F.C. Kelly, died of wounds, 9th August 1917

Gr. W.L. Cairns, killed, 6th September 1917

2nd A/M E.A. Snelling, killed, 6th November 1917

Gr. J.J. Lebrache, died of wounds, 6th November 1917

Gr. J. Taylor, killed, 21st April 1918

Gr. J.L. Cleary, died of wounds, 27th May 1918

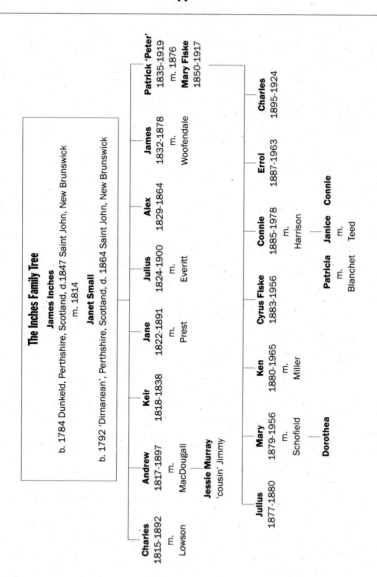

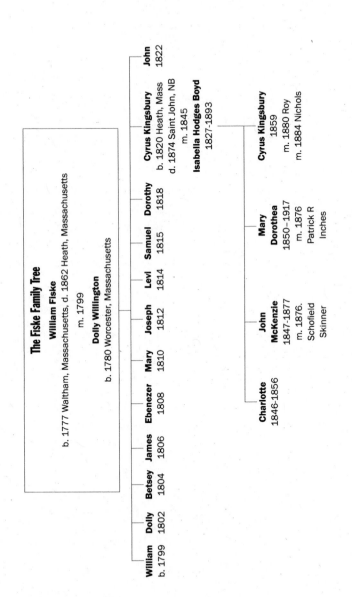

The Fiske Family Tree

William Fiske
b. 1777 Waltham, Massachusetts, d. 1862 Heath, Massachusetts

m. 1799

Dolly Willington
b. 1780 Worcester, Massachusetts

| **William** b. 1799 | **Dolly** 1802 | **Betsey** 1804 | **James** 1806 | **Ebenezer** 1808 | **Mary** 1810 | **Joseph** 1812 | **Levi** 1814 | **Samuel** 1815 | **Dorothy** 1818 | **Cyrus Kingsbury** b. 1820 Heath, Mass d. 1874 Saint John, NB | **John** 1822 |

m. 1845

Isabella Hodges Boyd
1827–1893

| **Charlotte** 1846-1856 | **John McKenzie** 1847-1877 m. 1876. Schofield Skinner | **Mary Dorothea** 1850–1917 m. 1876 Patrick R Inches | **Cyrus Kingsbury** 1859 m. 1880 Roy m. 1884 Nichols |

Acknowledgements

First of all, I have to acknowledge Cyrus Fiske Inches for his important contribution to the literature of the Great War. I am also grateful to the family recipients and heirs of his war letters for their accidental foresight in keeping the letters safe and sound so that I, a curious great niece-in-law, could find them ninety years later and bring them to light.

A nod must go to catalyst, Bob Dallison, who contacted me looking for a picture of Colonel James Inches to use in his book *Turning Back the Fenians*, another of the volumes in the New Brunswick Military History Series. I found the photo of James Inches, Uncle Cy's uncle, and showed the letters to Bob. He suggested I had a book in the making for this series.

Brent Wilson endorsed the suggestion and facilitated the process all the way through. Thanks, Brent.

Appreciation goes to my nephew, Benjamin Fitch, whose experience in writing his master's thesis on politics and recruitment in the Maritimes during World War One enabled him to fill in details of the War and to provide tips on historical writing.

I also thank my husband, George Teed, for his patient and continuing support of yet another of my mammoth, time-consuming transcription projects. Maybe he should thank me. This is his family!

Lastly I acknowledge my Dad, the late Commander Ray Bowditch. He, like me, would have seen the discovery of the letters as a rare opportunity and would have encouraged my efforts in producing the book — despite the fact the subject was Army and not Navy. All clear on the starboard side, Dad.

Selected Bibliography

Morton, Desmond. *When Your Number's Up: The Canadian Soldier in the First World War.* Toronto: Random House, 1993.

Nicholson, G.W.L. *Canadian Expeditionary Force 1914-1919: The Official History of the Canadian Army in the First World War.* Ottawa: Queen's Printer, 1964.

————. *The Gunners of Canada: The History of the Royal Regiment of Canadian Artillery,* vol. 1, Toronto: McClelland and Stewart, 1967.

Swettenham, John A. *McNaughton*, vol. 1, Toronto: Ryerson Press, 1968.

Photo Credits

Unless otherwise noted, all photos are from the Cyrus Inches Collection. The photos on pages 11 and 14 are from the *Saint John Globe* (public domain). The envelope on page 32 is from www.footnote.com. The photo on page 51 is from the *Daily Sketch* (public domain). The photos on pages 77 and 94 are from *The Daily Telegraph* (public domain). The photo on page 128 is from the *London Gazette* (public domain). The photo on page 181 appears courtesy of the C.F.B. Gagetown Military Museum. The map on page 184 appears courtesy of Mike Bechthold. The photos on pages 186 and 199 appear courtesy of the Provincial Archives of New Brunswick. The photo on page 226 appears courtesy of the New Brunswick Museum.

Index

Pozières France 161
Prest, Jane (Inches) 284
Pritchard 170
Prowse 197
Puddington 102
Puddington, Miss 136
Purves 177

Q

Quebec QC 17, 19, 21, 23
Quebec Harbour Commission 22
Quiévrain France 260

R

Rainnie, Andy 253
Raismes France 255
Rankine, Mrs. 190
Ray, Colonel 209
Raymond, Reverend W.O. 93, 237
Reading England 41
Red Cross Fund 53
Reed 49
Renrod 117
Rexton NB 187
Rhine 261, 265, 266, 278
Rhyl Wales 269, 273, 281, 282
Richebourg France 279
Ring, Ray 190, 239
Ritchie, Colonel 226
Ritchie, Dr. 79
Ritchie, Judge 22
Ritchie, Mrs. 226
River Ancre 142
River Lys France 114
Roberts, Field Marshal Frederick
    Roberts, 1st Earl 36
Roclincourt France 250
Roeux France 251
Roeux Chemical Works 253
Rosborough 273
Rosburgh 248

Roseburgh 245
Rosenorn, P.E.M. 237
Rothesay NB 79, 128
Rouen France 97, 242
Royal Air Force 276
Royal Automobile Club 228, 229, 256,
    268, 270
Royal Club for Officers Beyond the
    Seas 228, 256, 268, 270
Royal Military College 23
Royal Flying Corps 228
Royal Navy 33
Royal Overseas Officers' Club 225
Royal Trust Company 38
Ruffeinstein, Captain 74, 80, 83
Russian Army 146
Ryan, Lieutenant Jack 38, 47, 48, 58,
    74, 80, 83, 101
Ryan, Mrs. Jack 38, 48
Ryder, Lieutenant 88, 95, 150, 192, 195
Ryder, T.E. 237

S

St. Andrews NB 150
Saint John NB 8, 10, 17, 18, 20, 22, 26,
    37, 39, 41, 46, 55, 65, 68, 76, 86, 87,
    90, 93, 95, 96, 98, 102, 113, 116,
    117, 126, 148, 153, 165, 173, 199,
    202, 203, 208, 214, 232, 235, 240,
    256, 273, 281, 284
Saint John High School 10
St. John River 165, 207, 272
St. Nazaire France 57
St. Pancras Scotland 173
St. Saulve France 260
St. Vith Belgium 265
Salisbury England 37, 45, 49, 226
Salisbury Plain England 11, 17, 22, 31,
    33, 34, 35, 36, 37, 38, 40, 42, 44,
    49, 80, 81, 200, 270
Saltwood England 90, 102

The New Brunswick Military Heritage Project

The New Brunswick Military Heritage Project, a non-profit organization devoted to public awareness of the remarkable military heritage of the province, is an initiative of the Brigadier Milton F. Gregg, VC, Centre for the Study of War and Society of the University of New Brunswick. The organization consists of museum professionals, teachers, university professors, graduate students, active and retired members of the Canadian Forces, and other historians. We welcome public involvement. People who have ideas for books or information for our database can contact us through our website: www.unb.ca/nbmhp.

One of the main activities of the New Brunswick Military Heritage Project is the publication of the New Brunswick Military Heritage Series with Goose Lane Editions. This series of books is under the direction of Marc Milner, Director of the Gregg Centre, and J. Brent Wilson, Publications Director of the Gregg Centre at the University of New Brunswick. Publication of the series is supported by a grant from the Canadian War Museum.

The New Brunswick Military Heritage Series

Volume 1
Saint John Fortifications, 1630-1956, Roger Sarty and Doug Knight

Volume 2
Hope Restored: The American Revolution and the Founding of New Brunswick, Robert L. Dallison

Volume 3
The Siege of Fort Beauséjour, 1755, Chris M. Hand

Volume 4
Riding into War: The Memoir of a Horse Transport Driver, 1916-1919, James Robert Johnston

Volume 5
The Road to Canada: The Grand Communications Route from Saint John to Quebec, W. E. (Gary) Campbell

Volume 6
Trimming Yankee Sails: Pirates and Privateers of New Brunswick, Faye Kert

Volume 7
War on the Home Front: The Farm Diaries of Daniel MacMillan, 1914-1927, ed. Bill Parenteau and Stephen Dutcher

Volume 8

Turning Back the Fenians: New Brunswick's Last Colonial Campaign,
Robert L. Dallison

Volume 9

*D-Day to Carpiquet: The North Shore Regiment and
the Liberation of Europe,* Marc Milner

Volume 10

Hurricane Pilot: The Wartime Letters of Harry F. Gill, DFM, 1940-1943,
ed. Brent Wilson with Barbara J. Gill

Volume 11

*The Bitter Harvest of War: New Brunswick and
the Conscription Crisis of 1917,* Andrew Theobald

Volume 12

Captured Hearts: New Brunswick's War Brides,
Melynda Jarratt

Volume 13

*Bamboo Cage: The P.O.W. Diary of Flight Lieutenant Robert Wyse,
1942-1943,* ed. Jonathan F. Vance

About the Author

Valerie Anne (Bowditch) Teed was born at Pointe à Pierre, Trinidad and Tobago, to a British naval officer and a Nova Scotian mother. She graduated from the University of King's College and Dalhousie University and attended the Institut de Touraine in France. Teacher, writer, copywriter, voice talent, and researcher, she has produced several book compilations of letters and material discovered among her husband's family keepsakes. His Scottish Inches ancestors, in particular, left a large collection of correspondence dating from 1814 to 1925, which includes the war letters of Cyrus Fiske Inches, transcribed in this book.

Valerie is currently newsletter editor for the New Brunswick Branch of the United Empire Loyalists Association of Canada, program writer for the annual Empty Stocking Fund broadcast, and a partner in a family tree research business called Ancestors New Brunswick.